Samuel Reynolds Hole

A Little Tour in America

Samuel Reynolds Hole

A Little Tour in America

ISBN/EAN: 9783337187408

Printed in Europe, USA, Canada, Australia, Japan

Cover: Foto ©Andreas Hilbeck / pixelio.de

More available books at **www.hansebooks.com**

A
LITTLE TOUR IN AMERICA.

BY

THE VERY REV. S. REYNOLDS HOLE,

DEAN OF ROCHESTER.

EDWARD ARNOLD,

Publisher to the India Office,

LONDON: NEW YORK:

37, BEDFORD STREET, STRAND.   70, FIFTH AVENUE.

1895.

TO
HIS EXCELLENCY
THE AMERICAN AMBASSADOR IN ENGLAND,

THE HON. T. F. BAYARD,

THIS BOOK
IS MOST RESPECTFULLY DEDICATED

BY ONE
WHO KNOWS HOW GREATLY HE IS BELOVED
ON EITHER SIDE OF THE ATLANTIC.

THE AUTHOR.

THE DEANERY,
   ROCHESTER,
      November, 1895.

INTRODUCTORY NOTE.

"Hope told a flattering tale" that, having written a prefatory chapter to this book, no further prologue would be required; but I have just received an intimation from headquarters: "*No Preface. Please send at once.*"

I hate Prefaces. The writer always seems to magnify or to minimize his merits; and the reader resents his self-conceit, or infers from his humility "that his deserts are small." Who cares to know what an author thinks about himself or his books? The fond mother does not love her small boy the less because he has an appalling squint; and she describes as "a lovely auburn" his hair of brilliant red.

And why does he, the author, always assure us that he has done his best? Of course he has. He knows that the critic is waiting to crown him with laurel or with foolscap, that the public are waiting to nod in approbation or in slumber, and that the publisher is waiting to send him a condolence or a cheque. They do not desire information about his *modus operandi*, they want to see the *opus*. They are not anxious to be introduced to the cook, but to taste his dishes; and no ornamental *Menu* nor devout Grace before Meals will alter the organization of their palates or improve the flavour of their food. Let us omit the Preface.

S. REYNOLDS HOLE.

The Deanery, Rochester,
December, 1895.

CONTENTS.

CHAPTER		PAGE
I.	Preparatory	1
II.	Progressive	22
III.	Arrival	31
IV.	New York	43
V.	Clubs and Theatres	69
VI.	The Parks	75
VII.	Flowers and Florists	92
VIII.	The Culture of the Rose	99
IX.	The Political Crisis at New York	113
X.	Education	122
XI.	The Theological Seminary	133
XII.	The Churches	151
XIII.	Railways	163
XIV.	Newspapers	175
XV.	The Neighbourhood of New York.—Worcester City	193
XVI.	Niagara	213
XVII.	Toronto, Detroit, Whitewater, Milwaukee	232
XVIII.	Chicago	249
XIX.	Cincinnati	272
XX.	Virginia	277
XXI.	Washington	302
XXII.	Philadelphia, Pittsburg, Baltimore	322
XXIII.	Universities and Colleges	333
XXIV.	Hartford and Albany	347
XXV.	Rochester	357
XXVI.	Cleveland, St. Louis, Denver, and the Rocky Mountains	365

LIST OF ILLUSTRATIONS.

	PAGE
STATUE OF LIBERTY	*Frontispiece*
SUNNYSIDE: HOME OF WASHINGTON IRVING ...	11
THE LOVERS' WALK IN CENTRAL PARK	77
BISHOP POTTER OF NEW YORK ...	85
THE VICTORIA REGIA	109
SON AND WIFE OF AN INDIAN CHIEF	137
DR. MORGAN DIX	155
NIAGARA IN WINTER	227
ARMOUR'S SAUSAGE MACHINE	257
DRESSING BEEF AT ARMOUR'S ...	259
MASONIC TEMPLE, CHICAGO	267
AMERICAN MIDDLE-WEIGHT HUNTER	291
PURE-BLOODED AMERICAN HOUNDS	293
AN EMBRYO M.F.H.	295
OLD QUAKER INN AND PINE-TREE CLUB-HOUSE	297
THE CAPITOL, WASHINGTON	309
INDEPENDENCE HALL, PHILADELPHIA ...	325
WASHINGTON STATUE, BALTIMORE ...	329
CLIO HALL, PRINCETON	335
YALE UNIVERSITY BUILDINGS	337
YALE BOAT-HOUSE	339
OLD BUILDINGS, HARVARD UNIVERSITY	343
CAPITOL AND SOLDIERS' MEMORIAL, HARTFORD ...	349
BISHOP DOANE'S WORK, ALBANY	352
BISHOP'S THRONE AND OLD CROZIER, ALBANY ...	353
THE MOUNTAIN MONARCH, COLORADO	375
BALANCE ROCK, GARDEN OF THE GODS	376

A LITTLE TOUR IN AMERICA.

CHAPTER I.

PREPARATORY.

WHY should they, who have the opportunity, make a tour in the United States of America? Because they will see such results of political and industrial progress as have never been achieved, according to all the records of history, in the same period of time. Where, but fifty years ago, there was silence and desolation, or where the only inhabitants were wild men and wild beasts, the Indian and the buffalo, they will find great cities with their churches and capitols, colleges and schools, libraries and institutes, museums and galleries, and parks. Where, little more than thirty years ago, all joy was darkened, and all work was stayed by the tragic interruptions of civil war, they will find universal peace; and where, before that awful fight, the negroes were sold as swine in the market, were branded and whipped, and manacled, and hunted down by bloodhounds if they tried to escape, there is freedom alike for all. They will find an organization of government, designed by statesmen of consummate wisdom, vast information, and laborious thought, which, while it maintains the separate independence of the individual States, preserves the unity of the nation and the integrity of the common weal, through the recognition of a superior federal authority, and a final court of appeal.

The scheme is complex, but the success has been so far complete; and it will advance the admiration of Englishmen to note, that although free America could not, of course, condescend to copy the Kings, Lords, and Commons of the Old Country, there remains a pleasing resemblance in her President, and her dual Chambers, in her senators and members of Congress. There is a very striking contrast between the simplicity of the White House and the ceremonial splendour of Buckingham Palace, but

> " 'Tis not the balm, the sceptre and the ball,
> The sword, the mace, the crown imperial,
> The inter-tissued robe of gold and pearl,
> The farced title passing 'fore a king,
> The throne he sits on, nor the tide of pomp
> That beats upon the high shore of the world;"

it is not these, but the man, the woman, who, representing and concentrating the will and power of the people, commands our homage. Nor are we anxious to discuss the relative advantage of hereditary or elected authority, so long as " the throne of our queen is in Englishmen's hearts," or so long as *noblesse oblige*.

With regard to the members of Congress, they

may seem to be somewhat inferior to our representatives in the House of Commons, outwardly and intellectually; but I must dissent from the cruel distinction, made by a quaint gentleman of Denver, when he said, that as the cream was formed upon the milk, so in England the best men were sent up to Parliament, but as in boiling potatoes the scum rose to the surface, so in America the worst men were sent to Congress. Many causes combine to deter the cleverest and most energetic men from offering themselves for election. Congress does not make millionaires, and £1000 per annum, with travelling expenses, and £25 for stationery, is not such an inducement in a country where great fortunes are sometimes quickly made, as it would be in ours. It is said that further enrichments are accessible to the member of Congress who will hold out his hand to take them, and will give his vote upon certain specified measures in accordance with the donor's interest; but while it is generally deplored that bribes have been, and are accepted by the weaker brethren, it is confidently affirmed that the number of those who yield to the temptation is grossly exaggerated. Nevertheless, Mrs. Mary Livermore, a well-known public lecturer in America, made the startling announcement at Detroit, in November, 1894, "that the English House of Parliament could not be compared with the lower legislative body of the United States, because the former was invulnerable to bribery, while $200,000 would insure the passage of any bill in Congress." We accept the compliment, but not without a qualm of apprehension that if the censorious Mary came to England, she would have something to say about our Acts for the suppression of bribery, intimidation, and other corrupt practices, not quite annulled in this our virtuous isle.

Reverting from aberrations to inducements for a tour in America, I would assure the tourist that he will find himself in a land of infinite beauty and of inexhaustible resources, amid scenery which will delight him in all its varied forms, from the tree-clad slopes of fair Virginia to the stern grandeur of the Rocky Mountains, from rippling streams and silent rivers to the thunder and the glory of the "Falls." He will be reminded of the "land of wheat and barley and vines, and fig-trees and pomegranates, a land of oil-olives and honey, a land wherein thou shalt eat bread without weariness, thou shalt not lack anything in it, a land whose stones are iron, and out of whose hills thou mayest dig brass."

Herein, moreover, is "a vein for the silver and a place for gold." The coal-fields are said to extend over a third of the continent. The forests occupy millions of acres; and to prevent the enormous demand for timber exceeding the supply, a national organization, known as the American Forestry Association, composed of delegates from all the States, meets annually. The President is authorized to make public forest reservations; and the individual

States have striven to encourage the growth of timber by appointing a certain day in the year—the second Wednesday in April, to be known as *Arbor Day*—for the voluntary planting of trees by the people.

The wealth of the United States is an amazement. As each successful worker "makes his pile" in rapid succession, "hills peep o'er hills, and Alps on Alps arise." An interesting American census, recently issued, and quoted in the *Times*, April 8, 1895, shows that if this wealth could be realized and equally divided, there would be a sum of £200 for each inhabitant. The actual valuation of all real and personal property is $65,037,000,000, or £13,000,000,000. The total has multiplied ninefold in forty years, and the increase of wealth is faster than the increase in population. In 1850 it was only equal to £60 per inhabitant. Of this wealth 60·8 per cent. is real estate ; railways, 12 ; machinery, 4·6 ; agricultural stock, 4·1 ; mining, 2.

Nor must we forget how large a portion of this wealth has been won not only by patient labour, but by that inventive genius, which has done so much to accelerate the operations of our hands, and to diminish the burden of our toil in the factory and on the farm. What a development there has been, what a progress towards perfection in the crafts and skill of the workman ! One hundred years ago Eli Terry made wooden clocks at Plymouth, Connecticut, which cost £5 apiece. Then Chauncey Jerome manufactured them entirely of brass, bringing down the price to a few shillings; and then the process of making watches was brought to its present excellence at Roxbury, and Waltham, and Waterbury. The total production is said to be about 10,000 a day!

Again, it will be good for the English traveller to visit a nation, which, in the prevision of the seer and the prescience of the thoughtful, will be hereafter, from its wonderful intelligence and wealth, from the fertility of its soil and the treasures beneath it, the unbroken continuity of its possessions, the identity of its language, and above all from that righteousness, for which men hope and pray, because that only exalteth a nation, a queen among the peoples. It can be said no longer that England holds the balance of power, or a supreme priority in commerce; and if it should be her destiny to recede, and her fate be the common lot of all great dynasties—

"Assyria, Greece, Rome, Carthage, where are they?"

—what greater consolation can she have than that the heir-apparent is bone of her bone and flesh of her flesh? And so, *parva componere magnis,* as the aged sportsman rejoices to contemplate from the back of his steady cob, like himself well stricken in years, his grandson gallantly charging and clearing on his pony "really quite a respectable fence," or in later years hitting a cricket ball into the pavilion at Lords, or better still to read his name at the top of some competition list; or as the eyes of some fair mother glisten, and her cheeks glow, as she marks the homage of admiration which is paid to her daughter's charms and "*O matre pulchrâ filia pulchrior*" is whispered wherever she goes; so may John Bull say, "Jonathan was an audacious child, and cut himself free with his long bowie knife from his mother's apron-strings, and made himself generally unpleasant, but he is going to be a first-class man. He was a cantankerous colt, rearing, and jibbing, and kicking himself clear of his harness, but he has grown into a grand horse. If ever I have to climb down and take a back seat, Jonathan is the man for the box."

Moreover a visit to the States will assure the visitor that this affection is reciprocal. They who sail over seas change their climate, not their character; the old interests are entailed in the Anglo-Saxon heart, and will be always paramount above all other strains. There are everywhere bilious and discontented men, who love to stir up strife; but the American instinct is homeward bound, and thinks of England as Wendell Holmes when he wrote of her—

> "Our little mother isle,
> God bless her!"

"We are brothers," so Tennyson wrote to Longfellow, "as no other nations can be." Northamptonshire, in England, takes precedence of America in the biography of George Washington, and the mention of his name recalls an incident to my mind which charmingly and conclusively corroborates that which I have said.

While at New York I received, through Bishop Potter, an invitation from the Regent of "the

Daughters of the Revolution," whom I had not then the privilege of knowing, to attend a meeting to be held on the 5th of January, to commemorate the anniversary of the wedding of General Washington. I gladly accepted the summons in the kindly spirit which inscribed it, repeating to myself the motto of our Free Forester Club of Cricketers, " United though untied." I received a gracious, genial welcome, which I shall never forget, and when I was asked for the inevitable " few words," I acknowledged it *con amore*. I told that brilliant convocation of ladies and gentlemen—for there were sons as well as daughters met together, all lineal descendants of those who had taken part in the War of Independence—that my appearance in their midst was appropriate and opportune. That when the Generals of the Great Roman Emperors returned with their victorious armies from the battle-field, they were wont to include in their triumphal processions some huge barbarians who walked in chains behind their chariots of war, and testified to their conqueror's overpowering might. I at once confessed my complete subjugation to the irresistible influence of a foreign power, and was proceeding to express a willingness to hug my chains when it fortunately occurred to me that such an expression might be misconstrued and denounced as unbecoming an aged Dean. Whereupon I proceeded to express my gratification that their gigantic prisoner was not to be turned into a gladiator, *more Romano*, and introduced to famished lions and bears, but was to be exhilarated by beauty and enlivened by wit; that "grim-visaged war had smoothed his wrinkled front, and now instead of mounting barbed steeds to fright the souls of fearful adversaries," and subsequently dragging them ignominiously through the streets, to derision and dungeons, he was satisfied with *Batailles des Fleurs*, and his captives rode in carriages with grey horses, instead of walking behind them, American gentlemen overcome by English ladies, and *vice versâ*.

These nuptials suggested, of course, the occasion and the man whom we met to honour, and when I had assured my hearers not only that we had forgiven his somewhat rude behaviour, but that (in all seriousness) we revered him as one of the greatest and best of heroes, I was *decoré* by the Regent with the badge of the society, with a miniature flag of the stars and stripes, and with a large rose named "American Beauty" placed over my heart; and I went back to my astonished wife to inform her that "Europe was superannuated, and that my return was doubtful."

In the country, around the haunts, and it may be in the homes of those American authors who have impressed and instructed us from childhood until now, we are refreshed by pleasant memories; and the times and the scenes in which we read them, and the thoughts which they induced, are presented to the mind once more. Again, as I stood before the home of Washington Irving, on the banks of the Hudson,

I felt something of the implicit faith, and of the thrilling awe, with which, sixty years ago, I read his *Tales of a Traveller*. At Albany I grasped the hands of the grandson * and the great-grandson of Fenimore Cooper, and afterwards, in the places of which he wrote, I renewed the excitement which enthralled my boyhood, as I read by day, and dreamed by night, of "The Spy," "The Pioneer," "The Pilot," and "The Last of the Mohicans."

In Virginia and in Vermont, where Washington was born and died, I paid my homage to that ἄναξ ἀνδρῶν, not forgetting in the former place the honour due to that noble Christian soldier, General Lee, or his patriotic farewell to his defeated army, "*I have done the best I could.*"

"See, the conquering hero himself comes" before our imagination as we enter Ohio, the State in which General Grant was born, and as we travel elsewhere by many a battlefield, and thank God that America has passed the ordeal of that most tragic war.

In Kentucky, with a reverent admiration, we remember President Lincoln, how he said in his youth, when he saw the slaves sold in the market, "If I have ever the power, I'll hit this business hard," and how he lived to strike the death-blow; and that tyranny was overpast.

* He told me that his grandfather, who lived at Cooper's Town, a village belonging to his family, did not wish at first to be known as the author of his books, and, to promote the concealment, presented them to his sister as " new publications, which he thought might interest her."

SUNNYSIDE: HOME OF WASHINGTON IRVING.

In the State of Maine, "the manifold soft chimes" of Longfellow float on the air like bells at evening pealing, and the exquisite songs of the Chief Minnesinger, with their solemn sweet vibrations, dignify our ambitions, soothe our sorrows, and sanctify our hopes. Here also we shall have in fond remembrance—for he was born at Waterford, Maine, a fellow of infinite jest, who has so often refreshed our spirit, from the merry heart which doeth good like a medicine—Charles Farrar Browne, better known as "Artemus Ward, Showman."

Seven cities contended for the distinction of Homer's birthplace. Massachusetts boasts of seven Homers, seven wise men, of her own—Bryant, Prescott, Emerson, Poe, Holmes, Motley, Lowell—four of these, Emerson, Poe, Holmes, and Lowell, born at Boston. And it may be noted that the year 1809 was *annus mirabilis* in the history of American worthies, as introducing to the world a triumvirate, Abraham Lincoln, Oliver Wendell Holmes, and Edgar Allan Poe.

The Englishman can view the splendid conquests of the engineer without leaving England, and, when he visits other lands, will find the handiwork of his fellow-countrymen attesting their mechanical skill; but he will be delighted, none the less, with the magnificent accomplishments of American science and labour, in their great viaducts over valleys and rivers,[*]

[*] The Suspension Bridge between New York and Brooklyn has a clear span of nearly 1,600 feet, and, including the approaches,

their railways amid precipitous rocks; and, again, in their application of electric power, so far more extensive than with us, to locomotion and to light in the street cars, the public buildings, and private houses of their principal cities. Especially, he will find at Niagara a gigantic and momentous experiment, which promises results of a new and almost infinite force; but of this I would speak more particularly, when I come to the "Falls." He will be brought face to face with the inventive genius to which I have already referred, and which has done so much to diminish the drudgery of manual labour, in the improvements, for example, which were first made by Mr. McCormick in the reaping-machine, and in countless instances of minor importance.

A large number of my compatriots might derive much benefit from visiting a land in which the men and women are almost universally engaged in work. I believe that there are more idlers in Bond Street, London, than in all the city of New York—more lazy, tattling, maundering loiterers, who only live for the gratification of instincts which they share with the animal world, and have not a word of justification or apology to offer for their limp and silly existence. The Americans despise these dummies, whose literature is limited to the latest "scratchings" and "odds;" whose chief correspondents are trainers and touts; who shoot pigeons, and call it sport; who

is 3,455 feet in length. This, and the Niagara Railway Bridge, will be easily accessible to the tourist.

regard their dinner as the supreme object and occupation of the day; who have no love but for themselves, and no fear but of their tailor.

On the other hand, the Englishman will bring back over the Atlantic, with all this sympathy and praise, a more thankful appreciation of many advantages which he enjoys in his native land. America may be compared to a magnificent palace rising in the midst of a fair ground, of which the boundaries are too distant for the eye to see; but the edifice is as yet but a few feet above the soil, and the design of the landscape-gardener is little more than outline. England is a venerable mansion on a much smaller scale, but complete without, and comfortable within, from parapet to basement, tastefully and abundantly furnished from the attic to the cellar-bin; and all out of doors is garden. The surface of the land, and therefore the scenery, is more varied, and we have no long monotonous continuance of prairie desolation. The humidity of our climate gives us, as some small compensation for rheumatism, lumbago, sciatica and chronic catarrh, a luxuriant verdure, which seems to keep our "fields ever fresh, and groves for ever green," and which beautifies alike the pleasure-grounds of the rich and the cottage gardens of the poor.

Returning from the new to the old country, we regard with a more earnest reverence our cathedrals and other churches, our ancient colleges and schools, our hospitals and almshouses, remembering what

Christianity has done for us before and since those days of which Lord Macaulay wrote that, if there had been no monastic institutions, the country would have been divided into two companies, beasts of burden and beasts of prey.

Dilapidations do not excite me, and I have no sympathy with the gushing girl who informed the unmarried proprietor of a castellated home with fallen towers that she "was awfully gone on ruins." I am convinced that "not to the past, but to the future looks true nobility, and finds its blazon in posterity;" but I venerate, nevertheless, these ancient fanes and fortresses as teaching and illustrating history, as preaching sermons in stones, and as asking each generation, "Are you true sons of your fathers, who made those sacrifices and fought those battles, who said, 'I will not give to God that which costs me nothing,' and who went into the fight with this thought in their hearts—

'How can a man die better than facing fearful odds
For the homesteads of his fathers, and the altars of his Gods?'"

And then there is the joy of return and re-union, the sight of those who care for us most, the sound of the voices which have been praying for us.

"And oh, the joy upon the shore
To think of all our perils o'er!"

I had other inducements, personal, to visit the States—genial invitations from ecclesiastics and florists promising fraternal receptions and financial successes if I would give public lectures. This pecuniary incitement was decisive. Our funds for the restoration of Rochester Cathedral were exhausted, and if I could bring home a substantial sum, I might evoke new generosities, energies and hopes, and should feel that, while I was enjoying my excursion, I was not neglecting my work and duty. And so, having the promise, " Where thou goest, I will go," from one whom I could not leave, and two dear friends having agreed to accompany us, I engaged berths on board the *Majestic* and commenced preparations.

Then arose a commotion, which I had not foreseen— protests and prophecies of evil from kinsfolk and from friends. These were uttered, in my presence, sweetly and with smiles; but I detected from time to time, amid their playful banter, a severe rebuke of my temerity, and a sad commiseration of my ignorance; and I heard, from those loquacious makers of mischief, who exult in repeating that which " perhaps they ought not to tell you," that in my absence their denunciations were remarkably fierce and free. " Had the amiable, but slightly obtuse, old gentleman forgotten that he was no chicken ? "—as though any man in his seventy-fifth year should liken himself to a cockerel !—" had he never noticed that the Atlantic beat the record for rolling and pitching, fogs, icebergs, tornadoes, collisions, and wrecks ? The idea was preposterous, and suggested softening of the brain, for an old man to leave his comfortable home for perils by land and water, like the crazy old king in the play. As soon as he landed at New York, he would be the dupe of the covetous, and the laughing-stock of the scornful. The Americans would jeer at his gaiters, and would classify him with that community whom Dickens has described as 'a variety of humbugs in cocked hats.' Every one knew that the railway trains in the States were attacked and robbed almost daily by armed brigands, to say nothing of their falls from embankments and topplings into streams." They seemed to anticipate for me the reception which the cowboys gave to a tourist who had excited their anger, whom they denuded, tarred and feathered, gagged, and tied to a tree, and then questioned, with mock politeness, "How he liked travelling in the West?" They were credibly informed that in some of these Western States—they didn't quite know where—the Indians were still agile with their tomahawks and poisoned darts, and that the custom of scalping and cooking strangers was by no means obsolete. They regarded my exodus with melancholy forebodings, and with the tearful eyes of sad imagination they saw, thousands of miles away, a long, large, lonely grave!

Publicly, as well as privately, my project was criticized, and while it was commended by several journalists as courageous and deserving success, it was denounced in all kindness by a foremost London morning paper as objectionable, because such restorations should be made at home as a national duty, and that there was a jarring sense of incongruity in asking subscriptions, in sending round the hat, abroad. I can see no impropriety in Christians exhorting one another, wherever they may be, provoking to love and good works, in inviting the children on one side of the Atlantic to help in repairing the churches which their forefathers built on the other, and which many of them love as dearly as we do. We had done what we could, and I saw no signs of "national duty" coming forward to complete our unfinished work. Moreover, as a matter of fact, I did not "ask subscriptions." Two offertories, one at New York and one at Albany, were given to me after I had preached: all other money was paid by those who came to hear my lectures, in which there was no reference to the restoration, and was therefore at my own disposal. In preferring to spend the surplus of £500, which I brought home, upon the cathedral rather than in appropriating it to myself, I fail to apprehend that I have acted "hardly in consonance with the dignity of the nation and of the National Church."

A wise man, before he visits America, will read a reliable history of the country, such as Bryce's "History of the American Commonwealth," or Goldwin Smith's. He will carefully study a good modern map; he will try to obtain introductory letters to citizens of credit and renown; he will provide himself with such a strong portmanteau as will resist the notorious "baggage-smashers," with a smaller one for use on the rail; with a good supply of clothes, which are so much dearer in the States that I heard an

American gentleman affirm that by laying in a large stock of garments in London, and partly wearing them, as duty is chargeable on brand new garments, he had defrayed the cost of a voyage; and with a camera and field-glasses.

The ladies have, of course, more extensive needs. My wife secured from an eminent purveyor in Oxford Street two huge wooden tenements, described as "Saratoga trunks," which were about the size of the mysterious cabinets in the possession of Messrs. Maskelyne and Cook, and would have furnished ample accommodation for the plate of some wealthy peer. Nevertheless, I was severely repressed when I ventured to doubt the rapid portability of these structures without the introduction of levers and cranes, and was distinctly informed that the man who made them, and was therefore supposed to know something about them, regarded them as of medium size.

One more preparation remains for those who propose to visit America—the preparation of self, the elimination of prejudices, theories, verdicts pronounced without evidence, mere sentiments, opinions formed from circumstances which no longer exist. Charles Dickens, in the postscript to his "American Notes," expresses his great astonishment at the changes which had occurred between his first and second visit to the States, and ever regretted that on the former occasion he had made such an unfavourable and extreme selection. There cannot be a more disastrous mistake, the joint offspring of self-conceit and ignorance, than to frame from hearsay or from a brief and partial acquaintance, dogmatical convictions, laws unalterable as those of the Medes and Persians. If Froude could revisit America, he would hardly repeat his suggestion that "Washington might have hesitated to draw the sword against England, could he have seen the country as we see it now."

There are, nevertheless, not a few travellers who seem to measure and weigh everything by standards and scales of their own manufacture. They pare and they pad. They ignore that which exceeds or opposes their expectation, and they add from their own inventions that which they do not find. They fling all the material they collect, like pig-iron, into the heated furnace of their imagination, and pour it molten into their own mould. They bring home the impressions which they took abroad. If their conception of Hamlet is not Shakespeare's, so much the worse for Shakespeare. They confidently undertake to produce a striking portrait from a single sitting. It is striking. It is about as like the original as the small schoolboy's mural fresco in chalk of the master whom he loves the least—" the Reverent Mr. Juggins, he is a bewty."

We must go as disciples, and not as teachers. Jonathan will only amuse himself with the stranger who lectures him as though he were *in statu pupillari*. He will fool him to the top of his bent. He will seem to be profoundly impressed, to drink with

parched lips into his thirsty soul these showers of
blessings, and when he has exhausted such enjoyment as may be had from galloping donkeys, he will
despise and forget him. One of our demagogues
came to the States while I was there, and informed
the Americans that their Constitution was obsolete,
and ought to be discarded ; but though I remained
some time in the country after he had left it, I did
not hear that either the President or the people had
commenced any reconstruction.

CHAPTER II.

PROGRESSIVE.

THE Mersey is glittering in the midday splendour of the sun, and the *Majestic*—well-named, for she is every inch a queen—walks the waters like a thing of life as she steams out of Liverpool docks. She glides, she moves with a stately grace, like "a daughter of the gods, divinely fair, and most divinely tall," dancing a *minuet de la cour*. There are pale faces trying to smile, tremulous voices trying to cheer, hands waving snowy handkerchiefs which will never clasp each other again; but the motion of the ship, the breeze from the sea, and the surroundings of the shore refresh and exhilarate, and the apprehensive passenger gains confidence as he treads the deck in his new tweed suit, his fur-lined coat and cap, or reclines on his elongated chair with a guide-book or a novel in his hand, and a gay rug over his knees. How gratified he is to find, when the trumpet summons him to dine in the bright beautiful saloon, and he has adroitly inserted himself in his revolving chair, that he can thoroughly appreciate the excellent fare so artistically cooked and so attentively served. Yes, he will have a pint of Perrier Jouet, and then he begins to fancy, good, easy man full sure, that his greatness as a sailor is a-ripening, and that he must be a lineal descendant of those hardy Norsemen whose home was on the ocean wave. Alas—

> "Heaven from all creatures hides the book of fate,
> Except the page prescribed, the present date."

And no one disputes the veracity, however they may deplore the conduct, of the cruel hawk who prophesied, "when he heard the robin redbreast a-singing round the corner, that if he knowed who was a-coming, he would soon change his note."

Next morning, the sea, which seemed to be sleeping peacefully as an infant, awakes, as babies often do, to make itself most disagreeable. Its wavelets develop into billows, and that gentle breeze into a gale. The *Majestic* goes on her way bravely, as steady as ship can be, but you cannot travel over hills and valleys without ups and downs, and the enthusiastic passenger becomes painfully conscious that he has left the level road. He ceases to identify himself and to claim affinities with the hardy Norseman. There are no "notes of fatherhood," no traces of family likeness between that ancient mariner and himself, as, leaving the cabin, he clutches the balustrade of the stairs, reels to and fro on the deck, and finally stumbles, with a sudden lurch, upon a stout, elderly dame looking over the side of the ship as though he were a fond, affectionate son, who had just discovered his long-lost mother. He apologizes with a sickly simper, which is intended to announce that, though he has lost the control of his legs, he retains the command of his temper, and again pursues his devious course, as one who essays with his eyes closed to delineate the outlines of the cat or pig. Finally, he does the wisest act he can do under the circumstances, he betakes himself to the berth from whence he came, and resigns himself to the inevitable. With an expression of green and yellow melancholy he gazes on the closely packed life-preserving belts in the case over the end of his bed, and though these and the keel of the boat, which he sees through the round window of his cabin, are dismally suggestive of wreck, he feels helplessly, hopelessly indifferent.

Now he watches listlessly a pair of slippers and a shoe gliding from beneath the opposite berth, and then retiring with the roll of the vessel, like skirmishers, to be followed by the main army, in the form of a smooth portmanteau, which comes forth to assure him that it is "waranted solid leather," and then recedes, reminding him of a gentleman performing in the quadrille the *pas seul* always so hateful to the bashfulness and awkwardness of youth.

Then he hears with an angry disgust the loud and vulgar voices of his fellow-men pacing the deck outside, preposterously robust, offensively cheerful, smoking like limekilns while he shrinks from the whiff of cigarettes, voracious while the very thought of food distresses him—literally *usque ad nauseam*. He supposes that those boisterous, blustering snobs must be encased in oak and lined with metal, like the individual of whom Horace wrote, "*robur et æs triplex circa pectus erat;*" that they must possess the *dura messorum ilia*, of which the same poet speaks.

And then those execrable boys, prancing all over the ship, or playing their ridiculous quoits, instead of being well caned at school; and that stout little man, who is manifestly attempting something quite impossible "against time," and "goes thrashing round the deck like a short-tailed bull in fly-time."

Amid all these aggravations of his woe, the sad invalid lies supine, changed as Cæsar when that voice of his,

> "Which bade the Romans mark him,
> And write his speeches in their books,
> Alas, it cried, give me to drink Titinius,
> Like a sick girl."

But he can neither drink nor eat, and, powerless to retain the chicken-broth and other aliments kindly brought to him by the pitiful steward, he resembles the bath-room opposite his cabin, which, by an ingenious arrangement, announces itself on the bolt now as "occupied," and anon as "empty."

We were a representative crew. Two millionaires from Chicago, one of whom was said to "turn over" double the amount which goes through the same process of evolution at our Army and Navy Stores, and also to be the most beneficent of men. Others in business on a smaller scale, whose talk was of bi-metallism, free-trade, and ship canals. There were importers of corn and cattle; there were authors in search of new subjects, and artists in search of new scenes; there was a dramatic contingent of planetary stars; there were architects and engineers; there were comely widows, and compassionate, middle-aged men; there were young men and maidens, who admired the moon a little, and each other much.

We had a great variety of politicians, from the red-hot Tory to the howling Radical. The red-hot Tory declared that his heart was breaking, and that his existence was made intolerable—although no signs of premature decay were observable in his roseate face and hilarious demeanour by the howling Radical with his villainous crew of demagogues, dynamiters, and other assassins, incendiaries, teetotalers, vulpecides, wire-fences, and foreign meat. He dated the decline and fall of England from the introduction of the Ballot and the School Board, the substitution of retrievers for pointers, croquet for cricket, and cigarettes for cigars. The howling Radical announced himself as filled with joy—though he did not look it, being in countenance gloomy and in manner grim—as he foresaw the imminent abolition of crowns and creeds, armies and navies, nobility and gentry, sports and games. Neither was his behaviour quite consistent on the subject of the peerage. When my lord was absent he alluded to him as a birkie, a baboon, figure-head, hyæna, soap-bubble, stuffed peacock, etc.; but he seemed in his presence to be oppressed with a sudden awe, behaved as though he were in a place of worship, and was of all the company the most obsequious.

There was a funny man, with a comic and chronic grin on his countenance, who seemed always about to put his hands into his pockets, with "Here we are again," and, "How do yer don't?" A few members were present of the rowdy brigade, inclined to cards, coarse language, and perpetual pipes, but restrained from making themselves offensive by the higher tone of morality which pervaded the ship. They never opened a book save that in which they recorded their bets, and the subject of their conversation, so far as I was favoured with fragments, was always the race-horse and his rider, except when the daily mileage of the ship was made a topic for pecuniary speculation, for lotteries, and "sweeps." Asked somewhat impudently to take part in these proceedings by a principal promoter, I replied, "Sir, I do not want your money, and I will take care that you don't have mine." These were the only companions of our voyage who did in no wise add to its enjoyment, unless we include two loquacious ladies, who, with an utterance that was high and harsh, persisted in shouting to a deaf brother, when we were seated close by in the delightful library, and were desirous to read or to write, or to have "forty winks" in peace.

It was my privilege on the Sunday to say the prayers and to preach. The lesson was read by the captain as the Holy Scriptures should always be read—from the heart as well as from the lips, reverently, distinctly, the intonation varying in concord with the meaning of the words, and not restricted to a single note, as with some of our more feeble brethren. The purser acted as precentor, found us an excellent amateur organist, and led the congregation, which formed itself into a voluntary choir, the best of all choral associations, promoting unity of worship on earth, and rehearsing, as it were, "the sound of many voices" which will be heard in heaven. We had an offertory for the Seamen's Orphanages in Liverpool and New York, and our contributions, with those made two days afterwards from a miscellaneous entertainment, amounted to £50.

The latter performance was undoubtedly miscellaneous, inasmuch as an oration by the Very Reverend the Dean of Rochester, D.D., was followed by a song from a young *prima donna* of the music halls, entitled "Little Tottie's Half-crown Shoes;" and it was made entertaining by some good music and recitals, and especially by the delicious humour of the purser aforesaid, which, communicating itself without apparent change of feature to his countenance, fascinated at once with its subtle power, and prepared us for an enjoyment which never failed. Another performer pleased me much, although the joy was brief. He was announced to repeat the first speech of King Richard III., and, having approached and occupied with ostentatious and pompous deliberation a chair upon the platform, which represented his throne, he uttered the words, "Stand all apart," then rose, and, with undiminished dignity, returned to the audience, who received him first with amazement, and then with loud applause.

A startling incident occurred in our mid-voyage, and at midnight. One of our propellers came in sudden collision with some massive obstruction, and for a time the motion of the ship was irregular and spasmodic. It was said next morning that a vessel laden with huge blocks of mahogany had gone down in that locality, and that we had struck the derelict; but an elderly lady confidently affirmed that we had cut through a whale, because at the time of the concussion she could smell the oil! All who heard were politely derisive, but the statement notwithstanding was founded upon fact. The crew of a vessel following in our rear saw the great leviathan, with a terrible gash in his side, dying on the surface of the waves. The sceptic will jeer, as we did, and will repeat our brilliant observation, "Very like a whale," but the evidence has satisfied those who were the most incredulous before they heard it. It was a rare occurrence, a strange sight, to see this monster—*monstrum, horrendum, informe, ingens*—dying in a red sea, by his own blood incarnadined!

The floating derelict is, of course, a much more frequent and formidable cause of collision. A committee appointed by our Board of Trade on the subject has recently issued recommendations that upon arrival in British ports all incoming vessels shall report any derelict or ice passed on the voyage, and that the information thus obtained shall be published on a special form, a copy of which is to be promptly distributed every week, free of charge, to all mercantile marine officers and to masters of foreign-going ships. The committee does not propose to issue a monthly chart, such as is published in the United States, because they are of opinion that a map showing the position of wrecks reported some weeks previously can be of no possible utility, and may create needless apprehensions.

CHAPTER III.

ARRIVAL.

As we entered the harbour of New York, I thought of St. Luke's words in the Acts of the Apostles, "We came unto a place which is called the fair havens, nigh whereunto was the city of Lasea." It is indeed a fair haven, as picturesque to the eye of the tourist as it is complete in its depth, extent, and security for the exigencies of peaceful commerce or of naval war. Pleasant country homes, and, as we advance, huge cities, Brooklyn and New Jersey, appear to the right and left, and, dominating all, a statue of "Liberty Enlightening the World," one hundred and fifty feet in height, and two hundred and twenty tons in weight, rises from a small island about midway from the shores. This gigantic image was presented to the United States by the French Republic some ten years ago, in commemoration of the one hundredth anniversary of the Declaration of Independence. If one of the objects of this presentation was, as I am constrained to suspect, to depress the Britisher with a sense of awe and aversion, I frankly own that "our lively neighbour the Gaul" has achieved considerable success. It *is* awe-ful to the Englishman; it does make his heart sad, but not, as was intended, with the shameful memory of defeat—that wound has been healed long ago, and John Bull knows that he was well and wisely beaten—but with a dread and dislike of its ugliness, and of its cumbrous incongruity with the scene around. I was informed that by ascending the spiral staircase, which was formed in the granite pedestal and in the skirt of the goddess (if I may be allowed the expression), I could obtain a beautiful view from the head of the figure, which was capable of accommodating forty persons, but I pleaded my age and size and weight, and that I was more than satisfied with that which I had already seen.

I remembered a delightful engraving in *Punch*, which represented the ghost of Napoleon Buonaparte contemplating the equestrian statue of Wellington—not a thing of beauty, then recently erected at the entrance of Hyde Park—and saying, "After forty years I am avenged." So might the spectre of some vanquished hero of the Revolution stand before this cumbrous erection, which doth bestride its narrow world like a Colossus, and say, "I am comforted by this caricature of Liberty, and by its independence of all good taste in Art."

We had a disagreeable incident at the Custom House, which may serve as a caution to others. A young lady of our party had kindly undertaken to

convey two trunks containing clothes and other gifts
to the relations of another lady, who sent them, one
locked, without a key, the other with a key but with
a broken lock, which could no longer be opened.
After much perplexity and delay, the revenue officer,
relying upon the assurance that the garments had
been worn, and that there was nothing in the boxes
prohibited or liable to duty, allowed his benevolence
to overpower his discretion, and his strict obedience
to the laws of his service, and marked them as
examined and passed. A "detective" was watching,
and not only insisted on forcing the locks and
searching among the articles, which, of course, were
found to have been correctly described, but immediately reported the misdemeanour. Shortly afterwards the officer, an intelligent man, with attractive
manners, came to tell me, with a quiet, brave sub-
mission which commanded all my sympathy, that he
had been dismissed. I wrote to the authorities a
simple statement of the facts, and pleaded as earnestly
as my head and my heart could dictate for his
restoration. I do not know whether my intercession
had any influence, but I am sure that their ultimate
decision was wise and kind and just. They were
bound to punish, they had no desire to be cruel.
They fined the offender heavily—I think the amount
was one hundred and twenty-five dollars—and, after
a brief suspension, restored him to his place. He
appeared to be much more gratified by the results
than I was, when, on my return to England, I was

D

informed of a report, by one who had heard it gravely
announced as a fact, that the Dean of Rochester had
been fined fifty pounds by the revenue officers at
New York on their discovery of chemicals used in
photography, after his solemn declaration that he had
no excisable articles in his possession. Well, it is a
merciful provision that though for a time men will
lie with such volubility that you would think Truth
was a fool, they soon run themselves out of breath,
and the adversary whom they had despised and left
behind awhile, sound in wind and limb, well trained,
and in good condition, passes them in an easy canter,
and, in sporting parlance, "romps in."

Major Pond, whose vocation is to make arrangements for those who propose to give lectures in the
States, and who is not only the most successful
expert in his business, but a genial companion and
trusty friend, met me on landing, and informed me
that a conclave of journalists were waiting to interview me at his office. I may say here that before
I left America I was visited by more than two
hundred reporters, and found them, almost without
exception, clever and well-informed, pleasant in
manner, and accurate in their records. The majority
took no notes, and yet repeated almost verbatim a
long conversation. A few came at inconvenient hours
—when I was making myself a C.B. in the morning,
or arriving late at night in my hotel. One young
gentleman I found calmly seated in the drawing-
room of a friend with whom I went to dine. Several

met me at the railway stations, and some came into the train. The latter brought to mind the story of the Baptist minister who, having missed Dean Stanley at the station, wrote to express his disappointment, and "his hope to meet him on the Resurrection Morn, where there would doubtless be a much better opportunity for conversation than they could have had in the cars." Occasionally their queries are somewhat too crowded or abstruse for immediate and complete solution. A clergyman of high position in New York told me that he was visited by a pressman, and consented to see him upon the assurance that he would not detain him for more than one minute. "I only wish to ask"—he said, on admission to the clerical study—"why you belong to the Episcopal Church? What is your opinion of the Old Testament characters compared with those of the New? Whether you expect to meet your friends in a future state of existence, and, if so, on what foundations you have formed this expectation?"

At the same time their thirst for information seems to be quickly satisfied. The spirit of inquiry is not disheartened by reticence, nor offended by brief, evasive, or incongruous replies, if they are made in good humour. For example, when, on my first introduction to these ready writers and speakers, I was asked, "Are you a Home Ruler?" and I made answer, "So far as my wife permits," I evoked no protest of displeasure. The married men tittered their sympathies, and the bachelors laughed loud their scorn.

As we entered our apartments in the hotel, we were gladdened by graceful gifts and genial words of welcome. Boxes of beautiful flowers—roses, carnations, chrysanthemums, violets—came to us, not only in New York, but in all the great cities of the States. I knew, from fifty years' of happy experience, that in my own country there was no sympathy more sure and generous than that of the true florist—the man who loves flowers not because they are ornamental to his grounds, his rooms, or his coat; not because his specimens are so rare and costly—he "really would be ashamed to tell you what he gave for that orchid," and is bitterly disappointed when you don't seem to care—but who loves them because they are beautiful. No vocation so honourable, no apron so old, no brotherhood so gentle and true as that of the "grand old gardener."

On the table with these bouquets were letters announcing honorary membership in several New York clubs, invitations to dinners and receptions, offers of private boxes and stalls, and a pack of visitors' cards.

The hotels in New York and in the larger cities are very superior, excepting the small cluster of splendid inns which have been recently built in London, and their provincial satellites, to our own—on a larger scale, and of a more costly material, marble being largely used, and the charming varieties of American wood elaborately carved. They have, generally, large halls, in which men do mostly congregate to talk, read the papers, and smoke; spacious drawing, reading, and dining rooms, with electric light.

In many of these hotels the waiters are negroes, and upon a first introduction one almost expects a walk-round or a break-down, to hear a conundrum from "Bones," or an exhortation from the head waiter to his troupe, "Sing, darkies, sing." A black thumb on a white plate is but a brief surprise, and its proprietor is attentive and prompt, with a marvellous memory of every order given. He is cleanly and honest, in no instance suggesting the similarity which has been traced between him and Shakespeare's soft south wind, as "stealing and giving odour." The food which they bring is excellent in quality, abundant in variety, and well cooked. The Britisher does not at once understand the glass goblet of water and ice, which Mark Twain affirms to be the only distinct Americanism, and which invariably accompanies his breakfast, luncheon, and dinner; but the drier climate and the warmer rooms not only expel his aversion, but tempt him to excess.

The Americans begin their first meal with some refreshing fruit, such as the delicious grape fruit or shaddock from Florida, oranges, apples, bananas, peaches, melons, etc., and I quite believe in the opinion expressed to me by one of their clever physicians that this wholesome habit was a powerful antidote to gout. The bread, white, from the finest wheat flour, or brown, "Graham bread," from the meal unrefined, the cakes, and the pastry are all of the best quality. I counted some thirty preparations of corn—that is, maize—and of wheat, including hominy, a most agreeable food.

The beef, corn-fed, is as good as our own; the mutton, which rarely appears on the *menu*, quite inferior. The fish is not so good as on our side the Atlantic, though there are some very palatable varieties, *e.g.* of blue bass, and there is a great admiration of our English soles among those Americans who have crossed the sea. They have a fish which they call "the lake lawyer," from his ferocious looks and voracious appetite, even as on the coast of New Jersey they have a bird which they describe as "the barrister," from the enormous length of his bill. Oysters are good, plentiful, and cheap, and from a tiny crab found therein, in shape no bigger than an agate stone on the forefinger of an alderman, hitherto thrown away as unedible, the *chef* now makes for the epicure an expensive soup. The sturgeon known as "Albany beef" is excellent.

Other delicacies are prairie birds (the American grouse), quail, "ragout of antelope," venison (not to be compared with our park-fed fallow deer), the canvas-back duck, and terrapin. The canvas-back duck inhabits the Chesapeake Bay and the contiguous streams, feeding upon the wild celery which grows upon their banks, and by its delicate flavour acquiring that high regard, of which the author of "A Pictorial Picture of America" was inspired to sing—

> "That all the folks who love good eating,
> And think of little else but treating,
> With pleasure oft their lips will smack
> When speaking of a canvas-back."

The terrapin is a species of small turtle, or tortoise. It is said to be common in Connecticut, and in the Atlantic States south of New York, but the demand makes it a rare and costly dish. "It is found," as I read in "Bartlett's Dictionary," "exclusively in the salt water, and always in the neighbourhood of marshes. The most celebrated is the *diamond-back*; there are also *yellow-bellies*, *red-bellies*, *loger-heads*, and *snuff-boxes*." I do not know to which denomination the specimens belonged which were presented to me in pretty little vessels of embossed silver, expressly made for their reception, but I liked none of them, and I endorsed the verdict of an illustrious visitor from Rome, though I condemned the ungrateful rudeness of his words, when, in speaking of this viand to a friend, he said, "They are always giving me *that disgoostin' hash*."

One, to me insoluble, mystery I must mention ere I leave the *table d'hôte* of the hotel, in the hope that some kind philosopher may suggest a cause—the fact that the sharpest people use the dullest knives in the world. Babies and lunatics might be safely allowed to play with them.

Passing from solids to fluids, a stranger, who made his conclusions from the customs of the *salle à manger* in the hotels and restaurants, might infer that Jonathan had changed his name into Jonadab, and that he had been brought up, as Mr. Richard Swiveller said, with a tone of sad compassion, of the Marchioness, "in ignorance of the taste of beer;" but the illusion is dispelled by the first dinner-party in private, where he finds, as in his own country, the wine that gladdeneth the heart of man, and by the numerous saloons and bars, of which it was said by the only comic teetotaller I ever met, "There the wild asses quench their thirst."

In no country have nobler efforts been made to diminish the temptations, to prevent the shame and the misery, of a vice which stupefies the head, petrifies the heart, cripples the limbs, and disfigures the face of the vicious; but common sense, at the same time, has never failed to see that which zeal has hid from the eyes of the enthusiast,—not only that alchohol has its use and abuse, but that the latter will never be suppressed by prohibition, parliament, or pledge. Constraint exasperates, evokes opposition, and suggests defiance or deceit. Brandy is served in teapots. "You'll find a little tap under your dressing-table, Major, which will put you into communication with 'the old Rye,' and you can take what you please for yourself and your friends, for there is a meter on the other side of the wall." The child is father to the man, and the schoolboy who enjoyed his clandestine pipe has been known in his manhood to fill his flask with whisky before he entered the watery waste of prohibition, and to find a strange, revengeful relish in its surreptitious joy.

Smugglers, driven from the seas, have reappeared in the cities, and eggs, which have been sucked and filled with ardent spirits through a tiny aperture cleverly concealed, were at one time largely imported into the State of Maine, and met with a ready sale.

Of course the law must punish those who transgress it, but it must not condemn the guiltless, nor uproot the wheat with the weeds. It might, in my opinion, deal far more severely with the "drunk and disorderly," and with those who make them so, but it must not prohibit temperance. It must not classify a Christian virtue among the sins of the flesh, as those fanatical bigots who say that the moderate drinker is the best friend of the drunkard. It must not persecute those who, as Milton bade—

> "Observe
> The rule of not too much; by temperance taught,
> In what they eat and drink, seeking from thence
> Due nourishment, not gluttonous delight."

The punishment, I repeat, might justly be more formidable. The daily reports from our police-courts prove that the five-shilling fine is not a terror to the evildoers, and suggest that a whipping, or a week in gaol, might be more efficacious: but no penal, no human laws will abolish drunkenness. They may help, but they can never originate or sustain that self-respect and self-command which are taught by the religion of Christ, communicated by the Holy Spirit, and strengthened, through our prayers and the means of grace, by Him, who alone can order the unruly wills and affections of sinful men.

CHAPTER IV.

NEW YORK.

THE ears and the eyes of the stranger, as he leaves his hotel for a first inspection of the city, are astonished and bewildered by the sounds and sights of eager and incessant work. The roar of London seems to him as a faint murmur compared with the thunder of New York, and Oxford Street and Regent Street and the Strand and Fleet Street as by-ways and country lanes in contrast with its main thoroughfares.

If any man would realize Keble's "loud stunning tide of human care," or Whittier's city, "ever swinging its ponderous iron flail," let me advise him to secure an apartment on the ground or second floor of a house in Sixth Avenue. An elevated railway runs through the centre of this lively spot, with trains passing and repassing at brief intervals, with bells clanging and engines puffing and screaming. Below, on either side, there is not only a tramway for the cable cars, but outside of these a road for carriages drawn by horses. The "side-walks" are generally crowded by pedestrians, so that if the lodger will open wide his parlour window, and look out, he will be in a position to know what business means. Should these surroundings become at all irksome—to timid people from quiet habitations they have suggested softening of the brain—he can at once diversify his experience, and add to his information, by entering and occupying, say for half an hour, one of the tram-cars or omnibuses which go by his door.

The proprietors and conductors of these vehicles are men of such large benevolence, and so anxious to promote the closest fellow-feeling among their neighbours, that they welcome all who desire to travel with them. It is a New York proverbial saying that "there's always room for one on a Broadway car." The result is that not only the sides but the centre of the conveyances are crowded, chiefly with men, who almost invariably surrender the seats to the ladies, and who jolt against each other with polite grins whenever there is a sudden stop.* Believers

* Sometimes the results are more serious, as recorded in the following extract from an American daily paper:—

"FAINTS WHILE HE HOLDS THE STRAP!
"AGED MAN PAYS FARE ON A STREET CAR, BUT IS GIVEN NO SEAT!

"S. D. Hinman is little more than 80 years old. That fact however, does not entitle him to a seat when he pays a fare on a Cottage Grove Avenue car. At six o'clock last night he clung to a strap and gasped for breathing room from Madison Street to Twenty-second, and then fainted. He was wedged in the mass of humanity so tightly that he could not fall. A considerate conductor stopped the car, and Mr. Hinman was carried into a drug store, where he soon revived, and walked to his home at No. 2336, Michigan Avenue."

in the ancestral ape may readily imagine, as they hold on by the leathern straps suspended from the roof for their support, that they have reverted to type, and are chattering once more among their brother-monkeys, as they cling to the branches of primeval trees. I ventured to remark to an American friend that we had tried this system, this truck system, with our cattle upon the rail, and with a complete success, but that it did not seem to commend itself as a method of locomotion to my brother-men. Mr. Starey, a famous coachbuilder at Nottingham, took for his motto, "Stare super antiquas vias," but his customers were always seated. My friend made no answer, but I saw from the expression of his countenance that he did not think much of "my brother-men."

Everywhere there is the throng of busy life. I remember that when I went in my boyhood with our gamekeeper, whom I revered as being, next to my father and our clergyman, the most honourable and important of living men, to fetch for the young pheasants which he was rearing their favourite food, the eggs of the ants, and we came to the edifice which they (the ants) had reared, and he thrust in his cruel spade,—I remember how the hillock swarmed with myriads of these tiny insects, hurrying to and fro. I thought of them as I watched the rush and concourse of this larger life, and thought also of Donne's simile—

> "Methinks all cities now but ant-hills are,
>   Where, when the several labourers I see
>   For children, house, provisions, taking pains,
>   They're all but ants, carrying eggs, straw, and grain."

It is this manifestation of industry—*semper ubique et ab omnibus*—this nobility of labour, which commands an intense admiration of New York as a city of working men. As a thing of beauty, a panorama picturesque to the eye, it cannot be compared with London or Paris, Edinburgh or Oxford; but there is a grander design than architect ever drew, a fairer sight than cloud-capped towers and gorgeous palaces—man going forth to his work and to his labour until the evening, in obedience to the immutable law of his Maker, "In the sweat of thy face shalt thou eat bread."

Of course the pessimist and the cynic, who, true to his name, grins like a dog and runs about the city snarling and biting when he dare, will say, "It's only a race and scramble for money, it's only the worship of the almighty dollar;" but the accuser of the brethren is also the father of lies. Thousands of these workers are earning their daily bread, providing for their own house. And what is life but a race and a struggle? Are we not bidden so to run that we may obtain, so to fight not as one that beateth the air, to strive for the mastery, to contend earnestly? The idle men are the cowards and deserters, the children of Ephraim, who, being harnessed, and carrying bows, turn themselves back in the day of battle. It is the sluggard of whom Solomon spake as ever sighing, "Yet a little sleep, a little slumber, a little folding of the hands to sleep. So shall thy poverty come as one that travelleth, and thy want as an armed man." And what divine injunction is there forbidding men to make money? On the contrary, he was commended by the Master who had gained by trading, and he was condemned who had not only made no effort to improve his property, but would not even put his talent in the bank. It is not the possession but the abuse of wealth which is denounced. Dives was tormented, not because he wore purple and fine linen, but because he never clothed the naked.

> "I dressed, as the nobles dress,
>   In cloth of silver and gold,
> Silk and satin, and costly furs,
>   In many an ample fold;
> But I never remembered the naked limbs,
>   That freeze with winter's cold."

He suffered, not because he fared sumptuously every day, but because he never fed the hungry.

> "I drank the richest draughts,
>   And ate whatever was good;
> Fish and flesh and fowl and fruit
>   Supplied my hungry mood;
> But I never remembered the wretched ones
>   That starve for want of food."

No man is more beloved than the American or English millionaire who is rich in good works, ready to distribute, willing to communicate; he has the blessing of him who was ready to perish, and he causes the widow's heart to sing for joy; he has dispersed abroad and given to the poor, and his righteousness remaineth for ever. Endeavouring to promote the spiritual and temporal welfare of his fellow-men, he not only exalts their hopes and relieves their necessities, but he confirms their faith in our Christian brotherhood, teaches them by example to be tender-hearted, and so does more for the unity and happiness of his nation than all the scribes and disputers, who make paper programmes and grandiloquent promises of universal prosperity and peace.

No one is more despised than the American or English millionaire whose Bible is his banker's book, to whom worship is a bore, sorrow a nuisance, and poverty a crime. He is marvellously shrewd, never outwitted (my friend Nye, of whom more anon, refers to a report that a burglar once broke into the house of Jay Gould and was robbed of his tools before the police could be summoned), but he is contemptible. He who might do the most good does the most harm to the community. He is a monopolist and a Juggernaut who will crush all that comes in his way. He will persecute all competitors—undersell and ruin them if he can. Several thoughtful men of business with whom it was my privilege to converse while I was in the States denounced these sordid churls as enemies to progress, and as the objects of a bitter indignation, which might have disastrous issues.

I recall a charming picture of two street boys. The larger boy is eating an apple, the smaller boy asks for a bite. The reply, " Shan't," is followed by a further supplication, " Then please give us the core ; " but all hope is extinguished by the prompt announcement, " *There ain't going to be no core.*" But retribution will come sooner or later : the core will choke him.

I have a few more words to say about money, because I have heard some of my compatriots affirm of the Americans that their one object of reverence was an idol of gold, and that, after the manner of the Ephesians, they fell down and worshipped at silver shrines. Beyond the fact, which I am bound to admit, having visited the chief marts of commerce in both countries, boards of trade in America and exchanges in England, that Jonathan makes more noise than John over his business—" gives tongue " more freely, as a huntsman would say, in his chase— I see no difference between the nations in their high estimate of the precious metals, or in their methods of appropriation.

Alike on either side of the Atlantic, the prophecy of the wise man is daily fulfilled : " He that maketh haste to be rich shall not be innocent." I am inclined to think that, in proportion to our numbers, we have a majority of knaves and rogues in England, because we have more dupes and fools—more foxes because we have more geese. I do not mean that we are less honest, but we have more young men who,

E

inheriting instead of earning money, do not know its value, and, according to the adage, are soon persuaded to transfer it.

Again, I have heard it said that the American only values his possessions according to the price which he has paid for them, and that he will give an extravagant sum not for the beauty but for the rarity of his purchase. The infirmity exists. I have positive proof. A rich gentleman in New York was a collector of valuable tapestry, carpets, and rugs. A friend, inspecting, noticed on one of these textile fabrics a conspicuous white card, and, as he stooped to read the writing upon it—"$1000"—the proprietor expressed his angry surprise that it had been overlooked, and he unfastened and removed it. The visitor was suspicious, and when he related the incident, a few weeks after his visit, he was not unprepared for the loud laughter which it evoked from his companion, who at once exclaimed, "I was with him yesterday, the ticket was again conspicuous, and was banished with the same expostulation!"

Have we no small manœuvres of this sort in England? And do they not pale their ineffectual fire, as the glow-worm when the sun is up, before our undisguised manifestations, private and public, in proof of a general belief that "the worth of everything is just as much as it will bring?" In May last I attended a magnificent exhibition of plants and flowers in the Temple Gardens. The great attraction was a cypripedium, not because it was the most beautiful

specimen in the show, for there were lælias and
cattleyas lovelier far, and the queen of all flowers,
the rose, but because the owner had been offered
eight hundred guineas for his orchid.

As to the proportion in either country of those
who admire that which is admirable in nature and
in art for its own sake, I see no difference. In both
we have men of culture and refinement coming home
from dusty lane and wrangling mart to books by the
best authors, pictures by the best painters, to sweet
music, intellectual discourse. From both, especially
from America, we have intelligent persons going
forth to gaze upon the wonders of the world. Some,
it is true, from mere curiosity, and not so much for
the sake of seeing as in order to say that they have
seen. We have heard of tourists "knocking off St.
Peter's and doing the Vatican" before lunch; and I
remember that I displeased an elderly spinster at
Cadenabbia, who informed me that she was occupied
in doing Europe, and asked me how long it would
take to do London, when I replied that an observant
mind might be able to form some adequate conception of the past history and the present affairs of our
metropolis in two or three diligent years.

Although New York has no Westminster Abbey,
St. Paul's, British Museum, Houses of Parliament,
or Buckingham Palace, it has an abundance of handsome and spacious buildings, official, commercial, and
educational—city halls, exchanges, colleges, hospitals,
museums, institutes, clubs, and theatres. Some of

these edifices, such as that of the American Tract Society, are three hundred feet in height, and have more than twenty stories. The Hotel New Netherlands has seventeen stories, and is two hundred and ninety feet high. The Waldorf Hotel has eleven stories, and a height of one hundred and eighty-two feet.*

Our shops are no more to be compared with New York stores than hawks with eagles. "As well you might compare," I heard the principal of my college, Dr. Gilbert, afterwards Bishop of Chichester, say in a sermon, "the solid masonry of University with the meretricious architecture of Queens!"

There is one establishment in Broadway which seems to cover more ground than our Army and Navy Stores, and the capital employed in the latter emporium is said to be only half the amount which is "turned over" by Mr. Marshal Field, of Chicago.

I was delighted with the offices of the *Century Magazine*, with its large, bright, cheerful rooms, story upon story, so commodiously furnished with comfortable chairs, spacious tables, and ample apparatus for the writer that it seemed as though one might sit down, and that the hand would spontaneously "make copy" without study or strain of thought. The president, Mr. Scott, and the chief editor, Mr. Gilder, received me with the kindest courtesy, and showed me the most interesting collection of original

* The position of New York upon an island demands this economy of space.

pictures, drawings, and photographs which have been used as illustrations. Of these there is a selection circulated, through the kindness of the proprietors, in different parts of the States for the instruction of young artists. The *Century Magazine* makes at the present time a monthly sale of one hundred and seventy-five thousand copies, and has reached two hundred and fifty thousand.

On the other side of Union Square is "Tiffany's," the famous depôt for precious stones, bijouterie, and silver work. Here, too, I had a kindly welcome, and saw the venerable head of the house, in his eighty-third year, and, in the penetralia, such costly treasures as a necklace of diamonds of different tints, and another of pearls, each valued at £20,000, a yellow diamond at the same figure, and two black pearls £2000. There is some exquisite china, and a most interesting collection of armour, English, German and Italian, with crossbows, matchlocks, halberds, spears, swords and shields.

At Scribner's there is a grand book-room recently built, and here—again admitted into the treasury department—I saw yet more precious things, which cannot be gotten for gold, neither shall silver be weighed for the price thereof, which cannot be valued with the gold of Ophir, with the onyx, nor the sapphire; no mention shall be made of corals or of pearls, for the price of wisdom is above rubies. Here I was shown the original edition of Herrick's "Hesperides," 1648, the first edition of Butler's

"Hudibras," 1663, and fourth, 1678; the first edition of the "Vicar of Wakefield," which Johnson took to the publisher and sold for £10, when the author dared not leave his lodgings for fear of arrest; Hawthorne's first book, "Fanshawe," suppressed by the writer; Charles Lamb's manuscript of "Cupid's Revenge," published in *Harper's Monthly*, 1858, and Charles Dickens's copy of the first edition of Thackeray's "History of Samuel Titmarsh."

Of all the stores in New York, the one which seems to have a supreme fascination—though it is small in comparison, and much resembles an English shop—is conducted by Mr. Huyler on Broadway, for the sale of candies and chocolates and other confections which the Turks describe as "delights for the throat." I have never seen such a concourse of purchasers, making their exits and their entrances continuously, as there at Christmas-time. They are chiefly young ladies and children, but there comes forth at intervals a young man with a bashful countenance, under an apprehension that every one suspects the design of his purchase, and that the public survey with a derisive gaze the parcel which he carries—"sweets to the sweet"—unto his lady-love. I fear that the American maidens, and not a few of the American matrons, love these candies, peppermints, and gums "not wisely but too well;" that that excessive enjoyment is injurious to health and complexion; and that the most accomplished dentists in the world owe their success to their experience, and their experience very largely to the premature decay which issues from an intemperate fondness for "goodies."

But who, with a clear conscience shall pronounce sentence of condemnation? Who passes the pretty *bonbonnière* without making an extract? Who does not take home with affectionate care the beautiful box of preserved fruits which, after certain City dinner-feasts, is presented by the generous hosts to speed the parting guest, prizing the generous gift, not for its own sake only, but because he knows that its mediatorial presence will at once suppress any conjugal remonstrance concerning the lateness of the hour.

I pity the man who has no happy memories of a time when he stirred with perspiring zeal a delicious bubbling compound of sugar, butter, and treacle, tasting (always prematurely, that he might have an excuse for tasting) its progress towards completion by dropping small portions into cold water, "to see whether it would set."

When I told Charles Dickens that as a schoolboy I had devoted half my income, which amounted to sixpence a week, to the purchase of the monthly number of "Pickwick"—and this in defiance of a wily confectioner, who always presented himself with a basketful of temptations in our hour of emolument—the great author was pleased to say that this small incident was a greater compliment than most of the infinite and elaborate eulogies which had been written and spoken in his praise. It was, at all events, a victory of mind over matter, of literature *versus* lollipops, and suggests the possibility of more books and fewer *bonbons* to those of my younger brethren who are passing through the ordeal of choice. They are not incompatible, and Horace assures us that he wins all points who blends the useful with the sweet.

Happy and instructive hours may be spent in the American Museum of Natural History and in the Metropolitan Museum of Art. Indeed, I could have enjoyed days in one department of the former—the charming and complete collection of North American woods given by a citizen, Mr. Jesup. The number of the exhibits, five hundred and twelve varieties of wood, and the artistic mode of exhibition, gave me a thrill of joyful surprise, and Solomon himself, who spake of trees, from the cedar tree which is in Lebanon even unto the hyssop which springeth out of the wall, would have gazed in an astonishment of delight. Every variety of tree, deciduous or coniferous, which I had seen or heard of, and many of which I had never sight or hearing, were here. Ash, beech, birch, catalpa, chestnut, cedar, dogwood, ebony, elder, elm, fir, larch, magnolia, mahogany, oak, pines, poplar, walnut, willow. One of the most beautiful examples was a polished piece of lignum-vitæ; and thereby hangs a tale. A country clergyman gave an order to the village carpenter, a skilful workman, but no scholar, for a set of bowls, and when they were completed they were sent home with the claim following: "The ravent master Jones to John Smith, A compleat set of lignum vitey bowels, 14s. 6d." About four feet was shown of each specimen, cut from the trunk in its full maturity. This was sawn at the top through the centre for a foot in depth, and, when half of this was removed by a transverse cut, the remainder was left partly in a natural and partly in a polished state. These have been arranged by the man of all best qualified for the work, Professor Sargent, of Brooklyn, and are accompanied with brief but adequate information as to species, habitat, habit, etc. There is a section of Sequoia Sempervirens, known more commonly in England as the Wellingtonia, having a circumference of ninety feet at the ground, measuring three hundred and fifty feet in height, and calculated to contain four hundred thousand feet of timber. Adjoining these specimens we find portfolios on stands containing Mrs. Sargent's exquisite pictures of trees, etc., and some excellent photographs here and there of trees remarkable for their beauty, size, or rarity.

Geology, entomology, ornithology, and archæology are profusely illustrated. The collection of stuffed birds, though it is inferior to that of our museum at Kensington, is extensive and well set up. The ostriches, with their large ball of feathers, and their long thin legs beneath, always remind me of tall children with their frocks tucked up around their waist for a paddle in the shallow sea.

In the Metropolitan Museum of Art there are many rare and some unique specimens of ancient and modern art, Egyptian, Assyrian, Greek, Roman, English and American. The first and the last, Old Egypt and New York, were presented to view in a most striking contrast by a lovely young damsel bending over a shrivelled, colourless mummy, and wearing the last sweet thing in bonnets! There was some beautiful sculpture, of which I only remember Story's "Semiramis," Farran's "Death of President Lincoln," and Benzoni's "Flight into Egypt." Armour and arms, rare treasures in pottery, laces, and glass; and a most extensive and interesting collection of musical instruments, beginning with rude specimens made from sticks and stones and skins, and displaying the intermediate improvements up to the elaborate and ornate piano of our own times.

I lingered so long in admiration before Rosa Bonheur's magnificent picture, "The Horse Fair," purchased by Mr. Cornelius Vanderbilt, for £10,000, and presented by him to the nation, that I had not time thoroughly to enjoy the Old Masters—(to tell the truth, I never thoroughly enjoy them—they always impress me, after a brief interview, with an irresistible desire to sit down, or to partake of refreshment)—and only stayed to examine in the Memorial Room a most interesting collection of engraved portraits, some fifty in number, of General Washington.

I visited the law courts under the courteous

auspices of one of the judges. To an ignoramus, the proceedings and arrangement appeared to be very similar to our own—courts with and without juries, courts of probate, court of common pleas, recalling Hood's irreverent lines—

> "Good Judges in the law are they
> Of champagne, claret, and tokay,
> And when their lordships deign to joke,
> And banish Littleton and Coke,
> They order that the best old port
> Shall henceforth be the rule of Court,
> That care shall be the fate of asses,
> Their only circuit be of glasses;
> So, happy on such terms as these,
> They seem a Court of Common Pleas."

There may be many differences, but two only came within my observation. There is no distinction, as with us, between barristers and solicitors; a lawyer can combine and conduct all the operations which in England are divided between the barrister and the attorney; and there are no wigs nor gowns. I did not miss the former so much as I anticipated, because most of the judicial and other forensic heads had the intellectual expression which usually accompanies brains, and does not require accessions; but I retain my faith in these becoming indications of authority and insignia of office, as conducive to dignity, order, and respect. "Some men," it is well said, "have native dignity, which will procure them more regard by a look than others can obtain by the most imperious command;" and these others, exceptions to the rule which I have mentioned, that the mind illustrates the countenance, may wisely call upon Art for such assistance, withheld by Nature, as it is in her power to give.

I was transferred by one judge to another, equally courteous and communicative, that I might see the police courts, over which the latter had authority, and in which one hundred cases are sometimes tried in a day, and also the prison known as "The Tombs," somewhat resembling the catacombs at Rome in their narrow passages and gloom. It was a horrible sadness to walk in "Murderers' Row," reading upon the wall the long list of prisoners on trial for homicide, some of the names having the awful words written in red ink against them, "Sentenced to execution." These miserable men are taken to the State prison at Sing Sing, and are there put to death by electricity. I could obtain no information as to the process, and I could but infer from this reticence that it was not altogether satisfactory.

It seems to be now the universal conviction that it was wise to discontinue public executions, but I remember to have heard from one, who had seen more deaths upon the scaffold, before a concourse of spectators, than any other man—the Rev. Mr. Davis, who was chaplain at Newgate for more than twenty years—that in his opinion the transfer of these terrible scenes from the outside to the inside of the prison withdrew from the community a very powerful influence for good. He said that while public executions produced many deplorable examples of human depravity, brought together a host of reprobates, having their conscience seared with a hot iron, who neither feared God nor regarded man, so that you heard on all sides the blasphemy of the multitude, the curses and yells of drunken men, and the idiotic laugh of the harlot; though there might be seen the disgusting spectacle of persons calling themselves noblemen and gentlemen, paying ten guineas for a window to glut a morbid curiosity and a craving for excitement—yet, when the crisis came, and the cap was drawn over the white, quivering face, and as the drop fell and the living man was changed into a corpse, swaying to and fro, there was a silent awe upon all, and even when there was no pity, the terror of death and "the fear of something after death" seemed to warn the vilest, "Be sure your sin will find you out," and "What will ye do in the end thereof?"

In the ward set apart for the young prisoners I was sorely grieved to see many who were mere lads, evidently ashamed and distressed by their degradation. As I anticipated, they had been led into debt by habits of extravagance, by corrupt women, and, after a vain endeavour to extricate themselves by gambling and betting, had been finally tempted to steal from their employers. When shall we see a sadder sight than this young life maimed and marred—the athlete, who started so strong and hopeful, down and stunned at the outset of the race. On some of their faces there was a wistful look, which seemed to say, Will no one give us a kind word—who will show us any good? and I longed to sit down with those lonely lads, to talk to them of better and brighter days, and of the Love which never fails.

Two sisters of mercy were conversing with the prisoners. Access is freely given to all who earnestly desire to help them; reformatories are open to receive them when they leave the prison; so that we have a good hope when we pray "Let the sorrowful sighing of the prisoners come before Thee, and preserve Thou them that are appointed to die."

Outside the prison I was shown, near the top of the high wall, a piece of recent masonry under one of the windows. The inmate of the cell within had secreted some instrument by which he had displaced and removed the stones, got through the aperture, let himself down by his bedclothes, which he had tied together and fastened to the window-bar, so as to reach a long waterspout, and, descending, finally succeeded in making his escape. It would indicate a laxity of moral principles to express a sense of satisfaction on hearing that the fugitive had not been found. It would not be kind towards those who lived in the neighbourhood of a lunatic asylum or a zoological garden to enlarge with admiration on the subtlety which had let loose a madman or a wild beast in their midst, but who does not feel a brief thrill of sympathy with such adroit and dauntless enterprise? Then comes the sad regret that such power should be perverted, and a blessing turned into a curse.

Here I may appropriately refer to the subject of "lynch law," and may enlighten the ignorance of some of my fellow-countrymen who think—as I thought before my visit to the States—that this method of summary punishment without judge, jury, or trial, is all but obsolete. Lynch law takes its name from Colonel Lynch, an officer of the American Revolution, who, living in a district in Campbell County which was infested by a number of reckless ruffians, robbers, and cut-throats, had some of their leaders apprehended and executed without the tedious and expensive interference of legal proceedings.

Of course, no rational man defends this process as a principle, but there are cases of brutal cruelty—of outrage upon women and children in districts where it is difficult to obtain immediate arrest—in which unanimous indignation could not, and cannot, be restrained from punishing the offender with death. This lynch law, however shocking it may appear to Europeans and New Englanders, is far removed from arbitrary violence. According to the testimony of careful observers, it is not often abused, and its proceedings are generally conducted with some regularity of form as well as fairness of spirit. What are the circumstances? Those highly technical rules of judicial procedure, and still more technical rules of evidence, which America owes to the English

Common Law, and which have in some States retained antiquated minutiæ, now expunged from English practice, or been rendered by new legislation too favourable to prisoners, have to be applied to districts where population is thin, where there are very few officers, either for the apprehension of offenders or for the hunting up of evidence against them, and where, according to common belief, both judges and juries are occasionally " squared " or " got at." Many crimes would go unpunished if some more speedy and efficient method of dealing with them were not adopted. This method is found in a volunteer jury summoned by the principal local citizens, or, in very clear cases, by a simple seizure and execution of the criminal.

It may be asked, "Why not create an efficient police?" Because crime is so uncommon in many districts—in such districts, for instance, as Michigan or rural Wisconsin—and the people have deliberately concluded that it is cheaper and simpler to take the law into their own hands on those rare occasions when a police is needed than to be at the trouble of organizing and paying a force for which there is usually no employment. If it be urged that they are thus forming habits of lawlessness in themselves, the Americans reply that experience does not seem to make this probable, because lawlessness does not increase among the farming population, and has disappeared from places where the rudeness or simplicity of society formerly rendered lynch law necessary.

Cases, however, occur in which no such excuse can be offered—cases in which a prisoner (probably a negro) already in the hands of justice is seized and put to death by the mob.*

However this may be, the Americans in this matter, as in all others, are perfectly competent to boss their own show, and to paddle their own canoe, and they rightly resent an insolence, or regard with a silent disdain the expostulations and prescriptions of bumptious Britons, the sort of people whom Nye describes as "having such enlarged consciences, that they are always ready to take in other people's," to whom the message of Luther to Melancthon might be oft and earnestly repeated. "Tell Philip Melancthon to leave off thinking that he is going to rule the world." It may be kind when a man thinks that he has attained perfection, or that he lives in a country which has attained perfection, to desire to communicate to others this immunity from sorrow and from sin, but the "others" do not seem to grasp and realize the joy. Mr. Pitt Crawley, although, as Thackeray assures us, he was always thinking of his brother's soul, or of the souls of those who differed with him in opinion, was never a favourite, and the interference of persons who are only wise in their own conceits invariably provokes distrust and opposition.

The form of lynch law, and the frequency of its administration will be seen from the following extracts. The four cases which I quote occurred

* "The American Commonwealth." (Bryce.) Vol. ii. 507.

within two months, and were reported in the *New York Herald*, *Chicago Tribune*, and other principal newspapers :—

"Mount Sterling, Kentucky, January 1st, 1895.— Thomas Blair, one of the men who killed J. L. Bowmar here nearly a month ago, was taken from the jail and lynched at two o'clock this morning. He had been acquitted of the crime, but tried to kill a man named Day last Thursday night, and was serving out a jail fine for this crime. The lynching had evidently been carefully planned, and was conducted in a very systematic manner. Jailor J. M. Best was awakened this morning, at 2 a.m., by three men, who, entering his room, seized him, and demanded his keys. These they obtained and passed to their comrades outside, who, to the number of twenty or twenty-five, joined them, took charge of Blair, hurried him to the trestle of the Kentucky and South Atlantic railway, and there hanged him. Upon the body they pinned a paper, on which was written: 'We find Thomas Blair guilty of the murder of Captain J. L. Bowmar, and hang him this January the first, 1895, to avenge the rights of law-abiding citizens. Friends of Captain J. L. Bowmar.' Blair was from Morgan County, and a desperate character. The mob was well organized, and went about its work so quietly that all was over before the citizens knew what was being done. Blair fought desperately for his life, and was beaten into insensibility before he was hanged."

The next example, which occurred only three days afterwards, is dated Wichita, Kansas, January 4th, 1895 : by telegraph to *New York Herald* :—
" News comes from Cantonment, a trading point in the Cheyenne and Arapahoe country, to the effect that a fight occurred there yesterday between vigilants and horse-thieves. Gus Gaskell and Sy Campbell, two of the vigilants, were wounded and three thieves captured. The prisoners were promptly run up to the nearest tree and their bodies filled with lead. The farmers have been robbed of cattle and horses to such an extent that they have determined to put a stop to it, and have formed vigilant committees. In this instance the thieves were chased into the Panhandle of Texas, back into Oklohama, and finally cornered."

The third case is from O'Neill, Nebraska, and is dated January 20th, 1895 :—" The body of Barrett Scott, the defaulting treasurer of Holt County, who, while riding out with his family on New Year's Day, was fired upon by a party of vigilants, and, after being wounded, was dragged from his carriage, blindfolded, and carried off by his assailants, was found last night in the Niobrara river. A new hemp rope was around his neck, and the end, about three feet long, was dangling in the water. Evidences showed that he was hanged by the vigilants and then thrown into the water. There was a slight wound on the side of the neck, where a bullet had grazed it, cutting through the lobe of the right ear. Coroner Hoover, of Boyd County, took charge of the body, and will hold an inquest."

The last of these strange, eventful histories of which I made a record comes from Kingston, Mo, February 17th, 1895. "A mob of masked men, supposed to be negroes from Hamilton, surrounded the sheriff's house and jail here at two o'clock this morning, caught and bound Sheriff Goldsworthy, whose deputy was away, took the keys from him, and gained entrance into the jail corridor, with the avowed intention of taking out and hanging George Tracy, a negro, who shot and killed his wife at Hamilton, in this county, the morning of January 30th. On the inside the mob was unable to get into the steel cell in which Tracy was confined with two other negro prisoners. Tracey crawled under his bed, and the mob began shooting through the bars of the cell, and succeeded in putting seventeen bullets into his body, killing him instantly. The sheriff made all the resistance he could, but was overpowered. The two prisoners in the cell with Tracy escaped unhurt. Tracy was a bad character, and had lately served a full sentence for shooting a negro. He had some years ago lost both his legs just below the knees, being run over by a train he was trying to board to escape some Kansas officers."

CHAPTER V.

CLUBS AND THEATRES.

OUT of the dark tunnel, out of the smoke and the smell, into the fresh air and sunshine—from ignorance to culture, from rogues to respectability, from "the Tombs" to the clubs of New York! An honorary member for a time of several of the societies, I had only time to visit two of them—the Century and the Lotos. The Century is a charming institution, ample and complete in all its accommodations, uniting size with comfort, and surrounding its members—who seemed to be the *élite* of the city, professional and commercial—with things pleasant to the eye and good for food, books and pictures, nourishment for body and mind. This association is not designed for the mere enjoyment of easy-chairs, cigarettes, scandal, chaff, *menus*, wines, and whiskies, but it is a club "with brains, sir," and can talk about science and art, politics and statistics, having moreover weekly lectures by experts on some interesting and instructive matter, followed by an intellectual discussion and an intelligent debate.

There is so much white marble in this beautiful

building that when I was divested of my overcoat by the attendants, Balfe's lines from the *Bohemian Girl* came to my thoughts,

> "I dreamt that I dwelt in marble halls,
> With vassals and serfs at my side,"

and I recalled a small incident in my Oxford days: how one evening, when we were at dinner at the Mitre, in High Street, important business in the rural districts having made us too late for dinner in college, the leader of a street band came up to inquire if there was any particular music the "gemmen" would like to name, and on my replying *Bohemian Girl* (then in its first bloom of success, *circa* 1842), turned immediately to his subaltern waiting at the bottom of the stairs with the brief but adequate intimation —" Marble 'Alls, Jim."

The Lotos Club was established some twenty-five years ago for the social intercourse of those who had literary or artistic inclinations. It is famous for its hospitality, good taste, good speeches, and good dinners. It has entertained J. A. Froude, H. M. Stanley, Wilkie Collins, Charles Kingsley, Richard Monckton Milnes, Ferdinand de Lesseps, General Grant, Oliver Wendell Holmes, Henry Irving, Lieutenant Greely, Sir Edwin Arnold, F. Marion Crawford, and Dr. Conan Doyle. I was therefore somewhat perturbed in spirit—pleased at the same time to discover that I had so much modesty left—when I received a most kind invitation from the president and members to be their guest, and I assured them, when I rose to acknowledge the general sympathy with which the toast of my health had been proposed and received, that I resembled in my feelings, though not much in my features, the beautiful bride of Burleigh when

> "A trouble weighed upon her,
> And perplexed her night and morn,
> With the burden of an honour
> Unto which she was not born."

and I quoted from Hood's "Up the Rhine" the conversation which took place during a storm at sea between the Mate and a Lady of Quality:—"Can you swim?"—"Yes, my lady, like a duck."—"That being the case, I shall condescend to lay hold of your arm all night."—"Too great honour for the likes of me," said the Mate. But I was soon reassured by the hearty welcome and gracious reception, lost all sense of unworthiness, and was possessed by a delicious hallucination that I had said something, or done something—I knew not when, or what, or where—which marked me as a man of genius. It was a proud surprise, like that of the young soldier wounded in the battle, when the surgeon remarked that he could see the brain, and the poor patient exclaimed, "Oh, please write home and tell father, for he always said I never had any." There were some admirable speeches from the president, Mr. Lawrence, from the president of Cornell University, Dr. MacArthur, Mr. Joseph Hendricks, and General Swayne. The last speaker pleased me most when he said that my claim upon their esteem was my love for my fellow-men, and my endeavour to do them good.

The quaintest story of the evening was told by Dr. Greer, of a tedious, monotonous preacher, who had exhausted the patience of his hearers by an elaborate dissertation on the four greater Prophets, and when, to their sad disgust, he passed on to the minor, and asked, "And now, my brethren, where shall we place Hosea?" a man rose from the congregation and made answer, "You can place him here, sir. I'm off."

From the clubs to the theatres. I saw more dramatic performances in the few weeks which I spent in New York than in a dozen years preceding. It is my privilege to include among my friends two great actors, Mr. Beerbohm Tree and Mr. Wilson Barrett, and both sent me invitations. I repeat my conviction that Mr. Tree's "Hamlet," splendidly supported by Mrs. Tree's "Ophelia"—(by a curious coincidence, her namesake, Miss Helen Tree, afterwards the wife of Mr. Charles Kean, was equally successful in this most pathetic and difficult character) —is the happiest conception and presentation of the Prince of Denmark which has been seen by living man, and it was a very hopeful encouragement to the actors, and the audience and all outside, who deplore the sensual rubbish too often seen upon the stage, to know that when the prince of all playwrights, himself a player, had justice done to his plays, one of the largest of the New York theatres was overcrowded twice in one day! There are few plays except Shakespeare's (*longo intervallo,* Sheridan's?) which one cares to see or read twice, but Barrett's *Claudian* is one of the few, not only excellent as a drama, but as an impressive sermon upon the text, "Overcome evil with good."

I had also the gratification of seeing those popular favourites, Mr. and Mrs. Kendal, in *Lady Clancarty*, and was specially delighted with Mr. Denman Thompson in *The Old Homestead*. Towards the end of the play, his manager came to my box with an invitation to an interview, and I had the pleasure of thanking Mr. Thompson for his humorous, pathetic, bright, and wholesome performance, and of telling him how much he resembled in many ways the greatest comic actor of his day, Mr. Buckstone.

Next morning there appeared in the *New York Herald* a paragraph headed "*A Dean Behind the Scenes,*" and shortly afterwards I was gently rebuked by a brother clergyman as having imperilled the dignity of my office. As counsel for the defence, I made answer, "Reverend sir, in the play entitled *The Old Homestead*, two young fellows, who had been making fools of themselves and had gone to the bad, were brought back to a right mind—to their home and duty. They were shown the misery and degradation of vice, and then, in contrast, the happiness and the honour of a righteous life. I went behind the scenes to thank the teacher of that object-lesson, and if you, my brother, will prove to me that by one of your sermons you have persuaded two prodigals to get away from the husks of the swine and return to their Father's house, I shall rejoice to pay my respects to you in the vestry, or wherever we may meet."

CHAPTER VI.

THE PARKS.

I WAS most anxious to see the famous Central Park of New York, but as I have always lost my way in a strange country, on foot without a companion, and on horseback without a pack of hounds to guide me, and as I knew very little of the American trees and shrubs, which I chiefly desired to see, I was in perplexity, and almost in despair, when I received an intimation from the superintendent that he was as willing to show as I was to see the fair grounds in his charge. I welcomed the invitation as a mendicant, lone and hungry in the streets, would welcome the summons of some good philanthropist to come in and dine, and next day I was sitting by the side, and behind the horse, of Mr. Samuel Parsons.

As nearly as I can calculate, the time occupied in forming a friendship between men who really love trees and flowers—they are not numerous—is about five seconds. The heart goes with the hand. We do not gush at the age of seventy-five, and I make these annotations calmly, on the principle that old men should tell young men their experience of such enjoyments and sympathies as never seem to fail. We two had lived our lives three thousand miles apart; we differed in age, nationality, habits, and surroundings, and yet we were as happy and familiar as a couple of schoolboys out for a holiday before you could have boiled an egg. We had a delightful drive.

Little more than thirty years ago the site of this Central Park was a waste and desolation, with stagnant marshes and huge boulder stones. The landscape gardener came, and the wilderness and the solitary place were made glad, and the desert rejoiced and blossomed as a rose. The glory of Lebanon was given unto it, the excellency of Carmel and Sharon. Covering an area of eight hundred and forty acres, in length two and a half miles by half a mile in width, it is admirably planned and planted, upon the one true principle, *ars est celare artem*, to be as like Nature as it can.

Where it is necessary to economize space and to consolidate work, it is wise to build a city like New York in straight avenues and rectangular blocks, but when we go to rest the body and to refresh the spirit with pleasant scenery and purer air, we desire the open spaces, the varied outlines, the graceful curves which Nature everywhere supplies. And we have them here in glens and glades, slopes and steeps, groups of trees and large expanses of grass, the greenest which I saw in the States. There is water also in reservoirs, lakes, and pools, to the extent of one hundred and eighty-five acres, the larger portion being available for boats in the summer and for the skater in time of frost, the smaller being filled with aquatic plants, including large quantities, in great vigour, of

THE LOVERS' WALK IN CENTRAL PARK.

the Egyptian lotus, *Nelumbium speciosum*, Nymphæas, red and white, from India and Zanzibar, lilies from Cape Cod, water hyacinths, etc. There are trees, deciduous and coniferous, in infinite variety, groups of *Salisburia adiantifolia*, the maidenhair tree, named after Salisbury, an English botanist, and nearly forty feet in height.

But to me the chief fascination was my first sight of the foliage, which makes the splendid glory, the sunset, of the "Falls"—the sumachs, the oaks, the maples, the andromedas—the combinations of glittering gold and glowing scarlet and vivid crimson—let my poor British brother try to imagine a Poinsettia grown into a tree!—with the darker leafage, and the evergreens, notably the bright privet from California. I was just in time to see this vision of beauty in its wane and eve of disappearance; and if I were a younger man, I would cross the Atlantic again, early in October, for a longer and more complete fruition.

Before we leave the Central Park I turn to the superintendent, and, with my hat in my hand, and my heart in my mouth, congratulate him on the attainment of this supreme success. He modestly disclaims the honour, but when he declares that he could never have preserved the park in its present arrangement and condition, against innovations which would have disfigured its beauty and degraded its influence, had he not been generously and earnestly supported by gentlemen of refined taste, position, and means, as well as by that mighty coadjutor the Press, he admits that he has had a battle to fight, and that, in his position as a field marshal, he must have done much to win it. In a large city there is always a multitude who cannot dissociate beer and skittles from their conception of bliss, who prefer "the weed" to the flower, and believe the banjo and bones to be the most enchanting of all kinds of music. The only trees which attract them are those under which they can sit in the shade and smoke, but all others are disregarded except as "lumber." They are as abstemious in their admirations as a rough sailor who became lord of a great estate in our midland counties, and who, when a visitor remarked upon the beauty of the trees in his park, exclaimed, "Well, and what o' that? *They've got nothing else to do.*"

All managers of public grounds desiring not only to provide healthful recreation and harmless amusements, but to raise and refine the tastes and habits of the people, have to contend with the baser elements of humanity—with those who believe only in gross and sensual gratifications, and are as though they had neither mind nor soul. I remember that when young Sir Robert Clifton offered himself as a candidate to represent the town of Nottingham in Parliament, and some of the stockingers declared they would not vote for him because he would not permit them to fish in the Trent, which flowed through his estate, he first of all disarmed their hostility and put them in good humour by reproaching them for their ingratitude, because, having heard that some of them were unable to swim, he had done his best to keep them from the river, and the awful danger of a watery grave: that the mere thought of such a catastrophe occurring to any one of those whom he loved so dearly was almost more than he could bear; but that, if they still persisted in their desire, he could no longer oppose them: he would provide life-belts, and they should not only have free access to the stream, but he would build on either side of it for a couple of miles commodious public-houses, not more than a hundred yards apart. He was elected.

As we drove through the park I met with another novelty, which, though of very small comparative importance, much surprised and pleased me—the American trotting horse. He is an astonishment to the Englishman who has never seen him, who does not know what trotting means, and has yet to hear that "Pansy McGregor" and "Abdell," yearlings, have trotted a mile in two minutes and twenty-three seconds, and "Nancy Hanks," a six-year-old, in two minutes four seconds.

There is a striking congruity between the horse and his owner—the same energy and ambition to do their utmost, go ahead, get over the ground, and let no grass grow under their feet. In England we speak of the various *walks* of life that such an one is conducting, carrying on a concern, and making steady progress; but in America he *runs* a business. I have even heard said of a minister that he was running a church. He may gallop his business to death, but to the final gasp on its last legs it must *run*.

Not many of these fast trotters cross the Atlantic. Many years ago a great race for trotting horses was advertised to take place nigh unto a central English town, and a large number of competitors came from all parts. Among them was a gaunt, raw-boned, quadruped, wearing an old hood and rug, scanty and torn and patched, with his legs bandaged and his hair in places rubbed off, and accompanied by a biped, lean and ill-favoured also, in a tall hat and a long-tailed coat, with a look of stupid dejection, which seemed to indicate that he was thoroughly ashamed of his horse, himself, and his errand. So far from being offended by the ridicule and chaff of the spectators, he seemed to accept meekly their severe rebuke, and when one of them, on hearing that he came from America, inquired with all the brilliant humour of the race-course, "whether he had brought an old clothes-horse from Washing-town?" he answered humbly, "that his master had sent him, and had paid the stakes, and he guessed he'd have to go."

The time came for the race, and there was a sudden metamorphosis. Off went the soiled hood and rug from the horse, the long hat and coat from the rider, and as the latter in his cap and jacket, profusely embellished with stars and stripes, jumped into the saddle, the former seemed to start from his inert and pensive mood, as when the hunter hears in his quiet stable the sound of the coming chase.

G

"And faint, from further distance borne
Is heard the clanging hoof and horn,"

and, with a new light in his eye, and a new life quivering in every limb, he sniffs the battle from afar.

The English horses were strong and fleet, but they did not know their business. They had too much knee action, a superfluous curve, whereas the American seemed to propel himself straight from the shoulder and, "stretching forward free and far," to cover more ground. He went ahead from the first, and gradually extended the interval, the *hiatus valde deflendus*, between himself and his pursuers, until he had finished his course, and seemed to stroll in at his leisure.

The rider returned to weigh amid the cheers of the spectators, but with a solemn expression on his countenance which was almost funereal. Some thought they detected the ripple of a smile about his lips, and a close observer noticed a contraction of the left eyelid when its proprietor was met by a friend who, as it subsequently appeared, had been taking long odds against "Mr. Brown's Incog." The two departed in the direction of Liverpool, with a thousand pounds ($4900) in good English gold.

I admired "the Mall," "the Terrace," "the Bethesda Fountain," the countless drives and walks, bridges and arches. The statues are not so depressing as our own. England is represented by Shakespere; Scotland by Sir Walter Scott and Robert

Burns; Ireland by Moore; Germany by Schiller, Humboldt, and Beethoven; America by Daniel Webster.

In the Central Park you meet, as in the parks of London, every kind of vehicle, from the imposing drag with its "four spanking tits," to the wee conveyance which is drawn by goats. The American carriages are of much lighter construction than ours, the wheels being in some instances not much wider than those of a large bicycle. The draught, of course, is easier and quicker, but the wear and tear is sometimes too much for them, and it was a frequent occurrence, when the streets of New York were filled with frozen snow, to see them by the wayside minus a wheel. And this recalls me to the Central Park, for there can hardly be a more inspiriting or amusing spectacle than that which is there exhibited, when the snow is deep enough for the sleigh, and, in the bright sunshine and keen fresh air, the Kentucky horses, with their smart harness and coloured plumes, and their cinctures of merry bells, go swinging along with the grace and swiftness of a deer.

Here, in addition to every form of ordinary vehicle transferred from wheels to runners, you have the Russian and Norwegian sleighs, with numerous modern inventions of a fantastic and strange device. One of them seemed to represent a gigantic nest, and a mother with four children attired in fluffy white garments, a swan with her cygnets. The latest fashion was a graceful structure painted in imitation of a huge sea-shell, and lined with sea-green silk plush. It was called the "Columbia," because the original sleigh made on this design was first exhibited at the Chicago Columbian Exhibition, and was purchased by Mr. A. H. Moore, of Philadelphia, for $2400.

Reluctantly I leave the Central Park, a charming scene, where Art, by following her purest instincts, and by reverent imitations of the Creator's work, has won a sure success.

We passed by the hill which is to be crowned hereafter by a cathedral worthy of its sacred purpose. There could not be a more appropriate site, and the building, which is to cost some millions of dollars, will be seen from all parts of the city. The corner-stone of this cathedral church of Saint John the Divine was laid on the day of his festival by the Right Reverend H. C. Potter, LL.D., Bishop of New York, and an address was given by the Right Reverend W. C. Doane, D.D., LL.D., Bishop of Albany.

We inspected the monument of General Grant, not yet completed—a massive, square edifice in stone, to be surmounted by a dome. Whence the delay, where there is so much wealth and so much admiration? The coffin rests in a small building close by, and ten thousand times ten thousand come to see.

General Grant was of Scotch extraction, but his family had lived for several generations in the State of Ohio. He was the son of Jesse, and, like David, he slew a mighty and cruel giant. His name was

Ulysses, but, as with his illustrious namesake, the King of Ithaca, his superiority over his brother-men was not discovered until he became a hero through the fiery ordeal of war.

There is a story that he was sent by his father,

BISHOP POTTER.

when he was only eight years of age, to buy a horse, and that as soon as he met with the seller he accosted him with all the simplicity of youth—"Papa says that I am first to offer you twenty dollars, and, if you won't take it, twenty-two dollars and a half, and, if you still refuse, I am to offer twenty-five dollars;

but I am not to give more." The proprietor of the steed, having carefully considered the proposals, elected to sell at twenty-five dollars, and informed the purchaser, to whom he presented an apple with the receipt, that he hoped to see him again whenever his papa was buying horses. He little thought that this *ingenuus puer* was destined

"To witch the world with noble horsemanship,"

and to ride before victorious armies in all the panoply of war.

Young Grant was sent to West Point, "the Gibraltar of the Hudson," and the Military Academy of the United States, and there in the riding-schools, none better, except the hunting-field or the back of the buckjumper, he added to his equestrian skill.

He entered the army, and having seen some service in Mexico and California, he returned to face the fiercest and most subtle of all adversaries, to suffer for a while the saddest of all defeats—the degradation of manhood by intemperance—and then to achieve the grandest triumph of all—the victory over selfishness and sin. "Poor, much shattered, he essayed farming."* Carrying wood to St. Louis did not seem that for which he was created, neither did planting crops or raising cattle. Tanning is an honourable calling, and, to many, a road to wealth. Grant tried that, but found no gold in the tan-vat. Then he became a listless merchant, a silent, unsociable, and

---

* See "Eulogy of General Grant," by Henry Ward Beecher.

rather moody waiter upon petty traffic. Had Grant died at the tan-yard or behind the counter the world would never have suspected that it had lost a hero. He would have fallen as an undistinguishable leaf among the millions cast down every year. His time had not come. It was plain that he had no capacity to create his opportunity; it must find him out, or he would die ignoble and unknown. The opportunity came with that great and terrible war, in which an army of a million on either side met in more than two thousand engagements, and from which, reckoning all that died of wounds, exposure, and sickness, nigh upon a million perished.

His promotion and success were continuous. In June, 1861, he was colonel of the 21st regiment of Illinois infantry, in August he was brigadier-general of volunteers; in 1862 he was made major-general of volunteers, and in 1864, having been previously made major-general in the regular army for his victory at Vicksburg, which surrendered on July 4, 1863, with 31,600 prisoners and 172 cannon; he was promoted to the grade of lieutenant-general, and to the command of all the armies of the United States.

His supreme object was the maintenance of the union, which he regarded, and which all rational men who love America must regard, as inseparable from her national greatness. Happily this maintenance was also inseparably connected, although not in his mind the superior motive, with the emancipation of the slave.

Grant, like all true heroes, was generous to the vanquished. At the close of the war he sent them home with food, and with horses to use on their farms. When Richmond was conquered, he did not enter, but turned aside and went to Washington. When General Johnson, who succeeded Lincoln as president, would have General Lee apprehended, Grant protested against this revengeful spirit, and the proposal was withdrawn.

Clouds gathered round the setting sun. To increase his income—(how was it that the hero of a hundred fights was not provided with abundance?)—he went into a banking business, was defrauded by two of the partners, and suddenly, when he thought himself a millionaire, was a ruined man. Then he wrote his autobiography, which realized it is said, half a million dollars. Then cancer came to end this strange eventful history. Two generals of the federal army, Sherman and Sheridan, walked on one side of his bier, two generals of the Confederate forces, Johnston and Buckner, on the other.

It was my privilege to converse with officers who had fought against each other. I was deeply impressed by the reticence, which they made their rule whenever it was possible, with regard to the war, and I shall never lose my admiration of their mutual sorrowful respect when they were constrained to speak, and of the absence of all pride on the part of the victors, and of all bitterness on the part of the vanquished. There was a quiet solemn tenderness which was most pathetic, and which stirred the soul with pity. There was "the child's heart in the brave man's breast." I was reminded of that touching scene in the Sacred History in which the old prophet brings the body of the man of God for burial in his own grave, and they mourned over him, saying, "Alas, my Brother."

There are wounds which never cease to throb in lone lives and desolate homes, in the memory of widows, and fatherless children, and brotherless sisters, and maidens who were bethrothed to the slain—

"She only said, the night is dreary,
He cometh not, she said;
She said I am aweary, aweary,
I would that I were dead"—

and from these I heard, in one or two instances, a few hard, vindictive words; but from the men who went through that awful ordeal, who for four years bore the burden and heat of the battle— from the soldiers, taught by the suffering which they felt and saw to sympathize with all who suffer, there was no utterance which was not restrained, refined, and dignified by the anxious sense of a grave responsibility, and by the humble gratitude of a great deliverance.

Proceeding on our drive, and taking a turn to the left, we come suddenly upon the Hudson River. For me the Hudson,

"Broad and deep, and brimming over,"

has a life, a glory, a freshness and energy, which make it of all rivers king. Byron offered due and beautiful praise to the majestic Rhine, as an exulting and abounding river, making its waves a blessing as they flow, but the width of the Hudson is thrice that of the Rhine, and the antiquities on the banks of the latter stream—the crumbling ruins and the dear dirty old towns—are only to be preferred by lunatics to the pleasant homes amid the tree-clad hills, in the new verdure of the spring, the welcome umbrage of the summer, and the vivid splendour of the fall. As to

"Tiber, Father Tiber, to whom the Romans pray,"

it is difficult—*pace*, Lord Macaulay—to believe that the Romans, who were a sagacious nation, could ever have expected satisfactory results from their supplications to this narrow and discoloured stream; and the insignificant canal which flows through the capital of France, hardly deep enough to drown *les misérables*, who afterwards reappear in *la morgue*, can be regarded only as a subject for condolence; but what shall I say of our own great river our beautiful, bountiful Thames, which flows by the most famous school, the most famous university, the most famous palace, and the most famous city in the world—Eton, Oxford, Windsor and London—which passes hundreds of lovely gardens and parks:

> "The stately homes of England
> How beautiful they stand,
> Amid their tall ancestral trees,
> Through all the pleasant land.
> The deer across their greensward bound
> In shade and sunny gleam,
> And the swan glides past them with the sound
> Of some rejoicing stream,"

—which glides, through haunts of tranquil, happy peace, to dockyards crowded with the ships which sail on every sea, to the school of warriors and the factories of war at Woolwich. How shall we compare this river with the Hudson? Why should we compare them at all? Their charms, their associations are altogether different and distinct: they do not invite comparison. Some men lose half the enjoyment, the appreciation of the beautiful by their contrasts and measurements—"they have seen, or a friend has seen, larger specimens. There is an example, a hundred miles away, in a better state of preservation." I ask their leave to concentrate my admiration on that which presents itself to be admired. And though the glorious Hudson transcends in grandeur, and, so far as size is concerned,

"In vain fair Thames reflects the double scenes
Of hanging mountains and of sloping greens,"

yet has she charms and associations specially her own. I love them both; but this I am bound to say, that we have nothing in London — and I have seen nothing elsewhere—in the same class of scenery, so attractive, with such infinite capabilities of future development, as the New York river-side park, by which I returned with my friend, the superintendent, at the end of a delightful day.

CHAPTER VII.

FLOWERS AND FLORISTS.

> "Spake full well, in language quaint and olden,
>   One, who dwelleth by the castled Rhine,
> When he called the flowers, all blue and golden,
>   Stars which on earth's firmament do shine."
>   LONGFELLOW.

I PASS instinctively from the park to the gardens, because, as a rule, they adjoin each other, and because the forester and the florist are brothers, inseparable as the twins of Siam. And now my faith in compensation,

> "Good counteracting ill and gladness woe,"

is confirmed by the fact that, although we have not in our English autumn the vivid splendour, the golden, crimson glory of the American trees, and cannot vie—from want of sunshine—with our Transatlantic brethren in their production of perfect flowers under glass, we have sweet consolations in our cloudland, in our milder alternations of heat and cold, in our green fields and lawns, and in the infinite variety of efflorescence which we enjoy for nine months out of the twelve—from the first snowdrop to the last Christmas rose. Even in London, the mart of all things beautiful, the queen of flowers is not to be seen during the winter months, as in New York, in her royal beauty; but, from the end of May to the end of October, "there is a rose looking in at the window"—chiefly of Gloire de Dijon and the old China monthly—of the castle and the cottage alike.

And herein, when I am speaking of rich and poor, I find a further argument for my belief in compensation in the equal distribution of those gifts which are most essential to our real happiness, and in the just balance of good and evil. Not only in continents and climates and nations, but in our counties and hills and valleys, and to each individual man, to the lord of ten thousand acres and to the peasant with his "rood of ground," there is the same capacity—and however different the surroundings may seem—the same sphere of enjoyment. There are thousands of poor folks who love their tiny gardens and their window plants—having little else to love—more dearly than the rich their grand *parterres;* thousands who have as much delight in "the greenhouse"—about the size of a four-post bed—as could be had in the huge dome of glass which Mr. Jay Gould has raised on the banks of the Hudson, or in the Crystal Palace itself.

And now, having said so much, and having so much to say, in praise of my brother-florists, I must anticipate accusations of blind partiality by the confession that our community is human, subject to infirmities and to degradations from those who call themselves gardeners, but are unworthy of the name. My wife and a friend returned from their first inspection of the streets of New York with some beautiful chrysanthemums, suffused with a golden hue, unknown, unequalled. In honour of its excellence, so the vendor informed his purchaser, it bore the proud title of "Christopher Columbus," and it was indeed a new discovery in the world of flowers. We were admiring this treasure when, in appropriate coincidence, Mr. May, from New Jersey, one of the most famous growers of chrysanthemums in the States, was announced, and, as soon as we had exchanged civilities, we lost no time in introducing to our visitor, with all the pride of ownership, our new acquisition. We were surprised to see that Christopher evoked no signs of that respectful admiration which is usually expressed for the illustrious mariner. On the contrary, he was surveyed with a disdainful smile, which quickly developed into muffled laughter, and was followed by the brief verdict of condemnation, "Buncome!" Then the judge informed us that this flower, originally white, had been dipped in some chemical composition, and had emerged like a bubble blown from soapsuds, even as—

"prismatic glass,
Its gaudy colours spreads o'er every place;
The face of nature we no more survey,
All glares alike, without distinction gay."

Some of my English readers may ask, "What is Buncome?" Buncome—or bunkum—is humbug, sham, deception. Many years ago the member for Buncombe rose in Congress to address the House in a speech so vapid, pointless, so full of platitudes and vain repetitions, that there was a gradual exodus, which became general when the orator informed his audience that he should commend rather than censure their departure, as he "was only speaking for Buncombe," the place which he represented.

Judge Halliburton, of Nova Scotia, the author of "Sam Slick," has informed us that all over America the electors like to hear of their elected as taking part in Congress, and that if there is no report of his speeches they write to inquire whether he is still living, and they thoughtfully add to the direction, "To the trustees, if dead." Should he be still alive, and not in a sinking condition, they would respectfully intimate that silence does not become the representative of the most enlightened and illustrious city in the world, and that they do not propose to commit the custody of their homes and their property to "dumb dogs that cannot bark." Goaded by this pricking of the spur, and irritated by this shaking of the bit, the sleepy steed is roused into a snort, and feebly essays to prance. He fulfils Archbishop Whateley's definition of a bad speaker—"A man who has nothing to say, and says it"—*ex nihilo nihil fit*. He knows, and everybody knows, that he is talking *bunkum*.

> "Thus would-be Tullys pompously parade
> Their timid tropes, for simple *bunkum* made ;
> Full on the chair their chilling torrents shower,
> And work their word-pumps through the allotted hour."

Bunkum means also misrepresentation, imposture, and fraud ; and I read accordingly in the *New York Herald* of December 3, 1894, in gigantic capitals, that "CHICAGO ALDERMEN WERE BUNCOMED," "Confidence-man Howard impersonated George W. Turner, agent of the Cigarette Trust, and then got drafts cashed."

Applied to flowers this form of villainy may be regarded as comparatively harmless, but it is to the true florist a loathsome profanation, and he groans and writhes to read in a newspaper having a large circulation the solemn announcement that the women and the florists are discussing the question to what extent *green carnations* and *plaided chrysanthemums* should be manufactured and worn. A Buffalo "florist" declares that he shall continue to make them as long as the people will buy. He pleads that it is often impossible to supply flowers which exactly match in colour the dress of the lady who requires them, and that in such cases it is quite legitimate to dye the flower and produce similarity. What is the harm, he asks, of originating a sky-blue chrysanthemum, or a dappled rose ? Moreover, this barbarian, who

> "Would paint the lily,
> Or throw a perfume on the violet,"

proudly boasts that he can supply societies and institutions with their colours, however mixed, in flowers, and states that at a recent wedding the young couple were from two different colleges, and that in the floral decorations their colours were arranged in combination, each flower being divided into four parts, with their representative tints in alternation! Happily for the honour of Buffalo, the writer who makes record of this abomination goes on to inform us that other florists in the town, much to the disappointment of the women, who like fads, and much to the satisfaction of those who like flowers, object to these perversions, and decline either to daub or to drug.

There are, have been, and always will be a number of persons who regard themselves as specially qualified to touch up, improve, counterfeit, and change the workings of the Creator. Like the old Roman Topiarius, they transform their evergreen shrubs into ridiculous and impossible peacocks and other silly distortions. Designs in flowers, as a rule, are ludicrous. I read in the chronicles of the Massachusetts Horticultural Society,* of which I have the great privilege of being an honorary member, that when prizes were offered at an annual exhibition for the best floral design, there were displayed by the competitive candidates a temple, a Gothic monument, a Chinese

---

* From a most interesting address made by Mr. Marshal P. Wilder, ex-president of the society, at the Semi-Centennial Anniversary in 1879.

pagoda, each from fifteen to eighteen feet high, with smaller arrangements, such as a harp, a plough, and a *Newfoundland dog, covered with pressed black hollyhocks and grey moss, and carrying a basket of flowers!*

I had thought before reading of this monstrosity that no imagination could have dreamed of anything more disgusting in dogs than our British poodle, shaven and shorn in places, so as to introduce a series of penwipers on his shivering carcase, a tippet on his neck, and a tag on his tail, and to impart to his *tout ensemble* an expression of imbecile deformity which sickens the spectator, and makes the victim himself, as it seems to us, painfully aware of his degradation, but when I try to realize this awful hound, done in black hollyhocks and moss, and to see him, as he must have appeared when the fading of the flowers suggested a visitation of mange, and a general break up of the constitution, I at once give him precedence over all other deformities, and could almost find it in my heart to pat the poodle.

CHAPTER VIII.

THE CULTURE OF THE ROSE.

It was not possible to accept, as I longed to do, the numerous invitations which I received to visit the gardens of my brother florists, both amateurs and growers for sale, and the welcome which I received, and the sights which I saw, added largely to my regret. My first visit was, by ferry, over the Hudson, and thence by rail, to "The Summit," New Jersey, where Mr. John May has a charming home, which his family have occupied for three generations, and very extensive houses for the cultivation of flowers, roses, carnations, chrysanthemums, violets, etc., etc., under glass; and it was a most refreshing sight to find at the beginning of winter such a preparation and promise of beautiful flowers in abundance to brighten countless homes in New York and elsewhere, and to "cheer the ungenial day," when all the flowers of the garden lie lifeless beneath their shroud of snow;

"and on the rude and wintry soil,
 To feed the kindling flame of Art,
And steal the tropics' blushing spoil,
 To bloom o'er Nature's icy heart."

Roses in thousands, without an aphis or a leaf curled by mildew! The varieties which are best adapted for forcing are American Beauty—a grand, vigorous, and well-shaped rose, though it did not succeed in England, where it was known as Madame Ferdinand Jamain—American Belle, Bridesmaid, La France, Catherine Mermet, Madame de Wasteville, Niphetos, Mrs. C. Whitney, Perle des Jardins, Safrano, Kaiserin Augusta Victoria, Mrs. Pierpoint Morgan, a striking double tea-rose, a seedling from Madame Cusin, and many other hybrid perpetuals and teas raised by Mr. May.

Rosarians will be interested in the process by which, in consequence of the demand, climatic advantage, and cultured skill, their favourite flower is produced in the neighbourhood of New York during the winter months more successfully than in any other part of the world. The plants are struck from cuttings in the late autumn in a bottom heat of 65° to 70°, potted when they have made roots in three or four weeks, and, as their roots increase, and before they become "pot-bound," they must have more room, until in June or July they require a six-inch pot. They must be syringed daily, and fumigated weekly, to protect them from red spider, green aphis, and all manner of flies. They may then be transferred from the pots to the benches, which are filled with soil to the depth of five inches, placed four feet from the ground, and about six feet from the glass, and having a free drainage. I need hardly add that the soil must be the best which can be had, for the Queen of the Garden does not "prey on garbage," and should have a liberal addition of some approved fertilizing manure. The plants should be set about ten or twelve inches apart on all sides, and must be watered overhead and at the roots, in accordance with a constant and careful observation, which will prevent them from being sodden, as well as from being parched by drought. Tobacco must be used freely, by the usual fumigations, before efflorescence, and when the roses are in bloom, by placing it on the pathway under the benches, or in the evaporating pans over the hot-water pipes. It is desirable also to give these pipes an occasional coat of sulphur, the best antidote to mildew.

The Americans cut their roses with much longer stalks than we do, twelve to sixteen inches in length, and thereby obtain a much more varied and graceful arrangement.

Carnations are also grown at "The Summit" in the full integrity of their form, fragrance, and colour. These are struck from cuttings in the open ground, and brought under cover in October. A beautiful new yellow variety, not yet "sent out," was named, to my honour and delight, "Dean Hole."

The chrysanthemums were huge, incurved, recurved, quilled, native, Japanese, and their gay tints made them specially welcome for home decoration, when there is a dearth of flowers; but they become somewhat monotonous when you see them by the mile, in stacks, and it may be that recollections of " Christopher Columbus "—

> " Repressed my noble rage,
> And froze the genial current of the soul."

So I turned to enjoy the perfume of some splendid specimens of tree mignonette, and to other innumerable attractions in the houses around.

I saw everything, even to the cool, darkened room, in which the roses are retarded from a sudden development, which would diminish their value in the market; and here fond memories came to me of a time when, on the eve of some great Rose Show I cut and carried under an umbrella into dens and caves of the earth, outhouses and cellars, certain precious, but somewhat precocious specimens, with which I hoped to win the cup.

Then I rejoiced to find, in a bowling-alley and a reading-room, sure evidence that there were other attachments besides the paying and receiving of wages between the master and his men—recreation for the body and instruction for the mind. And then, after the genial converse and courteous hospitality of a happy Christian home, I bade farewell to " The Summit."

My next visit was to the oldest and most famous of the New York horticultural establishments, that of Peter Henderson, world-known as a king, a second Peter the Great, among gardeners. He was a man of very exceptional ability, with a strong taste for literature, and he not only originated and developed a most extensive nursery business, but was an accepted authority on practical horticulture, and author of "Gardening for Profit," "Gardening for Pleasure," and a comprehensive "Handbook of Plants." He detested humbugs, and when an impostor from Paris advertised and exhibited coloured plates of "blue moss roses," a brief visit from Peter was followed by an immediate rogue's march—*abiit, excessit, evasit, erupit.*

Henderson's denunciation of shams and counterfeits was exasperated by the fact that he had been himself a victim, "buncomed" in his youth. "Dutch Peggy" sold seeds in Washington Market, and persuaded him to purchase a packet of "the new red mignonette." It germinated and grew vigorously, and in due course presented the proprietor with a blooming little patch of robust red clover! All sense of shame or feeling of resentment gave way to his delight in the humorous, and with the inconsistency to which we are all so prone, he, whose severe indignation was aroused by the blue moss rose, made merry over the red mignonette. On matters of more grave importance he acted solely upon the evidence of facts. His good judgment and strong common sense would never permit him to accept without investigation the dictum of any man, however eminent, on any subject that properly came within the field of his profession. We therefore find him taking issue with Darwin's statement,* that certain plants, such as the *Drosera*, or Sundew, and the Carolina Fly-trap (*Dionæa Muscipula*), are fed by the insects, which their wonderful structure enables them to catch. He made a thorough and exhaustive experiment in his greenhouses with four hundred plants of the Carolina Fly-trap, one-half of which were so protected by fine wire netting that, while they had all the necessary light and air, it was impossible for them to receive any sustenance except that derived from the atmosphere and the soil. The remainder of the plants were not only regularly "fed" by hand with flies and other insects, but were also so exposed that any insects in the greenhouse were liable to be entrapped by them. The result was that the most careful comparison failed to show the slightest difference between those that were fed and those that were not fed, and this satisfied him that, if the plants digested the insects placed in the leaf-traps, the food was by no means beneficial.

Henderson also disputed Mr. Darwin's theory of what he called "graft hybrids," that there was an amalgamation of the stock and the graft, adducing this with other arguments, that during the past quarter of a century millions upon millions of pears and apples had been grafted upon millions of stocks, and yet to-day are as true as grapes or strawberries perpetuated by runners or cuttings, and not one of them in any way changed from what it was when it

* See "Memoirs of Peter Henderson," p. 30.

first appeared, unless by the temporary accidents of soil or climate. He expressed his conclusion thus— " I believe that the smallest or the greatest of God's creations has a separate and distinct individuality ; that they cannot be blended except by generation, and that the product of generation—whether in the lowest microscopic germ or on the highest type, man —has an individuality distinct and separate that it cannot attach to another."

I was conducted through the numerous houses, chiefly used for the propagation of plants and the cultivation of roses for the market, by the clansman and namesake of my old friend the Bishop of Brechin, Alexander Forbes, and afterwards presented with copies of Mr. Peter Henderson's books by his son Alfred.

The next adventure of my "love among the roses" was on the banks of the Hudson. Having lunched at Ardsley Park, the home in which Cyrus Field, the chief promoter of the Atlantic telegraph,* received so many distinguished men of his day, and which is still occupied by his daughter. We were conveyed through Irvington and by Washington Irving's house,† covered with ivy sent by Sir Walter Scott from Abbotsford, and stayed for a few minutes upon the spot where Major André, invited by Benedict Arnold, a traitor to his country, to visit the American lines, was

* In the Art Museum, Central Park, New York, the visitor will find a screen covered with most interesting delineations of the laying of the first Atlantic telegraph.

† See illustration, p. 11.

captured on his return, and was afterwards hanged as a spy. Arnold was a brave and accomplished soldier in command at West Point, but is supposed to have been in despair as to ultimate success, and to have distrusted the alliance with France. He therefore made secret proposals to Lord Clinton for the betrayal of his post, and Major André was sent to arrange the plan of procedure, which was found in his possession by his captors. His death was deplored with a lamentation which could not be comforted, seeing that he held a very high position in the British army, was universally beloved, and was denied "a soldier's death;" but his mourners seemed to forget the righteous indignation of those who punished him, not only as a spy but as a clandestine conspirator, as the chief ally of a base, despicable traitor, who was deliberately attempting the defeat of a great army in which he held high command, and the disgrace of a great nation which had the first claim on his love. In 1821, mainly through the intervention of Mr. James Buchanan, then British Consul at New York—I had the pleasure of meeting his grandson on board the *Majestic*, and of much interesting coversation—the remains of Major André were removed to Westminster Abbey, and a tablet erected to his memory. Another memorial which was raised on the spot by Mr. Cyrus Field, after a visit paid to him by Dean Stanley, met with a very different reception, having been shattered into fragments by some explosive material a few nights after its completion.

Leaving this scene of tragedy, we went on to Scarborough, to Mr. Pearson's nurseries, and all sad thoughts of grim-visaged war and the villainous smell of saltpetre were expelled by the beauty and the fragrance of his flowers; and we saw the Red Rose of Lancaster and the White Rose of York united in perpetual peace. Nine houses, each three hundred feet in length were filled with roses in various phases of growth, but all of them, in flower and bud and foliage, strong and clean; some twenty-five thousand plants, from which, last year, over a million roses were cut!

I have said enough to show that the cultivation of roses under glass during the winter months is, in America, a special and complete success, the result of a combination of sunshine with industrial skill, and impossible when either is absent.

In the management of the orchid, stove, and greenhouse, we have nothing to learn from our Transatlantic brethren, and in the variety and endurance of hardy flowers we have climatic advantages which they do not possess; but there is another form of floral production in which, though the capabilities seem to be equal, America takes precedence—the cultivation of aquatic plants. Their enterprise is all the more honourable because it is in most cases beset with difficulty and liable to disastrous issues. The artificial formation of lakes and ponds has not seldom been attended by results which have failed to gratify the organs of sight and smell. In times of flood they have overflowed their banks, and, retiring when the rains abated, have left slimy deposits on the surrounding flower-beds and lawns; and in times of drought they have gradually disappeared, until life was only possible to the eels in their moist residuum of mud.

Against these depressing liabilities my friend Mr. William Robinson, who has worked so hard and happily for horticulture, has done much to encourage and instruct those who desire to take up the subject, in his treatise on "The Bog-garden," and the culture of aquatic plants. In the parks, public gardens, and cemeteries of the great cities of the States we find them flourishing in ponds and tanks and basins, with all their charming attractions of colour, fragrance, and form. Of course there must be, first of all, the water naturally or artificially supplied without fear of failure; and then success depends upon obedience to the one immutable law—"in the sweat of thy face thou shalt eat bread." There must be a determination to overcome all obstacles, failures, and disappointments, a keen, continuous observation and patient work. Some aquatic plants are perfectly hardy if grown in congenial soil; some are half-hardy, like our "bedding plants," and must be taken under cover and "tubbed" in the autumn; some tender, and can only be placed "out of doors" during the warmest weather. To appreciate their exquisite loveliness, the grandeur, the fragrance of the *Nelumbium* and *Nymphæa*, the royal magnificence of the Victoria Regia, with leaves from five to six feet

THE VICTORIA REGIA.

across; and, to learn the best methods of cultivation, the traveller who loves flowers should visit from New York the nurseries of Messrs. William Tricker and Co., Clifton, New Jersey, and should obtain from Mr. S. C. Nash, Clifton, N.J., "Eighteen Views in a Water Garden."

The happiest hours which I spent in America were those in which I was entertained by my brother florists, who came not only from New York and the neighbourhood, but from distant parts of the States —the President, Mr. Barry, from Rochester, the Vice-President, Mr. Craig, from Philadelphia—at a dinner in the Savoy Hotel. The large room in which we met was a bower of roses. "The tables, they groaned with the weight not of the feast, for it was carved elsewhere, but of the flowers." The *menu*, supplied by Messrs. Tiffany, was worthy of their artistic fame—with roses in the foreground, and in the distance the old deanery of Rochester, and the cathedral roofs beyond.

I saw for the first time nearly all the faces which were assembled. Many of them were strangers to each other, but where the hands meet which have sown the seed and struck the cuttings, which have grafted, budded, inarched, and hybridized, which have pruned and watered, tended and trained; when the eyes meet which love to gaze with reverent admiration upon leaf and blossom and bloom, upon "all the green things of the earth," from the moss and the lichen and the hedgerow flower to the sequoia and the orchid—*the hearts meet also*. I make no claim for my brother gardeners of exemption from immoral debilities—" We are the sons of women, Master Page "—but I do affirm, from a life's experience, that among true florists—ignoring the crowd of pseudonyms—there is a reciprocity, sudden but sincere, which I have not seen in any other association.

I am only a dean, and therefore cannot speak with the infallibility of a pope, but I believe that there is more reserve and jealousy with authors, artists, and sportsmen than there is among gardeners, amateur and professional.

Moreover, as was said by Mr. Charles A. Dana, described in the published account of our meeting, as the leading editor and the leading horticulturist in America, "The zealous florist finds not only flowers but friends," wherever he may go. Enough to add that we realized from first to last how good and joyful a thing it is for brethren to dwell together in unity. Many genial words were spoken, and the most acceptable and appropriate compliment which kind feeling and good taste could have devised was gracefully offered, when Mr. Craig, with a lovely rose in his hand, informed the company that it was a new *debutante*—a seedling tea-rose raised by Mr. John H. Taylor, of New York—and that it was to be called "Dean Hole."* All too soon came the singing of

* I must here express my admiration of another recent introduction to the maids of honour and ladies-in-waiting in the court

"Auld Lang Syne," and the separation which was to be final here;—but no distance can dispel the memory or the hope—

> "You may break, you may ruin the vase if you will,
> But the scent of the roses will hang o'er it still."

---

of the queen of flowers—La Belle Siebrecht, in complexion of an exquisite vivid pink, graceful in form, with long, tapering buds, fragrant, vigorous, and distinct.

CHAPTER IX.

THE POLITICAL CRISIS AT NEW YORK.

" Once to every man and nation comes the moment to decide,
 In the strife of truth with falsehood, for the good or evil side ;
 Some great cause God's true Messiah, offering each the bloom
  or blight ;
 Parts the goats upon the left hand, and the sheep upon the
  right,
 And the choice goes by for ever 'twixt that darkness and that
  light."

On the eve of the Municipal Election at New York,* and of a most momentous crisis in its history, I was ruminating, as I drove along the banks of the Hudson, upon the recent revelations of tyranny and villainy, of corrupt and abominable wickedness in high places, which were not only tacitly acknowledged by the culprits, by the silence which gives consent, but by evidence as foul and nauseous in its details of guilt, as it was conclusive in its condemnation of the guilty. A system of corruption, bribery, and blackmailing, which had grown worse and worse. Both political parties had resorted to it so largely in the past that each was expected to neutralize the other, and it seemed as though men thought that the elections

* In the year 1894.

would become pure by an antithetical quality of crime.*

This open conspiracy and comfortable collusion was occasionally interrupted by the protests of honest men, but these were but as boulders in a stream, which divert for a moment the current of the water, but do not weaken its power. Sometimes a mistake was made in the selection for office of a man who unexpectedly developed a conscience, and made himself offensive by suggesting a certain amount of discrimination between good and evil, and by exhibiting a perverse disinclination to tell the more elaborate lies; but honour, as a rule, was considered to be squeamish, and the vilest stratagem was condoned by success. Fraudulent registrations, votes subtracted and others substituted by tampering with the ballot-boxes, were artifices in common vogue. Large sums were paid for appointments; but all this was harmless and venial when compared with the foul enormities which, when I arrived at New York, had raised the righteous disgust and indignation of all honest men, who had not hitherto believed in such rank atrocities, or had been deterred by their reluctance to take part in public affairs, or by some personal motives, from making ready for the battle. When they were convinced by the evidence given before the Public Committee of Inquiry that large sums were systematically received from those who

* From a speech made by the Hon. St. Clair McKelway at a dinner of the Chamber of Commerce in New York, 1893.

were violating the law, for immunity from its punishments by those who were authorized and paid to enforce them ; that levies were made by the police on those who kept houses of ill-fame ; that numerous warrants were issued by police justices and officials against persons who were accused of performing criminal operations, but that none of them were convicted or ever brought to trial ; that one doctor declared that he had paid $2,825 to extortioners receiving the wages of iniquity within six weeks ;* they awoke at last in an amazement of shame and fear.

The report made by the Lexow Committee, and adopted by the Chamber of Commerce of New York, not only affirms that in a very large number of the elections of the city, almost every conceivable crime against the election franchise was either committed or permitted by the police, invariably in the interest of the dominant democratic organization, commonly called *Tammany Hall*, but that they had been guilty of brutality, blackmailing, receiving bribes from disorderly houses, and abortionists, violating the excise laws, waste of the public money, and of connivance with almost every species of corruption and of crime.

So it had come to this, as Dr. Parkhurst said in one of the most eloquent and powerful sermons I ever read, and which he preached on the Sunday before the election, standing between the dead and

* Quoted in the *New York Herald*, November 4th, 1894.

the living, that the plague might be stayed, that "the election on Tuesday would be practically neither more nor less than a vote on the Ten Commandments." It was between God and Satan, Christ and Antichrist. It was not only a battle for the honour or dishonour of New York, of America, it was a contest between civilization and barbarism, rule and disorder, religion and infidelity, of tremendous interest and supreme importance to the world.

But what, or who, was Tammany? The Tammany society was named, no one knows why, after a famous Indian chief of the Delaware tribe, and was originally constituted for social and charitable purposes, assuming a dramatic form, having "sachems" and a "grand sachem," wearing their distinctive orders and insignia of office. Gradually it became political, democratic, a ring, a caucus, tyrannical, corrupt, unscrupulous.

Mr. Bryce, in his standard work on the American Commonwealth, gives an exhaustive history of its proceedings from its rise to its fall. It includes a remarkable illustration of the power which human genius possesses to exalt itself from the lowest to the highest positions. Fernando Wood, who became the most influential demagogue, and ultimately the Mayor of New York, was currently reported to have entered that city as the artificial leg of an elephant in a travelling show!

I was musing about these matters on the banks of the Hudson, and its weeping-willows reminded me of the trees by the waters of Babylon, with the silent harps of the children of Israel hanging upon their boughs. I was thinking of a captivity far more miserable than theirs—of prisoners tied and bound with the chain of their sins; when, looking onward and upward, I saw an eagle soaring above us, as though it had risen from the city, and was mounting heavenward, and it seemed to me, and to those who were with me, a most auspicious omen, and indicative of the victory which next day was won. The Bird of Freedom, released from his filthy cage, to return to his royal throne on the mountains—

". . . and unblenched,
Bathe in the bickerings of the noontide blaze."

The deliverance thus prefigured came on the morrow. The priests blew with the trumpets, and the walls of Jericho fell down. From the people and from the press there came a shout, so long suppressed, that it was like the roar of a lion, and Tammany Hall collapsed in ruin. "New York," in the words of one of its foremost newspapers, "was delivered from the most demoralizing and corrupt misrule that ever cursed a great city, and was emancipated from official abuses which have oppressed its citizens and blighted its material interests beyond the limit of endurance."

I shall never forget the solemn impression which was made by that election on the minds of thoughtful men. By mere partisans it was only regarded as a political success, and they exulted in the discomfiture of their opponents. The foolish shouted until they were hoarse, and drank until they were drunk;

but the wise were restrained in their rejoicing by the exposure of an infamous degradation, by their sudden escape from the thraldom of the oppressor, and by their responsibilities to amend and reform. They seemed to feel, as many of us have felt when we were brought by some strange accident face to face with death, and, when the peril was past we saw how near and terrible it had been in the light of the Love which had come to save.

I called on Dr. Parkhurst, having been assured of a welcome, to express my respectful sympathy. His character, his courage, his oratory, had won for him troops of friends; but adversaries, like fat bulls of Bashan, surrounded him on every side. He who goes in pursuit of skunks must be prepared for offensive odours; and it was not only the abjects at the corners of the streets, who were on the outlook for plunder, nor the knaves and rogues, who were already in enjoyment, who mocked and jeered and imputed evil motives—the only motives they know; nor was it only the sceptics and the sensualists, who affected, like Gallio, sublime indifference; not only those who declare that all men and women are vendible at a price, and that there should be free trade without protective duties in vice—but professors of religion, and virtuous philosophers, and citizens of the highest respectability, remembered engagements in an opposite direction when the trumpet called them to the battle-field.

Dr. Parkhurst anticipated the animosities, the

hindrances, and the disappointments which he was sure to meet—and he made his preparations. He knew that false witnesses would be suborned, who were not averse to perjury, and "would lie with such volubility that you would think truth was a fool." So he went, with a companion, and with a brave, sad heart, to see and hear for himself, into the haunts of the defiled and the drunken, that he might speak that which he had seen, and testify that which he knew, of mad orgies and filthy revels, which were permitted by the police and those who had control of the police, on payment of a bribe. His conduct was denounced as indelicate, unbecoming the dignity of his ministerial office; but he did not heed, remembering that he was the servant of One who sat down with publicans and sinners, and told His disciples to go out into the streets and lanes of the city, and seek that which was lost. As well might they have protested against a physician visiting the fever wards of the hospital, an advocate of temperance intruding into the home of the drunkard, a sanitary commissioner examining sewers, or an analyst detecting poison.

When the battle was won and the tyranny overpast—which had made the very name of Tammany a synonym throughout the civilized world for corrupt politics and riotous abuse, which had debauched the public service, blighted the material interests, and sullied the fair fame of New York—I had the privilege, as I have stated, of offering my congratulations to him who had been foremost in the fight. He was free, as I foresaw, from all pride of conquest, very thankful, but more anxious about the future than jubilant as to the past, confiding chiefly in the righteous disgust and indignation which this exposure should evoke in the hearts of all honest men, and especially in the nobler ambitions and purer morality of the rising generation.

I have referred to Dr. Parkhurst as the most prominent champion against the vile corruptions of the Tammany tyrants *at the time of the municipal elections in* 1894. I need hardly add that all true Christians were on his side. Bishop Potter, of New York, had long ago denounced the conspiracy with all the earnest, eloquent vigour of his zeal, and the clergy and laity of the Episcopal Church of America were of one heart and voice and vote.

My American friends well know, and I desire to assure my American readers, that I am not posing as a virtuous foreigner, startled and distressed by iniquities unknown in my native land. I am not oblivious of Acts of Parliament for the prevention and punishment of bribery; of elected members who have been unseated on account of an indiscreet and exuberant generosity to those who secured their election; of titular honours conferred upon stupid people, and lucrative appointments upon idle folks, because they were keen partisans. I affirm, nevertheless, and all the more boldly because the Americans have again and again made the same declaration—

that the reckless greed of political power and selfish appropriations had never wrought such infamous abasement; and that by both nations, and by the world, this history of the Tammany fraud should be remembered by all who, dressed with a little brief authority, are tempted to abuse and defile it.

CHAPTER X.

EDUCATION.

WE were taught, and it was one of our earliest and wisest lessons, that our faculty of criticism was designed for personal as well as for general application, and that householders who throw stones in a street imperil their own windows. John and Jonathan live in houses of glass, and if they take to missiles, to slings and catapults, "there will be the—glazier—to pay." We have no records of municipal corruption so gross as those of the Tammany Ring, and the members of our House of Commons have a fairer reputation than the members of Congress with regard to compensations in cash, but though the galled jade wince, our own withers are not unwrung, and we cannot present ourselves as accusers of the brethren when we remember the brisk business which we have done in the buying and selling of votes, appointments, and honours.

It will probably be affirmed by both nations that we have the higher political standard, that the Americans are not as a rule represented by their best men, because their best men have not the same ambition; but in other matters connected with morality there is, so far as my impressions convinced me, a strong family likeness. And if I am asked what my impressions are worth, I can only make answer that, although I was little more than four months in the States, I was continually where men most do congregate—in large hotels, at public receptions, on the rail, and on river boats—and that I kept my eyes and my ears open.

I do not accept as an absolute rule the maxim *fronti nulla fides*, having a large faith in physiognomy, but I did not draw my conclusions from superficial amenities, being aware that the case and face of a clock may be kept in a high state of polish, and that its hands may be accurately adjusted from time to time in accordance with the time of day, however worthless may be the works within; and as having known from boyhood that the big strawberry at the top of the pottle is not to be regarded as an exact sample of the contents of the cornucopia.

There are three special cases in which a visitor to New York might be deceived by hasty and partial observation. He might infer, from the absence of intoxicating liquors at the luncheons and dinners in the hotels and restaurants, a natural dislike and disuse of alcohol; he might suppose from the absence of military costumes—I do not remember to have seen a soldier in uniform when I was in the States— that the American knew nothing of war; and he might hope, when he saw, to the honour of this great city, no courtesans in the streets, that there was an immunity from sexual vice; but he must be convinced too sadly and too soon that the infatuation of drunkenness is poisoning the blood, enfeebling the reason, pauperizing the condition of multitudes alike on either side of the Atlantic; that no nation, unless it be France, has suffered so much in modern times from the horrors of war as America, and that, though she possesses but a diminutive army in proportion to her possessions, "it is capable"—as I once heard her ambassador to this country say, with just the suspicion of a smile upon his face—"it is capable of enlargement;" and he is compelled to bewail, had he no other evidence than that which was attested before the Lexow Committee, that the depraved, if they do not meet with temptation, will go in search until they find.

It must be added that no nation has been more vehement in its denunciations of drunkenness or more energetic in attempts to suppress it, and that although in America, as in England, the larger facilities for divorce seem to have increased the number of applicants, there is no country in which conjugal infidelity evokes a more fervid indignation, especially in the case of public men.

I came to the conclusion that, while taking into consideration the difference in our surroundings and temptations, neither of us could say, "Stand by; I am better than thou;" that in both cases the area for improvement is infinite, and that the method by which this waste can be reclaimed, and this desert made to blossom as the rose, is a system of culture which is the only one sure to succeed, and the only complete education. In this matter, the most important of all, there came to me the one great disappointment of my visit to the States. Christianity is not taught as a rule to the children of those who profess and call themselves Christians. Parents and teachers unite, like the Gadarenes, in beseeching the Divine Master to depart out of their coasts.

So far as secular education is concerned, the administration is admirable, and the appliances are perfect. It is delightful to visit the kindergartens, the public schools, the high schools, the technical schools, the normal schools for the training of teachers, the colleges, and the universities; but it is disheartening to find again and again that there is no religious instruction, no prayers, no place for worship.

There is a noble and generous enthusiasm for the mental and physical training of the young. In 1867 George Peabody established a fund of $2,100,000, increased in 1869 to $3,500,000, to be devoted to education in the Southern States of the Union. In 1882, Mr. John F. Slater, of Connecticut, placed in the hands of trustees the sum of $1,000,000 for the purpose of uplifting the lately emancipated population of the Southern States and their posterity. This is magnificent, so far as it goes; but if, as we Christians believe, man, made in the image of his Maker, has also a Trinity in Unity—his body, mind, and soul—this education is imperfect, and "a vast machine, supported at a public charge, is engaged in educating the children of the nation to ignore religion."

These latter words are of American utterance,* and I am thankful to express my convictions in the language of those who cannot be accused, as strangers might be, of ignorance, presumption, prejudice or haste. "The ignorance of the Bible among students in our public schools and colleges furnishes a curious illustration of the inadequacy of our educational machine to meet the requirements of life. It is significant also of a deeper miscarriage of our social and political life. We seem to be astonished that we cannot have public virtue without private virtue, and that a fair legislative and executive machine will not produce an honest and temperate community. We have got into a habit of looking to legislation for everything, and if legislation will not answer, then to a change of the organic or constitutional law. The first thought that occurs to us about any evil in the social body is that we ought to legislate about it, and it does not often strike us that the only real cure is personal and individual reform. We know, in an oratorical sense, that we cannot have a good state without good citizens, but at the same time we think that we can reform political corruption, the shameless traffic in votes and in offices, that we can cast out the lobby from our legislative halls, and stop

* The *Century Magazine* for June, 1895.

the members of the Legislature from taking money for passing laws or for rejecting bills, or for voting for senators and other officers, by some other method than by making voters and legislators honest and honourable. The reform of the individual must take place before there is any real reform. Nor can we escape the analogy between our political and educational schemes. There is a defect somewhere that is the common root of the lack in both. Take this matter of ignorance of the Bible—so great that the pupils are unable to understand many of the allusions in the masterpieces of English poetry and prose. The Bible is in itself almost a liberal education, as many great masters in literature have testified. It has so entered into law, literature, thought, the whole modern life of the Christian world, that ignorance of it is a most serious disadvantage to the student."* Disadvantage! Say rather darkness, with no lantern, no light upon the path. The time comes, Lord Bacon wrote, when every man must leave the pinnace of mere reason and embark upon the ship which has the true sea-needle. To take the Bible from the school is nothing less than to take chart and compass, helm and anchor, from the soul.

It is argued that the main object of education was to produce an intelligent vote, seeing that all alike are voters, and that it was the interest as well as the duty of a government to make the best of its citizens; but "if it is the primary right and duty of the State

* *Harper's Magazine*, March, 1895.

to give whatever education is necessary for good citizenship, it is self-evident that it is its primary right and duty to give education in moral principles, and training to the moral impulses and will. Few agnostics of any sort can be found who will aver that good citizenship can be developed by educating the intellect and leaving the animal propensities unregulated by the conscience and the will.*

Are we, then, to substitute morality for religion? Are we to revert from the revelations of the gospel to the reasonings of the philosophers on virtue and vice? Are we to exchange the creeds of the Church for the disputations of the epicureans and stoics, to leave the Saviour for "the unknown god?" Morality may be only a sentiment, an admiration without an effort, an armchair aspiration, which satisfies itself with a sigh. It may be a policy without a principle, mere worldliness, fear of exposure, or hope of recompense. Unless you have a very large income, or influence, you must have, or seem to have, a considerable amount of morals for success. You cannot be a member of Parliament, or a mayor, or a curate, or a butler, or a policeman without them. They are often constitutional, climatic, conventional. "What will people think? What will the world say? Is it genteel? Will it be in the newspapers?" Mere morality passes quickly from confidence to despair, because it is self-reliant. It lacks the high motives, the steadfast faith, the sure and certain hope, the

* The Reverend Lyman Abbott.

unselfish charity, the Divine instructions and communions which Christianity alone can confer.

I do not think that our kinsmen over the seas are less religious than we are, or less reverent at heart, though they may be so superficially, with regard to sacred things, but I am quite sure that on either shore there is an immediate and momentous need of the only education—Christian education—which can realize the design and dignity of our manhood, and can establish upon secure foundations the true grandeur and happiness of a nation. There are great difficulties because there are great differences in the minds of men as to matters of doctrine and discipline, but they are not insuperable, and might be removed by an equitable adjustment, organised, in a spirit of mutual forbearance, by those who were sincerely anxious that children should be taught, in the school as well as in the home, the vital truths of their faith.

Denominations are as numerous as with us. There are, for example, thirteen varieties of Baptists and seventeen of Methodists. Religious animosities are as rife, the *odium theologicum* as bitter. The following oath is taken by a new member of "The American Protective Association," which announces that it has two million names on its enrolment: "I do most solemnly promise and swear that I will not allow any one, a member of the Roman Catholic Church, knowing him to be such, to become a member of this order ; I will not employ a Roman

Catholic in any capacity if I can procure the services of a Protestant; I will do all in my power to retard and break down the power of the Pope; and I will not countenance in any caucus or convention the nomination of a Roman Catholic for any office in the gift of the people."

On the other hand, the Romans tacitly ignore all other Christians, on whom St. Peter, with the keys, has shut the gates of the holy city, and left them out in the cold, although we do not always find within the walls that perfect peace and congruity of which there is so much proclamation, nor behold how good and joyful a thing it is for brethren to dwell together in unity. I read in *The Denver Republican* of January 29, 1895, in a paragraph headed "Bloody Fight at a Grave," that a funeral party occupying seven carriages arrived at the Cemetery of the Holy Sepulchre, which belongs to the Church of the Blessed Sacrament at New Rochelle, on the preceding day, and that one of the mourners finding that the sexton, in consequence of some obstructions in the soil, had dug a temporary grave away from the place assigned to the family, denounced him so furiously that the man lost his self-command and struck his assailant, whereupon the funeral party pulled out the wooden crosses from the surrounding graves, and a general fight ensued. The combatants were finally separated by the drivers and other spectators.

There as everywhere we find extremists, from

those who misrepresent religion, and make it a burden which neither we nor our fathers were able to bear, to those who ignore all its obligations, and only accept its name; from the stern "gloom-pampered" Puritans, the descendants of "Bruise-them-with-a-rod-of-iron-and-break-them-in-pieces-like-a-potter's-vessel Jenkins," "Wash-our-footsteps-in-the-blood-of-our-enemies Smith," "Let-their-wives-be-widows-and-their-children-vagabonds Brown," to those who, if they dare, would make a jest of religion, and would say—

> "I du believe in special ways
> O' prayin' and convartin';
> The bread comes back in many days,
> And buttered tu, fer sartin;
> I mean in preyin' till one busts
> On wut the party chooses,
> And in convartin' public trusts
> To very privit uses." *

But between these extremes—between fanaticism and unbelief, between the Quixotes and the Falstaffs, between the wild skirmishers, the Bashi-bazouks, and the camp-followers who wait upon an army as sharks and sea-gulls on a ship, there is a great company of Christian soldiers; and it is that these may learn as recruits the only complete discipline, that they may be armed with the best weapons and know how to use them, that they may be indued with the only courage which has no fear of death, that

---

* Lowell's *Biglow Papers*, No. VI.

they may be more than conquerors, because their victory will win an eternal peace—it is for this that we desire in our hearts and demand from those in authority the one thing needful—a religious education.

CHAPTER XI.

THE THEOLOGICAL SEMINARY.

THERE are, of course, in America, as in England, a great number of theological colleges and Church schools. To the first in origin and importance of these institutions, "The Theological Seminary of New York," I was most kindly escorted by one of its professors on November 14, 1894—and I mention the date because, by one of those coincidences which occur not infrequently, but always seem phenomenal, mysterious, and strange, on that very day, ten years ago, my companion and I had met at Aberdeen to commemorate the consecration of his great-grandfather, Samuel Seabury, as the first bishop in the United States.

I have assisted at many interesting ecclesiastical functions, and I have witnessed the gorgeous ceremonies of the Romans at Rome, but I was never more solemnly impressed than when a devout multitude of bishops and priests, learned doctors of divinity and professors of theology, and noble lords of high degree and other earnest laymen were gathered together from all parts of the world—from Africa, America, England, Scotland, and Ireland—in the cathedral church of St. Andrew, at Aberdeen, to celebrate the centenary of the consecration, in the place where he was consecrated, of Samuel Seabury, the first American bishop. Men, whose homes were more than four thousand miles apart, but who had the same spiritual sympathies and the same instincts of brotherly love, met each other as though they had been friends for life. It was like a family party assembled at Christmastide. Brother clasped the hand of brother in that dearest of all homes—the church. Great was the company of the preachers: Bishop Doane, of Albany, who inherits the eloquence and energy of his episcopal father, George, Bishop of New Jersey, and of whom I have more to say; Bishop Whipple, of Minnesota, the apostle of the Indians; Bishop Williams, of Connecticut, the fourth from Seabury; Dr. Seabury, his great-grandson; Dr. Morgan Dix; and, among the speakers, the Bishops of Maritzburg, Winchester, Edinburgh, Aberdeen, St. Andrews, Gibraltar, Meath, Down, and Connor; Lords Lothian, Nelson, Aberdeen, and Glasgow.

The chief subject of thankful congratulation was the marvellous increase and organization of episcopal authority which had followed the consecration of Seabury. The Marquis of Lothian said: "There is not a square mile in any part of the United States, with the sole exception of a portion of Alaska, that is not embraced in the episcopal jurisdiction of a diocese or a missionary episcopate."

The Bishop of St. Andrews said, "In representing for the moment our Scottish Church, and looking to our daughter Church as it now exists in America, I fancy myself like old King Priam and his fifty sons, all married and each with a numerous and prosperous family—*quinquaginta illi thalami; spes tanta nepotum!* The *spes tanta*, the so great hope, has been more than fulfilled. The fifty *thalami* are represented by sixty dioceses, besides missionary sees. The number of *nepotes* has increased during the century to four thousand clergy and to four hundred thousand communicants; while in one *thalamus*, with which we feel the closest and dearest interest—I mean Connecticut—the clergy have increased to nearly two hundred and the lay members to upwards of sixty-five thousand. We may suppose that Priam was proud of his grandchildren; it is certain that we are proud of ours."

The Bishop of Minnesota testified that "five thousand miles away from Scotland, in the Western forests, there are congregations of red men under native pastors. Hundreds of those whom we met as painted savages are Christian men. The work of conversion had been made more difficult, as elsewhere, by the inconsistent living of so-called Christians—men who are the first to disparage the missioners whom they oppose. I have had Indians ask me if the Jesus I told them about was the same Jesus my white

brothers spoke to when they were angry or drunk.
It is not always easy to silence those who thus plead
our example. During our Civil War I was horrified
by witnessing a bloody scalp-dance near our mission.
I went to Wa-ba-sha, the head chief, and said, 'You
asked me for a mission; I gave it you. When I
come to see it, my heart is sick to find a horrible
scalp-dance. What does the Great Spirit think of
people whose hands are red with blood?' Wah-
ba-sha took his pipe from his mouth and smiled.
'White man go to war with his own brother—kills
more than Wah-ba-sha can count on his fingers all his
life; Great Spirit looks down and smiles, says, " Good
white man;" gives white man big book; keeps good
place for white man when he dies. Indian no book;
Goes to war, kills one man, has scalp-dance; Great
Spirit very angry—*Wah-ba-sha don't believe it!*'"

But Bishop Whipple, beloved by all, whatever be
the colour of their skins, has taught them that offences
must come, although woe be unto him by whom the
offence cometh—has convinced their reason, and has
won their hearts. A married man, like St. Peter,
he found a helpmeet for him in the Master's work;
and when he laid the corner-stone of a church at the
Birch Coulee Mission, the chief, " Good Thunder,"
brought him a paper, signed by all the Indians:
" Father, we were once wild men—we are Christians.
You led us to the light. You have been our father.
Your wife has been our mother. You are to lay the
first stone of a 'tipi wakou' (sacred house). We ask

SON AND WIFE OF AN INDIAN CHIEF.

you to name it after the woman we love so well, St. Cornelia." A few weeks after Mrs. Whipple died; and the church bears the name St. Cornelia. The incident is told in simple verse by "Elizabeth R. Burns"—

> "Like saints of old, she laboured
>   For the dear Lord above—
> She fed and clothed the needy,
>   She cheered with words of love.
>
> "She taught us and she helped us
>   With tender, loving care.
> We ask for her, O Father,
>   To name our house of prayer.
>
> "So on the Western prairie,
>   Where dwell the Indian bands,
> A church in loving memory
>   Of St. Cornelia stands."

One of the most affecting ceremonies of this happy congress was the interchange of gifts between the mother and daughter. The bishops being assembled, prior to a celebration of the Holy Communion, a magnificent chalice and paten of silver, exquisitely carved, was presented by an American priest on behalf of the clergy and laity of the diocese of Connecticut to the celebrant, as representing the Church of Scotland; and, having been solemnly offered upon the altar, it was used in the Eucharistic Service. On a subsequent occasion the Bishop of Aberdeen presented to the Bishop of Connecticut a pastoral staff of ebony and silver, beautifully adorned with sacred emblems and with figures of St. John, St. Andrew, St. Ninian, St. Augustine of Canterbury, and of Bishops Kilgour and Seabury. These mutual tokens of brotherly regard and unity were given and received with very earnest words and very evident signs of a pure affection; and every man who was privileged to join in the sacred and social intercourse of these two great nations went away, I am sure, with a stronger faith, a brighter hope, and a larger charity.

For many years, while America was under British dominion, and *was classified as belonging to the diocese of London*, the members of the Church pleaded oft, earnestly, but in vain for a bishop from England. Although Archbishop Laud was said to have designed a plan for planting the episcopate,* and Lord Clarendon had prevailed upon his royal master to appoint a bishop in Virginia, with jurisdiction over the other provinces, and he was named but never consecrated; and although early in the eighteenth century the efforts of the Society for the Propagation of the Gospel, supported by Archbishop Secker, obtained the heartiest sympathy of Queen Anne and the royal assent for the foundation of four bishoprics—two for the continent of America and two for the islands—all ended in failure. The queen died, political oppositions, financial difficulties, religious dissensions, worldly indifference, thwarted, and crushed.

* See Bishop Leighton Coleman's admirable "History of the American Church."

There was bitter hostility in America also from those who were no longer in communion with the Church of England, and who regarded bishops either as emissaries of the Pope or new encroachments and usurpations of British authority,* or feared them, because they foresaw in their spiritual jurisdiction and their apostolic claims to obedience a further development of the principles to which they were opposed. Puritans of an advanced type, with that exquisite sweetness of temper which shrinks from the prolongation of strife, and with that keen sagacity which discerns in a moment the quickest and most effectual solution of dispute, expressed their intention to submerge in the Atlantic any person of episcopal rank who proposed to visit their shores, and a well-authenticated account has been transmitted by Bishop Griswold of "a very intelligent and pious young man, who, while reading a newspaper, dropped it suddenly, and, turning to a friend, exclaimed, 'I am a dead man,' and when asked for an explanation, replied, in a state of great agitation and horror, 'Read that article.' The paragraph to which he pointed was in an English journal, and announced—as it afterwards appeared, without authority—that in the ensuing month a certain doctor of divinity would sail in a certain ship—both named—to discharge episcopal

* "The dread that the British Government might establish bishops among them was a vital apprehension, and such an establishment was regarded as a probable instance of the exercise of that tyrannical power which the writers and orators of the day were beginning to denounce."—*Life of Seabury.*

functions as the first Bishop of New England. 'But I do not see in this,' the friend said, after he had read it, 'any cause for your extreme emotion and distress.' 'No cause!' cried the Puritan. 'Why, I tell you that if that man sets foot on Long Wharf, Boston, as Bishop of New England, I will shoot him dead; and the next moment I will surrender myself into the hands of justice, with the certainty of being hanged. But I shall feel that I am doing God service.'"

Nevertheless, the craving for the primitive administration and universal polity of the Catholic Church increased its efforts and its power. The Mother Church seemed at first to be as anxious to bestow as the daughter to receive the gift, because both believed "that it was evident unto all men diligently reading the Holy Scriptures and ancient authors, that from the apostles' time there have been these orders of ministers in Christ's Church—bishops and priests and deacons." But it was not until the year 1783 that Samuel Seabury, elected by the clergy of Connecticut to be their bishop, sailed for England, bearing with him a letter of commendation, and urging his immediate consecration.* He had interviews with the two English archbishops and with the Bishop of London, and these all expressed their earnest sympathy, but they were extremely cautious. They could not act without the authority of the State, though we are not informed that the apostles

* "The Church in America," p. 819.

asked permission from the civil authorities to ordain elders in every city. They were not sure that a bishop would be popular in Connecticut, though St. Paul does not seem to have inquired whether Timothy would be a *persona grata* at Ephesus or Titus at Crete, and was not only the most unpopular man of his day, but persisted in going where he was most disliked. They saw no hope of an adequate income; the idea of a bishop without four horses and a coachman in a bag wig was preposterous. Lastly, they expressed their opinion that he could not be consecrated without such an oath of allegiance to the sovereign as he could not conscientiously take— although a majority of the judges and crown lawyers were of opinion that they might safely proceed—as if none but British subjects could hold high office in the service of the King of kings.

Seabury remained in England for sixteen months, but the timidity of the bishops, "letting I dare not wait upon I would," and the political oppositions and animosities of the State, at last constrained him to transfer his hopes, and to seek elsewhere for his church and nation that which England should have been proud to bestow. Application was made by him to the bishops in Scotland, and they, like Barnabas, the son of consolation, took him and brought him to the apostles, holding out to him the right hand of fellowship. On Sunday, November 14, 1784, Dr. Samuel Seabury (Oxford had conferred upon him the degree of Doctor of Divinity) was consecrated in the chapel belonging to Bishop Skinner at Aberdeen, by the Primus of Scotland. As a young man he had studied medicine in the famous Edinburgh schools, and from Scotland he took his diploma, and went forth like Luke the Evangelist, as a "beloved physician" of the soul. It was my privilege to attend the centenary meeting in commemoration of this joyful event, and, as I have said, there I met the great-grandson of the bishop; and ten years afterwards, on the very day of the consecration, we joined hands on American soil, and went to see the Theological Seminary of New York.

It began in the year 1817 with six students: it has now nearly one hundred and fifty, with a property of one million and a half dollars. Since the first permanent buildings were erected in 1825 it has matriculated over two thousand students, of whom forty-eight have been bishops,* and at the present time the applications for admission exceed the accommodation. The seminary forms a quadrangle of massive and stately proportions, with admirable arrangements for its educational purpose. It has a board of trustees, including forty-four bishops, and other distinguished clergymen and laymen, a most efficient staff of professors, instructors, and tutors, and numerous scholarships richly endowed by generous benefactors. Of all its donors the present dean, the Very Rev. Eugene Augustus Hoffman, has been, and continues to be, the most

* "History of the Church in America," p. 304.

munificent. The last precious gift which, with the liberal aid of Mr. Cornelius Vanderbilt, he has presented to the library, already containing twenty-five thousand volumes, is a collection of Latin Bibles, made by Professor Copinger, and believed to be the largest in the world. It consists of five hundred and sixty-five editions, in fourteen hundred and fifty volumes, which exceeds the number in the British Museum by ninety one; in the Bodleian Library, Oxford, by three hundred and seventy-three; and in the University Library, Cambridge, by three hundred and ninety-eight editions. Very many of these are extremely rare, and some are absolutely unique. In nearly every instance the books are in excellent preservation. Many of them are in the curious original bindings, with metal bosses and silver clasps, sometimes with leather tags to facilitate turning over the pages and protect the edges of the leaves. The old printing and paper are alike excellent in condition, and many of them are enriched with curious and beautiful woodcuts and engravings by such eminent artists as Bellini, Holbein, and others.

There is a school for music, wherein these candidates for holy orders may learn to sing and give praise with the best member that they have, and to teach and lead others also.

While I was in New York an excellent lecture was given to the students on "The Importance of Musical Knowledge to the Priesthood of the Church," by the Rev. James Levett Steel, who kindly sent me a copy. He argued convincingly that Church music comes not under the head Doctrine, nor under the head Discipline, but under the head Worship, and that with the matter of worship they of the priesthood had much to do daily; that they must bear in mind that music in the worship of the Church is to serve as the vehicle of man's adoration of God, and not as a pleasing accompaniment to an otherwise tedious formality; and that in the musical portion of our service we have an opportunity of expressing in relation to God and His worship every emotion and sentiment of the human heart.

And I would respectfully suggest to the University of Oxford, of which I am a member, that some similar instruction in the sacred harmonies might hereafter be as profitable to those who are preparing for the priesthood, and as conducive to the dignity of public worship, as the "Alcestis" of Euripides or the "Odes" of Horace. In my undergraduate days there were scores of us who had irrepressible instincts and talents of a remarkable order for music. Our teachers must have been conscious of these proclivities, because some of our solos and all our choruses were audible throughout the college, but they expressed no admiration of these melodious outbursts, and, instead of educating them to nobler adaptations, surrendered them to the praise of feminine beauty and the glorification of field sports.[*]

[*] We ought to have in our universities some such statute as that which was ordained in the Theological Seminary at Andover,

Again, as regards instrumental music, who can tell how much genius—discouraged and untaught—was stamped out, or, rather, blown out through long tandem horns, or in those abortive efforts to perform our National Anthem upon the cornet, which seemed, from their infinite repetitions, to satisfy the performer, but which well nigh drove his hearers mad—in one instance to a madness which was followed by great searchings of heart, by noble resolutions, by hard work and lofty ascensions.

There is a tradition at Oxford that a member of Queen's College was ultimately *made an archbishop because he had knocked down an angel.* The explanation was this: in rooms not far from his own another undergraduate, by name Angell, began to teach himself the key-bugle. The power of his lungs was abnormal, but his manipulation was dilatory and erratic. The results would have been eminently

Massachusetts, in the year 1817: "Sacred music, and especially Psalmody, being an important part of public social worship, and as it is proper for those who are to preside in the assemblies of God's people to possess so much taste and skill in this sublime art as at least to distinguish between those solemn movements which are congenial to pious minds and those unhallowed, trifling, medley pieces which chill devotion, *it is expected that serious attention will be paid to the culture of a true taste for Church music in this seminary, and that all students therein who have tolerable voices will be duly instructed in the theory and practice of this celestial art; and whenever it shall be in the power of either of the said professors, it shall accordingly be his duty to afford the necessary instruction; and whenever this shall not be the case, it is expected that an instructor shall be procured for this purpose.*"

successful, if they could have been utilized as a process of scaring away crows from corn, but considering

> "The cause why music was ordained—
> Was it not to refresh the mind of man?"

they were a failure. So far from having any "power to soothe the savage breast," they made it more savage than before, and attached a stomach-ache. I remember in my own Oxford days that, in the long vacation, I began to play upon the flute. I was supposed to be reading hard for my degree, but, as my small study was at the top of the house and my father's room far away, it never occurred to me that the dulcet tones would reach and announce to the parental ear that, to use a Midland saying, I had "run my job." He told me in after years—he was too kind to tell me at the time—that the resonance was heard distinctly; that my rendering of "Auld Lang Syne" was the most doleful and depressing performance within the range of his recollection; that he generally left the house after the first five minutes in search of outdoor relief, being convinced that ten minutes would soften his brain, and that a quarter of an hour would suggest suicide. He reluctantly confessed that on one occasion, during a special concourse of discords, he had bestowed a monosyllabic malediction upon "Auld Lang Syne"—(he spoke as though "Lang Syne" was a person of infamous character, a brigand or a fiend)—which he had regretted ever since, and that he never heard the melody without a transient qualm. Judge, then, if the distant utterance of the milder music could so painfully incense the cool tranquillity of middle age, how must the proximate intonations of sounding brass have fired the ardour of the youthful spirit sudden and quick in quarrel. And so, after angry interviews and vain expostulations, the exasperated hearer knocked the bugler down.

The musician, after a brief survey of his antagonist, who was of an athletic type, abandoned the idea of single combat in favour of an appeal to the college authorities, and as the offender happened to be at variance with his judges on certain questions as to discipline and study, he was severely punished and threatened with expulsion. This crisis induced serious meditation, and, reminding him that his future success depended mainly upon his present exertions, and that he was abusing his talents and wasting his time, evoked a new ambition. He took high honours in the schools, became a fellow and tutor of his college, a bishop and archbishop in the Church.

But it is time for me to return from Oxford to New York, and to pass from the music school in the Theological Seminary to the chapel—one of the fairest, because at present, sad to say, one of the rarest, sights to be seen in the States—a beautiful place of worship, consecrated and set apart in a place of education. It is a building worthy of its sacred designations—prayer and praise, the administration of the sacraments, and the preaching of the Word.

It inspires reverence with its altar of alabaster and its windows of coloured glass.

As we entered one of the professors was giving a lecture to some young students on the subject of sermons. I was asked, as an old preacher, to give my experience, and condensed it to the best of my power as follows :—That there was only one source of real success—hard work ; and that in the holiest and most responsible of all work they were bound to do their very best. That their best, preceded by prayer, would have the help which never fails. That they should always have some definite object in preaching, and, when their subject was fixed, should think, read, and write about it. That the best commentary on the Bible was the Bible itself, the marginal references attached to the verse of their text, and the further help of a concordance. That, after the Divine example, they should teach their hearers from the surroundings and incidents of their daily life familiar to them all, and this, like the greatest of human preachers, not with enticing words of man's wisdom, but using great plainness of speech. That, having committed their sermons to memory, they should speak, not read them. That, above all, the preacher should remember always that the best sermon he could preach was a good example, that the only true faith was that which worketh by love, and the only pure religion to visit the fatherless and widows in their affliction, and to keep himself unspotted from the world.

I spoke as anxiously and as earnestly as I could, because a new voice sometimes evokes a new interest, suggests a new meaning and importance to some truth which has been accepted as a precept, but not obeyed as a rule; and when I remember the eager, attentive look upon those bright young faces, I try to hope that my anxiety was not altogether in vain.

CHAPTER XII.

THE CHURCHES.

I WENT to the services in several of the New York churches; and though, as with us, there are diversities of gifts and differences of operations, I liked them all. The sacred edifices are not to be compared with our ancient or modern churches, but many are fair and stately, and all well proportioned and well built. The administration is excellent. The Episcopate maintains the high character which was assigned to it by Archbishop Trench when he said, at the time of a Pan-Anglican Conference, "The American bishops seem to me about the ablest body of men I have met." The priests and deacons are well-taught, well-trained kind pastors and able preachers; the worship is reverent, the congregations are devout.

The music is impressive—sometimes, as with us, too elaborate and sensational, sometimes inappropriate as an accompaniment, for example, to the Lord's Prayer* and the Creed; but, as a rule, sweet,

* The American who remarked, when he first heard this prayer said in monotone, "that if any child of his ever asked a favour in that key, he should let him have the stick," would have resented yet more the addition of music.

solemn, and impressive. This is the more honourable to those who originate, instruct, and sustain the choirs, because, owing to climatic influence, the material for their formation, the vocal power, is much less abundant in America than in England. More than one organist who has been in both countries has assured me of a fact which is indicated, even within the close boundaries of our little isle, by the eminent superiority of our northern to our southern people in their power of voice and in their love of song. In Yorkshire and Lancashire the factories resound with the sweet, clear voices of "the hands," the Nottingham stockingers make soft harmonies in catch and glee, the Midland farm lads sing and whistle at the plough; but no music comes to us from the hop-gardens and the orchards—from the hills and valleys of Kent.

I was surprised at a strange incongruity which exists in nearly all the American churches—even in those which have good music in abundance—the Psalms are read. I am aware, of course, that, together with the Canticles, they may be said or sung—may be said when they cannot be sung; but surely a psalm is, as Dr. Johnson defined it, "a holy song," and becomes a misnomer when it is not sung.

The chief differences in the American and English Prayer-books are, the use in the former of the Scotch Communion Office, which many of us prefer to our own, the exclusion of the Athanasian Creed, and certain alterations in the ordination of priests, and in the visitation of the sick which many of us deplore, and the additional title of Protestant, which has a sectarian, ambiguous sound, and is not to be found in our English Prayer-book.

Some of the churches have beautiful ornamentation. In that to which we went first, being the nearest to our hotel, the Church of the Calvary, there is a most impressive representation behind the altar of the Crucifixion. In many the reredos is of alabaster, exquisitely carved. In the Church of the Ascension there is a grand picture, by Lafarge, of that glorious Exaltation, and some windows of painted glass by the same artist, rich in colour, but inferior as to design and devotional treatment to those of our most successful experts, of whom I venture to assert that my friend Mr. Kempe is chief.

Until the new cathedral is complete, the Church of the Holy Trinity must be regarded as the mother church of New York, and it may well be said of her—

"Sons she had, and daughters fair,
And days of strength and glory,"

in the bright sanctuaries affiliated and under her care—sons, in the churches of SS. John, Luke, Paul, Augustine, Chrysostom, Cornelius, and a comely daughter in that of St. Agnes. Trinity Chapel, with its bright services and cultured choir, must also be included in the family circle, outside of which a multitude of poor relations have been and are most generously dealt with in the matter of building, income, education, hospitals, and other charitable undertakings.

Famous men, whose praise is in the churches, have been rectors of Holy Trinity Church—Charles Inglis, afterwards the first Bishop of Nova Scotia; Samuel Provost, afterwards consecrated in the chapel of Lambeth Palace by the two Archbishops of England and by the Bishops of Bath and Wells and Peterborough first Bishop of New York; Benjamin Moore, afterwards Bishop-coadjutor of his diocese; and John Henry Hobart, his successor and third bishop in 1816; but none more highly esteemed in love for his work's sake than the present rector, Dr. Morgan Dix.

The church has great size and dignity, but the east window is somewhat appalling, and altogether incongruous with the admirable altar and reredos offered by the Astor family in memory of their father. The ritual is solemn, without fantasy or ostentation; the music is reverently sung by a powerful and well-trained choir; and the best sermon which I heard in New York—as teaching the catholic faith, as the composition of a scholar, and the utterance of an earnest and tender heart—was preached by the rector. I have listened to preachers far more vehement and excited, who seemed, in the flesh, to occupy a pulpit, but, in the spirit, a balloon, carried about high above the heads of their congregations with every wind of doctrine, and altogether uncertain, aëronauts and spectators alike, when and where it would come down.

In one of the New York churches, wherein the altar was represented by a box or table about the

size of a Saratoga trunk, and the pews were so
narrow that it was almost impossible to kneel, I heard
Plato and Socrates and Carlyle and SS. Peter and Paul,
all bracketed together as co-equal; and in others I
was told there are, as in London and elsewhere,

DR. MORGAN DIX.

preachers who, not having faith by patient continuance and well-doing to seek glory, essay to make
themselves conspicuous by novel speculations, vague
theories, doubtful disputations; and, therefore, there
is the greater need of men to lead us on the old

paths where is the good way, and to assure us not only with their lips, but by their lives, that in quietness and confidence shall be our strength.

As St. Paul's Cathedral looks down on Lombard Street, so Trinity Church looks down on Wall Street, the two greatest money markets in the world, and both seem to preach the same "sermons in stones"— "If riches increase, set not your heart upon them;" "He that maketh haste to be rich shall not be innocent;" "To do good and to distribute forget not;" "He hath dispersed abroad and given to the poor, and his righteousness remaineth for ever."

> "And wisest is he in all this strange world
> Of hoarding and growing gray,
> For all you can hold in your cold dead hand
> Is what you have given away."

The melodious soft chimes of Grace Church were playing the tune of Keble's hymn, "New every morning," as we admired the goodly building from without and entered the pleasant courts within for a very helpful service and a very interesting sermon from Dr. Huntington. The day on which it was preached was known as "Prisoners' Sunday," and was originated by wise heads and tender hearts to enlarge that Christian sympathy with the inmates of our jails, which should visit, or appoint others to visit, them in prison, and should help them when their term of punishment is over to make a fresh start and earn an honest living.

Where shall we find a brother, as we call him, so

forsaken and forlorn as he who stands upon the steps of his prison door in the same blank despair which cried—" I looked on my right hand and saw there was no man that would know me. I had no place to flee unto, and no man cared for my soul." I doubt whether any of our Church workers are doing more good in England to-day than those who wait upon prisoners just discharged, convincing them with gentle words that God had sent them a friend, offering them a place of refuge, and the hope of restoration to the respect of their fellow-men. And in this goodly fellowship I would include those agents of the Church of England Temperance Society who attend at our police courts and reason with the drunkards, as Paul with Felix, of righteousness, temperance, and judgment to come.

At Grace Church I heard Bishop Bickersteth's sweet psalm of solace, beginning "Peace, perfect peace, in this dark world of sin," most affectingly sung, the first line of each verse by a female having great musical power and tenderness of tone—" tears in the voice "—and the rest by the choir and congregation. This hymn, so helpful to sorrow and so hopeful to faith, was written by the author on his return from visiting a sick friend to whom he had repeated the words of Isaiah, "Thou wilt keep him in perfect peace, whose mind is stayed on Thee, because he trusteth in Thee."

A great work, of the best kind which Churchmen can do for the Church, is making successful progress through the energetic zeal of the clergy and laity of the Church of St. George in New York. In the first place, they seem to be fully persuaded in their minds that the House of One who is no respecter of persons should not be made a house of merchandise for the accommodation of those who can afford to pay for it. They do not hold with Luther that St. James wrote "an epistle of straw," but that he was divinely taught to warn us against awarding precedence to gay clothes and jewellery, to those who love the uppermost rooms at feasts and the chief seats in the synagogues. Wherefore St. George has thrust his spear through the dragon of arrogance, and his church is "free and open," albeit his pews are somewhat narrow for those who kneel in prayer.

The rulers, believing that the labourer is worthy of his hire, and that they who preach the gospel should live of the gospel, rely upon their offertories to make good the loss of the pew-rents, to defray the expenses of their common worship, and so give something more than that which costs them nothing to Him who giveth all.

We precede our American brethren in these appreciations of Christian equality. We are ashamed of the wrong which has been done, of the bitterness and the estrangement which have been caused by exclusiveness in our Church; we are becoming more and more democratic, yearning, praying, and working that it may be said once more, "The common people" —the masses—"heard Him gladly," and that without money and without price the poor had the gospel preached to them.

Not only within the Church of St. George but outside its walls, not only on Sunday but through the week, these principles are in evidence. "The ministry of communication," on which I heard a sermon from the chief minister, Dr. Raynsford, is at work among the men and boys at the docks, in classes of instruction, and in social gatherings of all sorts and conditions of men.

I must add that although as to equality in our churches and missionary enterprise among working men we are somewhat in advance of our episcopal kinsfolk on the other side of the Atlantic, they are not to be surpassed in their kindness of heart, in their charity towards all. Let me just tell two little incidents in proof. I went one Sunday to the Church of the Holy Cross, in Avenue C, where the clergy, aided by some of our Clewer Sisters, are ministering in the slums, and as soon as the service—very reverent and real, though it might be too ornate for those who are strange or averse to "high ritual" —was over, a priest came and invited me to join them at their midday meal; and on the following Sunday, in "the little church round the corner"— the Church of the Transfiguration—subscriptions were invited towards a Christmas dinner for the poor, and an announcement was made from the altar —startling to the ear, but gratifying to the heart —that *three hundred turkeys had been already purchased!* These are small indications of a large benevolence which comprehends all classes, and has a special grace in entertaining strangers.

Always I shall remember with gladness of heart the genial words of welcome and compliment (though they tried my humility), and the generous hospitality (though it tried my digestion), which I received in the States, not only from my brother Churchmen, but from the members of other Christian communities. Among the Presbyterians especially I found gentlemen of great intellectual power, highly educated, and so courteous and amicable that I oft repeated to myself the words, "What is presbyter but priest writ large?" and longed more than ever for the time when Episcopus and Presbyter shall shake hands.

Of course I did not presume to look up, *de profundis*, from the depths of heresy, schism, and excommunication, for the faintest smile of Christian charity from the holy Romans, who—

> "Sit on a throne of purple sublimity,
> And grind down men's bones to a pale unanimity,"

if they do not fall down and worship. But I was abundantly consoled by the words of one of their own poets—

> "That the love of God is broader
> Than the measure of man's mind,
> And the heart of the Eternal
> Is so wonderfully kind.
>
> "*But we make His love too narrow
> With false limits of our own,
> And we magnify His strictness
> With a zeal He will not own.*"

And, more than this, I heartily admire their enthusiastic zeal, which has in America more than ten thousand churches, and more than six million members. Not only are their buildings the most beautiful—there is no church in New York to compare with the Cathedral of St. Patrick—but they are used far more frequently for their sacred purposes than the other places of worship. Although there were three American bishops at work before the first Roman bishop (John Carroll) arrived, the Roman Church has so far made ten times the progress of our own; and this in spite of various accretions to the Faith, infallibilities, immaculate conception, compulsory celibacies and confessions, with other fond things vainly invented, without the authority of an Œcumenical Council. With an encumbered creed, and among a people, so far as the Anglo-Saxon element is concerned, neither superstitious nor servile, they have established far and wide that form of Christianity which demands the most from imagination and credulity, an autocracy which insists on a severe obedience, not only to its local officers, but to a foreign potentate in Rome. This consummation has been attained by long, laborious, and united effort, by those noble sacrifices of time and money which rarely fail to succeed. When the clergy and laity of "the Protestant Episcopal Church of America" shall more fully realize and rejoice in the truth that it is Protestant because it is Catholic, and shall claim as their own, and not surrender to the Romans, that glorious title; that it is Protestant, because it is scriptural and primitive, and as such repels innovation; and when faith in the power, and thankfulness for the blessings, conferred upon their Church, are more practically expressed in self-denial and service, worship and works of mercy, we cannot doubt that, as being the more pure and apostolic, it will have the stronger growth, and will stretch out its branches unto the sea and its boughs unto the river.

That this development is making sure progress I had abundant proof from what I saw and heard as I went through the States; the belief in the Church as a Divine institution, in the apostolic succession, and the grace of holy orders, in the inspiration of the Bible, and the power of the Sacraments, which has always animated and encouraged the most enlightened and energetic of her sons, is everywhere increasing; and the hope grows brighter every day that, travelling in the greatness of her strength, she will be empowered to teach those principles which have made England, and can make America, the greatest nation of the world.

CHAPTER XIII.

RAILWAYS.

The American railways are on a much grander scale than ours. In extent of metal there are in America sixty thousand more miles than in Europe.* The engines and trains are much larger, more massive in construction, and run more smoothly. The speed is much the same as ours; and in the records of the fastest runs made by locomotive engines there is little to choose.

The compartments for passengers are much higher and longer than ours, elaborately ornamented with carving and gilding, and lighted by electricity. The parlour-cars are furnished with luxurious revolving chairs. Iced water is supplied from a tap in most of the carriages. Vendors of newspapers, magazines, books, candies, peppermint, and chocolates pass at intervals through the trains, but are not importunate, sometimes leaving a few volumes for inspection, and collecting them without comment.

There is a laudable custom of announcing the

* From Mulhall's "Table of Statistics of the Railways of the World."

name of a station on arrival, and shortly afterwards of that next on the line, and there is a custom strange to the Britisher of occasionally placing a ticket in the band of his hat to notify his destination.

The railway servants—I beg their pardon, there are no servants in America, I mean the lords-in-waiting—have been much maligned as morose and disobliging. They may not be quite so pleasantly attentive as some of our English guards, and certainly they are not given to superficial *politesse*. The word "sir" is not in their vocabulary, and they may not salute every man with a moustache as "General"; but they reciprocate kindly approaches, and the respect which is due to men on duty (even Napoleon could say, "Respect the burden," when they bade some poor man, heavy laden, to move out of his way); and I had pleasant converse with them.

More than once or twice I found in this vocation Englishmen who were "*born* gentlemen" (I have seen a great number of babies, but was never able to make this discrimination) who, having come to the States under the erroneous impression that, if you were nice looking and well dressed, and had a few hundred pounds, you had only to emigrate and you became a millionaire, had sorrowed over a dissolving view of their hopes and of their gold, and had finally been constrained to accept occupation which would keep them healthfully and honestly employed.

In the night intervals, when they had nothing to do, they were interested in anecdotes connected with the rail, told by one who had seen *Puffing Billy*,* the sire of all the iron horses in the world, and *The Rocket*, a marvellous improvement by George H. Stevenson, which, to the astonishment of the beholders, drew a carriage containing thirty passengers at the rate of thirty miles an hour; who remembered the opening in 1830 of the first important railway in England—the Liverpool and Manchester, and the sad death from collision with an engine of Mr. Huskisson, who had been Secretary of State for the Colonies; who, travelling in the dark, had become suddenly aware that the train had left the metals, and then, hurled down a steep embankment, in a carriage turned topsy-turvy, and within two or three feet of the flooded Trent, had awaited extrication; and who—this pleased them most—had a large acquaintance with working railway men, and had addressed them by hundreds in the railway sheds, with the lads perched on the rafters of the roof and singing hymns lustily and with a good courage from the white leaflets in their coal-black hands.

Apropos of accidents, I saw in some of the cars axes and hammers, available in case of a smash, and, like the life-belts on the *Majestic*, unpleasantly suggestive, the more so because in continuous journeys, sometimes where the construction of the line has almost baffled the skill of the engineer, there must be a contingency of peril, and it is out of the power of human wisdom to prevent the disastrous

* Puffing Billy is now in the Patent Office.

results of a mistake, of a flaw, a fracture, or, as in the instance to which I have referred, in the sudden subsidence of the soil. In spite of all the improvements and precautions, the number of deaths and injuries is appalling. It is stated in a "Report of Railway Accidents in the United States," made by the Interstate Commerce Commission, Washington, D.C., that in the year ending June 30, 1893, 7346 persons were killed and 40,393 were injured. The total number of passengers carried was 593,560,612.

But we were never, so far as we knew, within sight of danger, and were only incommoded at times by the excessive heat of the cars, and this was modified upon our courteous entreaty, although the American is not so sensitive on the subject of ventilation as we are, and they who have the care of the carriages and their costly furniture are of course unwilling to admit any smoke and dust that may be reasonably excluded.

Nevertheless, though I travelled so many hundred miles without danger and almost without discomfort, I passed through an ordeal of much mental and physical perturbation on the rail, and I shall never forget the first night which I spent in a sleeping-car. By ingenious adaptation and addition, the seats used by day are converted at night into an upper and lower cubicle, not unsuitable for those of moderate dimensions, but oppressively limited for a bulky giant nearly six feet four in height, and in weight over sixteen stones. Thus cabined, cribbed, confined,

I felt, as I drew my curtain, about as happy as a seagull in a canary's cage. More miserable, in fact, because a sea-gull has no gaiters with twelve buttons for each leg to put on or off, no small properties, moneys, letters, keys, watch, to transfer from his pockets he knows not where, no devotions to be said kneeling. I became involved, entangled, confused, oppressed, and when I was at last in a position to rest from my exhaustion, I found it impossible to assume the usual attitude of slumber, and I thought, reverently but ruefully, of Isaiah's words, "for the bed is shorter than that a man can stretch himself on it, and the covering narrower than that he can warm himself in it." Long time I traversed my couch in a vain pursuit of sleep, and then I dreamed that we were playing hide-and-seek as in childhood at the old house at home, and that in "the lumber-room," and in an old oak chest containing ancient family raiment, in which we delighted to "dress up" and to gratify the dramatic instinct, innate in all, I had secreted myself with a sure success, when suddenly the lid fell and the click of a spring lock amazed me with a terrible apprehension that I should perish like young Lovell's bride. Happily I awoke—while making frantic but futile efforts to communicate with my friends through the keyhole—like Childe Harold in his pilgrimage, "awaking with a start, the waters heave around me," not to mention a miscellaneous mixture of bright scarlet rugs with my customary suit of solemn black, sheets and shirts, hats and shoes.

The morning investment was quite as incommodious as the unrobing at eve, and whenever, to expedite the operation, I ventured to put out a leg some vulgar pedestrian rushed by, thrusting it aside, and then grunting his displeasure. I do not wonder that the potentates of the rail make very different provisions for their own comfort, that they prefer real beds to boxes and bins, and cosy sleeping apartments, elegantly and luxuriously furnished, to the ordinary sleeping-car, that they elect to have special trains of their own, or special accommodations, when they condescend to march with the ordinary rank and file. It seems to me, although complaints are made, that they have a perfect right, these presidents and receivers, managers and chairmen of the railway companies being as a rule among the ablest, the most energetic and enterprising, as well as the wealthiest of their nation. The chief management of one of these great American lines requires such a sagacity, diversity of information, keen, patient observation, coolness, and courage as are very rarely bestowed upon one man; but, as a rule, that one man is found. He is autocratic—of course he is; he is admired, he is famous, he wins golden opinions from all sorts of men—of course he does; but he is too wise (I was introduced to him), he has too much common sense to be bumptious. He does not propose to go into that business—he says it's overcrowded.

Different words are used in speaking of railways and their surroundings :—

RAILWAYS.

They say.	*We say.*
Railroad.	Railway.
Track.	Line.
Car.	Carriage.
Baggage.*	Luggage.
Depôt.	Station.
Engineer.	Engine driver.
Fireman.	Stoker.
Conductor.	Guard.
Switches.	Points.
Freight train.	Goods train.
Ticket-office.	Booking-office.

Here it may be opportune to notice some other idioms, differences in verbal descriptions of the same thing, set down in order as I heard them:—

In England.	*In America.*
Letters are *posted*.	They are *mailed*.
Tradesmen sell their wares in *shops*.	In *stores*.
Boots and shoes are *polished*.	They are *shined*.
We make *inquíry*.	*Ínquiry*.
We talk about *goloshes*.	They are called *gums*. "Mother is wiping her gums on the door-mat."
Our children are *born and brought up*.	They are *raised*.
We express astonishment with *Goodness gracious! Well, I never!*	They exclaim, *O my!*

---

* The American system is better than ours in this matter of baggage, though sometimes it is very roughly handled. Reserving such articles as you require during your journey in a portable box or bag, you transfer the rest of your belongings to the officials at the depôt, receiving checks, which you produce on reaching your terminus, and this luggage is sent to your hotel.

In England.	In America.
Beefsteak	Is *tenderloin*.
We *carry on*, we *conduct*, a business..	It is *run*.
We say *immediately, at once*.	They say *right away*.
First floor	Is *parlour floor*.
Biscuits	Are *crackers*.
Cut wood	Is *lumber*.
The lift	Is *the elevator*.
A good deal	Is *pretty much*. Quite a good deal.
Somewhat early	Is *pretty* soon.
Quick, nimble, clever	Is *spry*.
To *give*	Is to *donate*.
Racing	Is *speeding*.
A *Racecourse*	Is a *speed-track*.
A *commercial traveller*, or *Bagman*	Is a *drummer*.
Influenza	Is *grippe*, as in France.
Sweets	Are *candies*.
Street pavement	Is *side walk*.
The driving-reins	Are *the lines*.
We shall be there *in* time.	We shall be there *on* time.
A *wooden house*	Is a *frame house*.
To *make* a collection.	To *take up* a collection.
To *carry*.	In Virginia and elsewhere is to *tote*.

" De possum and de coon are as safey as you please,
Since all de hunting dogs was *toted* off by fleas;
De measles *toted* off all de cunning little Nigs,
And de soldiers of de army have *toted* off de pigs."

The chairman *opens* the meeting.	The chairman *calls* the meeting *to order*.
To *place*	Is to *locate*.
A horse *jibs*.	He *baulks*.
The man who is called a *spooney, greenhorn, nincompoop*.	Is known as a *tenderfoot*.

In England.	In America.
To aim *straight*	Is to *draw a bee-line*, straight as a bee returns to its hive.
Improvements in cultivation, etc.	Are *betterments*.
When we say *Indeed?*	They say, *Is that so?*
We say *What?*	They say *How?*
Bank notes	Are *greenbacks*, first issued during the Civil War; the Confederate notes were blue.
An *idle* man	Is a *loafer*. "I do not call him a thief, but if I was a chicken, and I saw that nigger *loafing* round, I should roost high—dat's all."
To *move away*	Is to *make tracks*.
Some time	Is *quite a while*.
Straightforward	Is *right away*.
A mean person	Is a *scrimp*.
Papa and *mamma*	Are *poppa* and *momma*.
A good many.	*Quite a few*.
A *cabby*	Is a *hackman*.
Hired carriages	Are *hacks*.
A travelling bag	Is a *grip*.
A *vicious horse*	Is a *mean horse*.
A *dandy*, or *masher*,	Is a *dude*.
He who does not vote with his party—a *turncoat*	Is a *bolter*.
A *deception*, a *sell*, *chouse*, or *swindle*	Is a *fake*.
To get into trouble	Is to *wake snakes*.
A *downright good fellow*	Is *clear grit*.

Reverting to the rail, I was sorry to see the same field advertisements so common at home. I am prepared for any number of announcements in the cities and towns of articles on sale, or performances on view, which "bang creation" and which "stump the world." I gazed with admiration at a huge banner, some twenty feet in length, rising from a gilded dome, and gracefully floating above the houses in Union Square, at first supposing that it surmounted some great national institution, or intimated the anniversary of some great historical event, but discovered on a closer inspection that it was only an invitation to purchase "the Crawford Shoes." I delighted in the solemn pedestrians who walked the Broadway attired in sacks, on which the public were informed in large letters that "Professors Jenkins and Moon, Chiropodists," were available for consultation. I was inclined when the snow was thawing in the streets to "Try our nobby Romeo Rubbers," though I had not noticed that Sir Henry Irving wore them when he appeared under the balcony of Juliet. I was glad as a father to know that *"Papa's Pants would do for Willie*, if they were altered and dyed with *Diamond Dyes*, the great home money-saver," and that " children's clothes —the faded cloak, wrapper, or dress—could be made to look like new at a cost of only 10 cents., and no experience needed." I never presumed to doubt the proclamation made on the outside of a store, that "The man who exclaimed, 'Oh, what a fall was there, my countrymen!' would have felt no surprise, and would never have uttered such an imbecile observation, could he have foreknown the *stupendous Fall in Prices which would take place in this Establishment* on Monday next, and during the week." I could not say with the tender-hearted elephant in the American "Æsop," when, having trod on the mother partridge, she beheld the wee chicks close by, "I am a mother myself," and sat down on the callow brood, but I did not question for a moment the powers of "*Payne's Celery Compound* to restore health in a few weeks to those daughters who, owing to rapid growth or absorbing study, have a waxy, bloodless look, and are suffering from nervous languor." I stayed to listen to the brass bands which preceded vociferous heralds of "Ruinous *Sacrifice!*" and "*Slaughter* prices!" I watched the procession of men with brooms which symbolized "the *Sweeping Sales!*" I assented to the statement "that if any lady or gentleman felt as if rats were gnawing the coats of their stomachs, these rodents might be quickly expelled by *the Shaker Digestive Cordial*, originally invented by the Society of Friends." And, finally, I beheld with almost a childish glee the illuminated letters traced in glowing lamps of crimson and gold, which defied the darkness of the night and all who passed through Madison Square to deny or disprove that "Paul Jones's Pure Rye has No Equal," or conferred elsewhere effulgent honours on "The Admiral Opera Cigarettes."

But I draw a line when I am *procul negotiis*—far from the madding crowd—and protest against these ugly innovations which, when I would forget the streets and the cars and the mart, and would enjoy the country and inhale the purer air, advise me, in letters big enough for Brobdignag, to take "Carter's Little Liver Pills," or "Schenk's Mandrake" ditto, while I simultaneously sucked "Adam's Pepsin Tutti-frutti as the best aid for digestion;" played on "Slanter's Piano," and smoked "General Bull Tobacco." I do not want to be told in hideous yellow delineations upon a black ground that "Children weep for Pitcher's Castoria," even as in England they mourn for Mr. Pears's soap and Mr. Ridge's nutritious food. It gives me no pleasure to be assured that "Julius Saul, of Albany, is the World-Beater for Children's Clothes," that "Dodd's Liquid Fish Glue Mends Everything," and that "Salve Cea Kills Chilblains and Frostbites, and Stops Itching at once."

CHAPTER XIV.

NEWSPAPERS.

The advertisements suggest the newspapers, and the newspapers—the American newspapers—suggest a perplexity. I have to express my hearty appreciation of the kind words which were written in them wherever I went, and simultaneously to declare my conviction that they are not altogether worthy of a great nation. I was interviewed by more than two hundred journalists of both sexes, old and young, and so far from being bored by their tedious dullness or exasperated by their inquisitive curiosity—as certain false prophets foretold—I was almost invariably pleased by their courtesy and instructed by their information. Surprised, moreover, by their retentive memories, which often, without making a note, would publish the details of a twenty minutes' conversation almost verbatim; and if, as in two or three cases, recollection failed, imagination, less accurate but always kind, built up the broken wall. The lady interviewers were especially bright in conversation and clever in eliciting the communications which they desired. The editors and sub-editors are, as a rule, men of superior ability and intelligence. Their articles on political, commercial, social, and international topics are thoughtfully argued and lucidly expressed; but they pander to that morbid craving for the terrible which, like the ghoul or the horse-leech, thirsts for blood, gloats upon the ghastly corpses spread out in the *morgue*, and makes a collection of murderers, robbers, and ruffians of all denominations, to which Madame Tussaud's Chamber of Horrors is by comparison a bower of innocence and beauty. I am emboldened to make this protest, not only because I know it to be in accord with the convictions of those Americans whose judgment has first claims on our respect, but also because, when I freely spoke my disappointment to the journalists themselves, none dissented or disputed, and only defended on the plea of expediency—the people loved to have it so—*populus vult decipi*.

When Charles Dickens first visited America he wrote the most severe and scathing denunciation of the corrupt portion of the American press which indignation could suggest or eloquence utter. He described it as a monster of depravity, accused it of rampant ignorance and base dishonesty. He ridiculed the "New York Sewer," the "New York Stabber," the "New York Family Spy," the "New York Private Listener," the "New York Peeper," the "New York Plunderer," the "New York Keyhole Reporter," the "New York Rowdy Journal," as containing "particulars of the last Alabama gouging case, the interesting Arkansas duel with bowie knives, and the extensive account of a flagrant act of dishonesty committed by the Secretary of State when he was eight years old — now communicated at a great expense by his own nurse." He testified, at the same time, to journals of character and credit, from which, conducted as they were by accomplished gentlemen, he derived both pleasure and profit. He said that among the gentry of America, among the well-informed and moderate, in the learned professions, at the bar, and on the bench, there was but one opinion of these degraded journals. He affirmed that these were, nevertheless, in an overwhelming majority, and that their name was legion; and yet on his second visit to the States, although he had made no retraction, he was invited to a public dinner by two hundred representatives of the press, and at the banquet itself only modified his railing accusation by saying that there had been "changes in the press, without whose advancement no advancement can take place anywhere."

One of these changes is happily manifest in the cessation of bitter, hostile, and contemptuous words about the mother country; and we read no more of the British lion having his talons eradicated by the noble bill of the American eagle, that he may be taught to play upon the Irish harp and the Scotch fiddle that music which is breathed in every empty shell that lies upon the shores of green Columbia. But there is less improvement with regard to accumulation from all quarters of criminal incidents and the minute exposition of their details; and the attempts to justify are as feeble as they are few.

It has been stated that these revolting particulars create disgust, aversion, and decrease of crime. The police reports bear evidence, on the contrary, that in many instances they have suggested imitation, and put sharp weapons in the madman's hand. It is said that the public will have these records, gruesome and unclean. What a charming home it would be in which the children were permitted to eat and drink whenever and whatever they fancied, and the youths and maidens to go where and with whom they pleased.

The press, with its infinite power, should elevate and not debase. Is there to be no praise of religion or virtue—even though it might evoke jealousy or annoy the worldling? There is room for more mention of the many benevolent societies, and the charitable work which they do. There is room for an outburst of righteous anger at villainy; for tenderness of pity towards those who suffer; for hope of remedy; for ideas of reform. As though you were serving on an inquest, you are to view the body —smashed, scorched, pierced by bullet or knife, without shroud or coffin—without a sigh or a tear. That I may nothing extenuate or aught set down in malice, I quote illustrations. The first five are the more remarkable extracts from a single copy of a daily paper, published in one of the largest cities:—

BENT ON BLOOD!

Man Shoots his Wife, her Sister, and Himself.

WIFE DIES, OTHERS WILL DIE.

Martin V. Strait, of Elmira, Commits Three Murders.

FIVE MEN COOKED!

Mud Drum Burst and the Contents Strike a Number of Workmen.

MUNCIE, Ind., Nov. 16.—The large mud drum under the boilers at the Muncie Muckbar Mill burst last night and five men were drenched with hot mud and scalding water. This stuck to them and cooked the flesh. The victims are: John Gainer, Valentine Gibson, John Curtis, Lenzie M. Tyler, and John Bowers—all over forty years and married. The flesh on their hands, faces, breasts, and legs is cooked. When Gainer's clothes were removed the flesh dropped off in places. He cannot recover. The other men are suffering terribly, but will not die. The mill was slightly damaged.

RAIDED!

Dozens of Houses of Prostitution Pulled.

HUNDREDS AT THE STATIONS.

Every Place in the 1st, 2nd, 3rd, and 4th Precincts Visited.

Supt. Bull gave the Order at Eleven o'Clock Last Night, and the Patrol Wagons were Kept Busy for Three Hours.—Women were Brought In by the Score.—Scenes at the Station-houses.

WHITWORTH IS DYING!

He is said to have been a Defaulter, and this may have been the Cause of his Crime.

NASHVILLE, TENN., **Nov. 16.**—George K. Whitworth, who killed Chancellor Allison, is not dead, but is sinking rapidly, and there is no hope of his recovery.

"RED DUCHESS" IS DEAD!

She Raced Horses under the Name of "Mr. Manton," and was a Notable Figure in the Racing World.

LONDON, Nov. 16. — Caroline Agnes Beresford, dowager Duchess of Montrose, known in the racing world as "Mr. Manton," and also as the "Red Duchess," is dead. The duchess died at her London house, No. 45, Belgrave Square, S.W.

The following are from other sources—samples from an infinite bulk :—

WITH A WRENCH!

Money-lender Short Murderously Assaulted in his Office.

Rest Charged with the Crime.—Motive was Robbery. —Short had $1800 in a Wallet in Front of Him.—An Exciting Chase.

KUKLUX CRIME.

Thrown Wounded into a Pit Sixty Feet Deep.

Rescued after Five Days of Terrible Suffering, and Returns to Bring his Assailants to Justice.—Remarkable Tale told on the Witness-stand.

TRIED A BIG JOB.

Desperado Waylaid and Attempted to Kill a Party of Thirteen People who were Witnesses against him.

DUEL IN THE SNOW.

Dr. Reigle Objected to the Attention His Wife Received from Her Cousin, William Bebler.

EMPTIED THEIR PISTOLS.

Each Fired Six Shots at the Other, and Both were Wounded, though Not Seriously.

CLINCHED ON A HIGH BANK.

The Doctor Fell to its Bottom, One Hundred Feet, but Landed in a Big Snowdrift.

(By Telegraph to the "Herald.")

BLOOMSBURY, N.J., Dec. 31, 1894.—Dr. E. Lear Reigle and William Bebler fought an impromptu duel here in the snow on Sunday morning. Each fired six shots, all there were in the revolvers, at each other at close range, and each was wounded, but not seriously.

Their pistols emptied, they clinched, and the doctor fell down an embankment a distance of one hundred feet into a deep snowdrift, and his antagonist fled. The affair was caused by a woman, and she the wife of Dr. Reigle.

HE KICKED MRS. MINNIE LEE.

Wine Agent Julius Kauffman First Knocked Her Down in the Park Casino.

BECAUSE SHE REPROVED HIM.

He also Struck at "Bud" Ellis and Missed, but Succeeded in Felling Landlord Isaacs.

AMID A WRECK OF DINNERS.

Grovelled for Mercy.

Eye-witnesses of the scene that followed speak eloquently of the details, but the policemen themselves are modest about it. Kauffman, flushed with the triumph of kicking a woman and pummelling a genial boniface, was promptly and effectively humbled.

Crusted with the remnants of overturned dinners, and bleeding from sundry swift blows on the nose, the humiliated Kauffman was finally dragged from the Casino like a bag of potatoes, and right across lots to the Arsenal. Landlord Isaacs, attended by a party of well-known gentlemen, witnesses of the disgraceful fracas, appeared there as complainant, charging Kauffman with assault, disorderly conduct, and drunkenness.

The diversity of subjects in these sensational paragraphs, sometimes in close proximity, are startling — as when "Stunning Bonnets at the Lyceum" are followed by "Fifty Persons Drowned in the Flood;" or "Fight between Corbett and Fitzsimmons to come off in Florida" by "A Meeting of the Roman Catholic Synod and the Pontifical High Mass." But rarely, in continued sentences, is such an antithesis to be found, such a swift transition from the pulpit to the playhouse, such a sudden association of the preacher and the pugilist, as in the following extract:—

TALMAGE A NEW YORK PREACHER.

Henry Eyre Brown, the organist of the old Tabernacle, and Prof. Peter Ali, who played the cornet for so many years in Dr. Talmage's Brooklyn church, furnished the music yesterday. As soon as Dr. Talmage left, the theatre carpenters went to work to set the stage for the regular Sunday night vaudeville show which Mr. Billy Brady, manager of Pugilist Corbett, gives.

Sometimes they are humorous. I select two examples from leading New York papers, which would mightily astonish the readers of the *Times*:—

SHE KILLED THE MOUSE.

The Captor Hurried Home from Church with the Creature Clutched Fast in her Dress.

Serious trouble arose during morning service

yesterday at St. George's Episcopal Church, in Rutherford-place, that fashionable house of worship presided over by the Rev. Dr. William S. Rainsford. The cause of the trouble was small, but it created much uneasiness until it was removed. Fortunately, the excitement was confined to two persons, and the creature to blame for it was forced to give up its life as a penalty for its boldness. St. George's Church was filled by the customary fashionable congregation at morning service. Among them was a woman-parishioner who is well known in social circles, and whose husband is a business man of prominence. During the singing of the *Te Deum*, she suddenly arose and made a hasty retreat. The ushers looked concerned, but the lady passed quickly through the door—which was held open for her—and asked no aid.

She went swiftly up the street convulsively grasping a portion of her dress, and, when she arrived at her residence, frantically rang the door-bell.

"Oh, Ann, Ann!" she exclaimed in tones of anguish to the maid who opened the door—"I came out of church with a mouse. I felt it while the Creed was being said, but it kept quiet through the Psalter and part of the First Lesson, and I had almost thought I was mistaken; but presently I felt it again, and I clutched it. I thought possibly I could manage to hold it fast, and remain throughout the service, because I wanted to hear the sermon. 'But suppose it should get away?' I thought. That decided me. I couldn't sit out the sermon, so here I am; and now, while I hold the horrid little animal tightly, you catch hold of its tail."

The servant declared she could see no mouse, and said she believed the animal only existed in her mistress's imagination. The servant continued her investigation, however, and, in a few moments, exclaimed—

" Why, sure enough it is a mouse, after all!—But you've squeezed the breath out of it. You must have gripped it awfully hard to have killed it." And she drew from her mistress's dress the little animal squeezed flat.

MANY OFFERS OF MARRIAGE.

Scores of Women Write to the Nine Unmarried Hatters who were Discharged in Watsessing.

The Postmaster of Watsessing, N.J., is seriously considering the propriety of asking the postal authorities for an increase of salary. His work has increased to such an extent during the last few weeks that he has great trouble in handling it. Curiously enough, most of the letters which make up the increased mail matter are addressed to nine young men who were recently discharged from the hat factory owned by the Ellor Brothers & Hall.

It became necessary not long ago to reduce the working force in the factory. The proprietors carefully considered the matter, and decided that the married men in their employ should not be disturbed. Then they told nine unmarried men that, as no one was dependent upon them, their services would be dispensed with.

The story of the sad fate of the unmarried men of Watsessing was widely published, and then the postmaster's troubles began. Many unmarried women read the story and sympathized with the unfortunates of Watsessing. They made known their sympathy in writing. So many women wrote letters that the mail pouches left at Watsessing, formerly easy to carry, became well filled and difficult to handle.

Nearly every letter received by the young men

contains an offer of marriage. In some of them, financial inducements are presented, which lend an additional attraction in view of the fact that the men are out of work. Four young girls who are employed in a factory in a Central Ohio town wrote a joint letter, in which they offered to become the wives of four of the unmarried hatters. They added a postscript, in which it was intimated that the railroad fare of the young men to the Ohio town would be paid if the hatters accepted the proposal without delay.

An Omaha girl, who wishes to aid one of the hatters, is not willing to take any of them " with her eyes shut," but has written that she would like to have a photograph of each from which to make a selection. Several widows have written that, in addition to marrying the young men, they will give them a half interest in their farms.

Most of the letters are written by girls and widows in western towns. The people of Watsessing will not be surprised if the nine young hatters leave within a short time, to select wives from among the charming letter writers.

Such chronicles may be regarded as silly and insipid, as beneath the notice of those who write, and as wasting the time of those who read newspapers; but beyond this they are harmless. The viands have not much aliment, but they are easily digested. They do not create those diseases of the heart and the brain—the acrid humours, the restless fevers, the bad dreams—which wait upon the rich sauces and highly seasoned dainties—composed to stimulate a morbid appetite no longer able to relish wholesome food. The public press should be prescriptions of a wise physician, advising healthful diet and exercise, not a *menu* wherein the palled appetite of the epicure may find new incitements to gluttony, indigestion, and gout.

Of these poisonous preparations I cite, in conclusion, that which seemed to me the most noxious of all, the description in a daily newspaper of last January, of a drinking bout of thieves and prostitutes held in the lowest haunts of vice and corruption, to celebrate the return of one of their gang from penal servitude. The proceedings are minutely detailed, in a spirit of facetious levity, as though crime were little more than a jest. A few sentences will demonstrate the shameless and offensive character of an article which occupied a column of the paper, and was accessible for perusal to all the wives and daughters in the city :—

IS BACK IN THE FOLD.

Reception to Minnie Williams on Her Return from Joliet.

Distinguished Company of People whom the Police Delight to Honour with their most Assiduous Attentions.—Some of those Present.

The guest of honour was Minnie Williams, formerly convict No. 3158 of the Illinois State Penitentiary, but now of Chicago. Miss Williams, after an absence of eleven months from the city, was joyously received by her old friends, who spent much good money and drank much questionable wine in expressing their welcome. The only drawback to the entertainment was the enforced absence of one of the most distinguished of Miss Williams's old friends. This was Miss Lilly Vale, who is now being cared for by the State on a sentence of seven years recently imposed.

We are then informed of the enthusiasm with which she was received, and a long list is given of *the names of the women present with a description of the dresses which they wore* :—

Among the men present were: "Dandy" Nugent, petty thief and "grafter"; Frank Quirk, known as Dora Donegan's right hand; Ed. Clancey, nothing in particular; Thomas Roach, ex-convict, burglar, and sneak thief; Ed. Newberry, petty thief; Charles Harlow, given to petty larceny and pocket-picking; James Johnson, undistinguished; Ed. Long, street-car "worker"; Charles Hanson, who says he has "thieved some"; Tom Allen, general thievery and confidence work; Tom Donovan, Highwayman; Charles Peters, "tin horn" gambler and race-track "tout."

After the guests had eaten and drunk their way through the *menu*, and had reached coffee, Miss Williams was called on for a speech. She is not accustomed to making addresses except in court, but her words were well received. She spoke of the accommodations at the county jail, and compared them unfavourably with those of Joliet. The jail, she said, was one of which Chicago people ought to be ashamed. In this view she was heartily supported by most of those present. After the speech, there was wine galore, and the popping of corks continued for several hours.

All who love America must protest against these

degradations, these abuses of a predominant influence, the power of the public press.

Facility of production has established a cheap and daily circulation of millions of newspapers. In a most interesting lecture addressed to the students of Cornell University, Mr. Dana, the editor of the *New York Sun*, informs us that, before the invention of the new printing machinery, an old-fashioned press that could turn out six or seven hundred copies a day was the best there was in the world, but that now it was possible to turn out at one impression large sheets of eight, ten, or twelve pages, and deliver twenty thousand papers in an hour. But the great revolutionary agent, he said, was the cheapness attained in the cost of paper. At first paper was made from rags, and the demand became greater than the supply. Then a Frenchman invented a method of making paper from rye-straw, and the value of that article rose in the State of New York from $6 to $20 a ton; but the paper thus made had a silicious surface, which in three months wore out the types. Then the inventor left the field for the forest, and now all printing paper that is used in newspapers is made out of wood, and when you pick up your paper in the morning the probability is that you are picking up a piece of spruce tree from Norway,[*] or taken out of the Adirondack country, or

---

[*] "In Norway a new industry, the paper pulp trade, has in a few years become extremely important, and the manufacture of it is carried on entirely by cheap water-power, derived from considerable falls on the glacier-fed streams."—W. C. UNWIN.

wherever in North America the spruce is grown. That which is now universally used is made out of spruce trees or pine trees, or almost any other soft wood. It is put into a mill and ground to powder as fine as flour, and then it is converted into pulp, and from that the paper is made by the mile and circulated by the million.

According to the latest statistics, the number of newspapers in the United States is now 1855 dailies and 14,077 weeklies.* The editors and their staffs are, as a rule, men of brains and culture, work hard, and well deserve their remuneration, stated to be on an average as follows—Managing editors $5000 per year, equal to the average salary of bishops of the various churches, and only $500 less than that of brigadier-generals of the army. In New York city the salaries are higher than anywhere else, because of the superior standard of proficiency, and partly because the cost of living is greater than in any other large city. The editor-in-chief has the same salary as the President of the United States, $50,000 per year, and others receive from $10,000 to $12,000, or more than members of the Cabinet; editorial writers (recurring to the average) $3500, equal to the salary of an Assistant Secretary of State at Washington, and more than the average salary of college presidents; city editors $2500, only a little less than the salary of a Secretary of Legation at one of the leading Courts; news editors, copy-readers, and space-writers

* From *The Forum*, January, 1895.

$1800, matching the pay of a captain in the army or a junior lieutenant in the navy; and reporters $1200, as much as the average income of those engaged in commerce. For cities of over 200,000 and less than 400,000 inhabitants these averages have to be lowered from 10 to 15 per cent., and for cities of less than 200,000 about 25 per cent. The average pay of journalists of all the dailies is to be put at $1500.

Such being their attainments, in capacity and income, there is no excuse for the piling up of the agony, for the proclamations in huge and hideous type of the most abominable crimes, for a procession of bad men and bad women on the front of the stage, as though these actors were of all the most important, and as though this rogues' march down hill to perdition were much more interesting to the public than the march of intellect, the progress of industry, the advancements of science, the ascents of religion and of truth. Moreover, this protrusive accumulation of horrors, with all their ghastly details, leaves a false impression upon the mind of the stranger, not taking into account the immense area from which they are collected, that America has precedence in the crimes so conspicuously and constantly recorded; and all of us who know and admire her true character must feel righteous indignation that it should not have the universal appreciation which some few of her children affect, but cannot afford, to despise. This sensational system, this appeal to the lower instincts will be discarded, and meanwhile it is consolatory to know that the effort, the ambition which inspired the fat boy in Pickwick when he said, " I wants to make your flesh creep," is defeating its own purpose—the appetite is sated to repletion, and the digestive organs are beginning to decay.

CHAPTER XV.

THE NEIGHBOURHOOD OF NEW YORK.—
WORCESTER CITY.

As the young rook before he flies abroad to the woods and fields exercises in brief migrations from twig to twig and from tree to tree his powers of volitation, as the jockey takes his preliminary canter before he rides his race, or as the bowler takes advantage of the "trial balls" before he attacks the wicket, so before I went forth to deliver my lectures in the great cities of the States, I had the privilege of addressing smaller audiences in the neighbourhood of New York, of encouragements from sympathetic hearers, instead of the frigid, silent stare foretold by false prophets, and also of instruction as to the subjects which pleased them most. For example, when I was informed by a clergyman who invited me to lecture in his district that the subject which I had chosen, "Fifty Years in the Church of England," did not evoke any sympathy, and that my audience had never heard of Pusey, Newman, or Keble, I did not repeat the offence, although in other places an affectionate interest was often expressed in the history, past and present, of the Mother Church, and even, on the occasion referred to, the kind approbation which the lecturer received excluded any signs of indifference to the subject.

One of my earliest and happiest experiences on the platform was at Brooklyn, where I addressed, by invitation, the members of The Twentieth Century Club. I did not inquire whether this title was chosen to denote that the society was somewhat in advance of the age, being abundantly satisfied with the fact that it was one of the charming coteries which had been formed in the chief cities for the social and intellectual intercourse of those who desire to unite the amenities of friendship with the acquisition of knowledge and the accomplishment of art. I have not seen brighter assemblies. They are held in large houses, with all the adornments of a refined and wealthy taste, amid things pleasant to the eye and good for food, amid faces beautiful and thoughtful, gay costumes, sparkling gems, pictures and flowers. The portly Britisher in his eighth decade is somewhat perturbed by a steep ascent to a bedroom on the second floor for the deposition of his hat and overcoat which he had been accustomed to leave in the hall, with a *da capo* movement when he departs suggesting a negro melody which we sang fifty years ago at Oxford, "Such a gettin' upstairs I never did see."

The most remarkable figure in the company at Brooklyn, the most unlike the others, yet admired

of all, venerable in the simple garb of widowhood,
with no decoration save the ornament of a meek and
quiet spirit, was Mrs. Beecher, the wife of the famous
preacher, the Spurgeon of the States. The greatness
and the goodness of Henry Ward Beecher were never
duly recognized in England, and his reception in this
country was rarely cordial, and was sometimes hostile.
The faithful members of the Church of England are
fully persuaded in their own minds of the truth of
her doctrines, and do not go to hear those who
contradict them, and for the more highly educated
portion of our countrymen there was a lack of the
reverence, refinement, and scholarship, which they
admire, in the sermons of Mr. Beecher. When the
Duke of Argyll and Mr. Gladstone were asked to
contribute to a volume of tributes to his memory,
they both declined on the plea that they had not
sufficient personal knowledge, although the former
testified to the noble work done by Beecher and
"his illustrious sister, my old friend, Mrs. Beecher-
Stowe," in the great contest against slavery, and
the latter referred to his undying fame. Archdeacon
Farrar was far more enthusiastic in his declaration
that it was impossible to hear him without being
struck by his great power, and that he had
rarely listened to any man who seemed to have a
more powerful hold upon his audience, or a more
generous sympathy with all sorts and conditions of
men of every race under the sun. The Rev. Newman
Hall expressed "his sorrowful and strong disapproval

of some of Mr. Beecher's theological utterances in later years," but he added that this in no degree interfered with his admiration of his genius, his unrivalled eloquence, and his labours as a philanthropist.

These are, I believe, the only contributions of eulogy from men of note in England to "the Beecher Memorial," whereas in America his death not only evoked the highest praise of his worth and his work from many of her most distinguished men, but a general, almost a national, grief.

Oliver Wendell Holmes remembered his visit to Pittsfield, thirty years ago, and how he had dispelled the gloom of a day which, though it was not known in his household by its Jewish name of the Sabbath, was observed in the old Puritan fashion. On Saturday all playthings were put away at "sundown," all voices were hushed, and all features subdued and sobered. When Mr. Beecher appeared, joyous and radiant, it seemed as if the leaden cloud which had hung over the day for so many years had given way to a burst of sunshine. No long faces, no melancholy tones, no fear of a smile, or even a laugh, no constraint, but, on the contrary, a wholesome, natural, cheerful welcome to the day of rest. In the pulpit he had a gift of fervid eloquence, which swayed the multitude before him as the wind sways the leaves of the forest. He never addressed men as if they were convicts, born rebels, and would-be devils, but as brothers to be helped, to be led, to be raised upwards. What a comfort it was, after hearing a bloodless invalid preaching "as a dying man to dying men," to hear a sound, strong-bodied minister of the gospel speak with virile force and ringing accents as a living man to living men. He was a mighty power in the land.

Whittier wrote: "Apart from his unequalled pulpit successes, our country owes to him, as a great moral and political force in his day and generation, a deeper debt of gratitude for his noble services in the dark days of the Rebellion."

The President of the United States, Mr. Grover Cleveland, expressed "his appreciation of the loss which he and his country had sustained in the death of the great preacher, whose friendship, based upon acquaintance and personal contact, had been to him a source of the greatest satisfaction. He never met Mr. Beecher without gaining something from his broad views and wise reflections."

Generals, and admirals, and millionaires brought wreaths and laid them on his grave. The famous soldier, Sherman, spoke of his most warm friendship with a national man, grasping all the thoughts and feelings of a continent, whose writings would carry hope and consolation to millions. Admiral Porter affirmed that, as a theologian, orator, lecturer, or citizen, his vacant place was not likely to be filled, and that as a speaker he could only be compared to Niagara, sweeping all before it; to the Himalayas, overtopping all other mountains; or to the leviathan, compared with whom the common herd are but as a shoal of minnows. Mr. Andrew Carnegie declared that in the death of Mr. Beecher America lost her greatest citizen, and the world her greatest preacher. That he resembled Shakspeare and Burns in this—that he was without prototype, and would remain without a successor.

Authors praised him—Will Carleton with a sweet, pathetic poem upon an incident in his life; Bill Nye with a bright, earnest encomium. Actors testified. It could not be said to Ward Beecher as by one of their community to a vapid preacher who inquired, "Why do I fail and you succeed with an audience?" "Because we represent fiction as though it were reality, and you treat reality as though it were fiction." Edward Booth remembered "that on one of the saddest occasions of his life Mr. Beecher had sent him such a message of hope and encouragement that he ever held him in grateful and affectionate esteem." Dion Boucicault, to whom Mr. Beecher had frankly confessed that he had learned, among other truths, how wrong he had been in the prejudice he had entertained, and the attacks which he had made, against the stage, suggested an epitaph :—" Beecher fills a grave; but no man can fill the grave which he has left in the world, above the sod, and under the sun."

If it be urged that they who write these obituary notices are tempted, sometimes from a desire to gratify the living, and sometimes from a desire to demonstrate their powers of composition, to be too effusive, and that the authors of these panegyrics are apt, as in the Himalaya simile, "to pile it up a little too mountainous," I would make answer, "Go to America, and hear, as I did, from those who knew Beecher best, what sort of a man he was." This, the strongest evidence of all, convinced me that, though he had, like all public men of superior talents, many jealous opponents; though, like all men who denounce vice and preach righteousness, he was derided by the sensual and doubted by those who, finding no good in themselves, cannot believe in its existence elsewhere; though he sometimes startled and sometimes irritated his friends—"was," as Wendell Holmes said, "uncomfortably hot to meddle with, shot up into extravagance," and, as General Sherman said, "occasionally kicked over the traces;" though he was attacked by railing accusations, and passed through a protracted and painful ordeal before he was acquitted; though he did not leave as monuments of his charity any great and costly institutions, such as the college and the orphanage established by Mr. Spurgeon; he was beloved and honoured by those who were the most closely associated with him, and was acknowledged by all as a man who, having extraordinary gifts, devoted them to the honour of his nation, and the benefit of his fellow-men.

No one, I believe, outside his own home, knew Mr. Beecher more thoroughly than his friend, and my friend—his agent, and my agent—Major Pond, of

New York. He was often with him for consecutive weeks, by themselves, and in company. He heard him preach and lecture, and listened continually to those revelations of the inner man which find utterance in private conversation. He was with him in seasons of great success and of great disappointment. He was with him in those dark years of terrible anxiety, when he was suspected, hooted, and reviled. He saw him re-established in the love and confidence of the people. For thirteen years he was the friend that loveth at all times, and the brother born for adversity. Then he was summoned to stand by his deathbed and to weep beside his grave. Eight years afterwards, when his friendship, if it had depended upon pecuniary advantage and mere mutual accommodations, would have been forgotten, Major Pond seemed to keep it perpetually " in memory's fondest place," and was constantly referring to Mr. Beecher's sermons and speeches, his patriotism, his philanthropy, his courage, his truthfulness and sincerity, his hatred of shams, his tenderness and gentleness, his love for the children, his cheery humour, his sympathy and sorrow, his delight in his flowers and trees,* his admiration of all things beautiful. The

---

* He was an enthusiastic and successful gardener. "I went to Indianapolis," he wrote, "in the summer of 1839, and here I built a house and painted it with my own hands ; here I had my first garden, and became bishop of flowers for the diocese ; here I first joined the editorial fraternity, and edited the *Farmer and Gardener*." He read Loudon and Lindley, even as in theology he read Barrow, South, and Butler.

major kindly presented me with some of his friend's sermons—full of common sense and striking illustrations—and his "Patriotic Addresses," containing memorable arguments and splendid eloquence.

The child was father to the man, and there was an early development of his wit. One day his sister took him aside to a private apartment, to drill him in the rules and definitions, which caused much perplexity. "Now, Henry," she said, "you must remember that *a* is the indefinite article, and must be used only with a singular noun. You can say *a man*, but you must not say *a men*." "Oh yes, I must," replied the boy—"at the end of my prayers. Father always says so." Then he was called upon to decline *he*—nominative *he*, possessive *his*, objective *him*. "You see, *his* is possessive; you can say *his*, not *him* book." "But I do say 'hymnbook,'" exclaimed the pupil with a merry grin, "and take it with me to church." Finally, when his attention was invited to an explanation of the difference between the active and the passive voice, and his sister remarked, "You see, Henry, *I strike* is active, because if you strike, you do something; but *I am struck* is passive, because if you are struck, you don't do anything, do you?" He promptly protested, "Oh yes, I do. *I hit him again.*"

I lectured in Flushing, a bright and pleasant town, "a goodly place," and we had "a goodly time" under the hospitable auspices of Mr. Robert

Parsons. He resides in a modern mansion with charming grounds, and with two of the tallest tulip-trees I ever saw, guarding, like gigantic warders, his entrance door; but he is also the owner of one of the most ancient—if not the most ancient—habitations in the States, the old Bowne homestead, which he inherits as representing the seventh generation in descent from him who built it. It is a privilege, I think, to live where our forefathers have lived for centuries; to play, and to see our children—it may be our children's children—play amid the same surroundings; to worship where they worshipped; and if, in our mid life, we have work to do elsewhere,

> "We still have hope, our long vexations past,
> Here to return, and die at home at last."

But beyond this I see no advantage in knowing the Christian names of our ancestors, unless they were men of renown; and, under any circumstances, rational people will smile at the claims of long descent, unless *noblesse oblige,* and honest men will have nothing to do with that fabrication of pedigrees which is not uncommon with our *nouveaux riches,* and is in some cases almost as ludicrous as the claim supposed—by a vivid imagination—to have been made by the Queen of the Sandwich Islands, "that she had English blood in her veins, because one of her forefathers had partaken freely of the remains of Captain Cook." Nevertheless, a genealogical tree with seven "rings" is, in these days of sudden splendour and eclipse, by no means common in the old country, and, of course, more rare in the new; and it was interesting to inspect "the house," not "with seven gables," but with seven owners, who were kinsmen in sequence, accompanied by the present possessor. It is one of those unpretentious but comfortable houses—with its low ceilings and small windows, its simple furniture, its cleanly sweetness, its huge fireplace—in which the American pines burned with an exhilarating glow and warmth which no other fuel gives; its snug recesses in the lower chimney, wherein, when the snow lay deep upon the Broadway, the goodman smoked his pipe and the good dame sat at her spinning-wheel; with doors on either side, through one of which the ox brought in his load of logs, and, having no room to turn, went round the long dining-table, and so passed in and out; such an abode as was occupied a hundred years ago by our substantial yeomen, before fine clothes, and mirrors, and bad champagne were regarded as essential to human happiness, and a thing, which sauntered about with its hands in its pockets, was supposed to be a gentleman.

There is, however, an explanation of the plainness, without and within, which involves a much higher principle than that of thrift or propriety. The builder was the leader of the Society of Friends, who were numerous in Long Island. He came from England in 1651, and in 1661 erected this house.

The British forces were encamped in the neighbourhood during the war, and I saw the aperture which had been made in one of the walls for the secretion of plate and other valuable articles. During their occupation of the place, it is recorded to their credit that, when they first approached the meeting-house, and found that it was the time of service, "with commendable courtesy they stacked their arms in the porch, and waited until the worship was concluded, before they took possession."

George Fox, the founder of the Society, who in his youth was a shepherd-boy like David, and passed his early years among our grand Leicester sheep, and who afterwards, when he went forth on his sacred mission, resembled in his costume one of the greatest of preachers, the Baptist, being known—I do not write in ridicule—as "the man with the leather breeches"; Fox "the Quaker"—the world is quick to disparage with derisive terms the enthusiasm, the zeal, the earnestness and piety which rebuke its apathy, and it was said of the Master, whom he served so truly, "He is beside Himself"—mistaken in many ways, as most of us believe, was, nevertheless, apostolic in his self-denial, for he left all and went forth with his Bible in his hand—more than apostolic, Christ-like, for there were times when he had not where to lay his head, and slept in the open air, Christ-like in his poverty, in his love of the poor, in his endurance of persecution, despised and rejected of men. George Fox visited Flushing some two hundred and thirty years ago, and Mr. Parsons showed me the site of the last of "the Fox Oaks," under which he preached, and which had perished little more than a year ago.

Mrs. Parsons related to me a catastrophe in her family history, so tragic and so strange that I asked and received permission to repeat it in her own words:—

"Theodosia Burr, daughter of Aaron Burr, married Governor Alston of South Carolina. A great sorrow came upon her in the death of her son, and her husband suggested that she should go to New York to join her father, hoping that the change of air and scene would be of service. My grandfather, Mr. T. R. Green, at that time practising as a lawyer in New York, was called south to consult with his brother, Dr. Green, at Columbia. After attending to his business, he passed on to Charlestown, whence he was soon to embark for New York; and being a friend of Aaron Burr, he was asked by Governor Alston to take charge of his wife. The vessel on which their passages were secured was called the *Patriot*. She had been a privateering cruiser, her guns being stored below. The voyage to New York took five or six days. The vessel started in the month of December, 1812, *and nothing more was heard of her*, until many years afterwards, so the story goes, a man, who lay dying in an almshouse in Michigan, expressed his desire to see a minister of the gospel, and to a Methodist, who complied with his request, he made the following statement: 'I was a lad about twelve or fourteen, and was employed on a pirate ship. Before the *Patriot* sailed, we noticed that she had a rich cargo on board, and it was known that Mrs. Alston was taking with her a great deal of silver and jewellery, which our captain meant to have. We sailed after her, overtook, and boarded her in mid sea. The captain, crew, and passengers were made to "walk the plank." Mrs. Alston was a very beautiful woman. She asked permission to go down into her cabin, and shortly returned, dressed in white, with her Bible clasped upon her breast. Sailors are superstitious, and she hoped to move their hearts. The command was given, but the man to whom it was spoken refused to obey, and I was ordered to tip the plank, and dared not refuse. I have never forgotten the look of that face; it has haunted me all my life. Mr. Green perished in the same way.'

"Aaron Burr and my grandfather waited, hoping against hope for tidings of those whom they had loved and lost, but though he lived for many years after that disastrous voyage—he died in 1836—no tidings came.

"In the house of one of the Burr family there was a portrait of the beautiful Theodosia Alston. One morning, when the family came down to breakfast, the picture was gone; it had been cut out of the frame. It was ultimately discovered, such is the tradition, in the cabin of a sailor."

Then, when my "young muse had waved her

joyous wing," I took a longer flight, to Worcester, in the State of Massachusetts, and of its cities the second in size, a fair city of well-built houses, and wide streets, and avenues of trees, which with their bright leafage and pleasant shade refresh the wayfaring man.

Here I had a most genial reception from the Rector of All Saints; and after we had knelt side by side in his beautiful church, two priests dwelling more than three thousand miles apart, but one in faith and doctrine, one in charity, and I had admired the arrangements not only for worship, but for education also in the large school attached to the church, and we had inspected some pieces of carved stone, which had been sent from Worcester in England during the restoration to Worcester in America, with the same filial love and reverence for her who is the Mother of us all, we had a delightful drive through the city, and then a charming panoramic view from the top of Newton Hill. We saw the public offices and institutes and schools, and a very effective group of figures known as the Soldiers' Monument. There are magnificent libraries, as in all the great cities of the States, the American Antiquarian Society and the Public Free Library each possessing more than sixty thousand books.

We had a sprightly little congress at dinner, including two members of the Senate, and some humorous talk about humour. We were of one mind that a majority of the most laughable stories were those of impossible exaggeration, solemnly narrated as established facts, which the most incredulous sceptic had never dared to doubt; or of a combination of disparities and juxtaposition of extremes, a fusion of the incongruous, of the minute with the magnificent, the silly and the sublime; of complications and accidents by which our dear fellow-creatures are suddenly brought into situations of discomfort painful and perilous to them, but ludicrous to the spectator; or of some adroit exposure of humbug, some rebuke and prostration of bumptious folk.

I should cite, as an example of exaggeration, the story of the affectionate dog who, when his blind owner stumbled and fell as they crossed a railway, saw the express in the distance, tore the red neckerchief from the throat of his master, twisted it round a forepaw, stood on his hind legs, and, with this impromptu signal of danger, stopped the train; or the statement made as to the intense heat in Arizona, which necessitated a constant supply of broken ice in the poultry yards to prevent the hens from laying their eggs hard-boiled.

Among contrasts which provoke our innocent mirth, all the more enjoyable because it may not be expressed, may be included a gigantic wife arm-in-arm with a tiny husband, a very fat man with a red face (I saw him in the booth of some strolling players at a country fair sixty years ago) playing "Romeo" in the tightest of "tights," strained to the uttermost, and evidently designed for a lover youthful and slim;

and I remember that at a great ecclesiastical function I, the largest person of the company, was told by an insane *ceremonarius* that I was to walk in procession with the smallest of my brethren, because he was a dignitary, and that I rushed at the most substantial curate I could see, and besought him not to leave me. Had I taken the place assigned to me, the effect would have been as though by some confusion a giraffe and a goat, a turkey and a tom-tit, had walked side by side into the ark.

Asked for proofs of the gleeful and unpardonable satisfaction with which we contemplate the sufferings of our fellow-men, I desire to mention those falls in the hunting-field, those submersions of the horse and his rider in the brook, which, without waiting to ascertain whether our brother's neck is broken, or helping him out of the water, we regarded with peals of laughter.

I met a gentleman once by "the sad sea waves" who, from motives of economy or privacy, had retired far from the madding crowd and the machines to bathe. Some naughty urchins had watched him from the cliffs above, descended, removed and secreted his clothes. He was furious. He forgot that his denunciations and anathemas, when he had nothing on, and was in a lonely place where there were no police, were not calculated to inspire awe. I lent him my overcoat, and shall never forget his language or his legs (they were in form of the order which I have heard a rustic describe as "bad uns to stop a pig in a gate," and resembled in substance those of a colonial bishop of whom it was said that he ought to have been apprehended as a vagrant having no visible means of support) as we walked together towards a cottage on the beach.

At intervals we were greeted with derisive sounds, which came to us from the rocks above, and increased in volume whenever my companion halted to look upward, and shake his fist, like Ajax defying the lightning, at his jubilant and inaccessible foes. Finally he was struck by the comedy of the situation, which from the first had oppressed me with an ecstasy—or, rather, with an agony—of enjoyment which was becoming intolerable, and he gave me the opportunity of opening the floodgates of a reservoir which had well nigh burst its banks.

Who does not admire the transcendent power of humour in the demolition of shams, in the pricking of windbags, in the removal of masks and wigs, the nudification and flagellation of rogues? Charles Dickens, the king of humourists, made a wise selection when he placed the representation of old Weller sousing "the Shepherd," after a long series of preliminary kicks, in the horse-trough, for in that history, as in the histories of Pecksniff and Uriah Heep, he preached, and preaches, to millions of men such sermons as have helped them all to despise hypocrisy, and to love sincerity and truth. In these various phases of humour it seems to me that, since Dickens died, the Americans have taken precedence, and when such brains as I possess are on strike, and I am wearied by work, I find alteratives and tonics not only in "Pickwick," "Nickleby," and "Copperfield," but in Artemus Ward, Mark Twain, and Nye—of the latter more when we meet.

The nations of the world do not yield the priority in imaginative power without a struggle. The Frenchman in whose family there had been so many field-marshals that their bâtons were used as firewood, the Irishman who saw so many hares in a field that some of them had to sit on the gate, and the Englishman who, on hearing a visitor from New York criticising—as well he might—the inferiority of our provincial hotels, inquired whether the traveller had seen "The Black Swan at Falmouth," and assured him, on receiving a negative answer, that after such an inspection he would certainly have modified his views, because the dining-room at this hotel was the largest in the world, and all the waiters went about on horse-back—these, all of them, were men of genius.

Moreover, we have some splendid artists in humour, such as Burnand and "Jerome," Rudyard Kipling and Lewis Carroll; nor has *Punch* a rival in the States; and yet I am inclined to believe that the first prize for terse, smart, ready wit in conversation and in public speaking must be awarded to Jonathan. Here is a sample:—A proud Britisher, who had forgotten history, was conversing with an American upon a subject then under discussion by the two nations, and, losing his temper, foolishly said, "If you fellows don't know how to behave yourselves, we shall have to come over and teach you." The threat only evoked two words of meek expostulation, "*What again!*"

CHAPTER XVI.

NIAGARA.

If I were asked to name, according to my knowledge, the most wonderful place in the world, I should make answer, "Niagara Falls." Wonderful, because no other sight which I have ever seen so surprises with awe and admiration, so subdues the spirit to a reverent adoration of Him, who, repeating the miracle of the Red Sea, has "made the waters to stand upon an heap;" so wonderful, that no poet, no painter, can present to the imagination or the eye the grandeur or the beauty of that scene; but also wonderful as being the site of a scientific enterprise, which promises to be the chief achievement of engineering skill in the creation and adaptation of electric power. Few subjects are more interesting than the discovery in the materials which surround us of a force, hitherto unknown, its transfer from natural sources, and its appliance to machinery, its introduction as a new and precious tool into the great workshop of the world.

What a development there has been in the last sixty years of this scientific success! What revelations to patient study, to the experiments of men undaunted by failure—to hard, persevering work. I remember in those blissful days of boyhood, when I went a-fishing on the banks of the brook to the old mill pool at Norwell, and my face flushed, and my heart throbbed in anxious ecstasy, as the new float, all aglow with vermilion and bright green, danced awhile upon the surface, and then dipped into the flood; I remember when that float was quiescent, in those opportunities for reflection which are so abundantly bestowed upon anglers, how impressed I was by the revolutions of the great wheel, notwithstanding the ravages which had been made in its timbers by damp and by decay; that I regarded this stoppage and subjugation of Nature as magnificent, but almost profane; and that I believed the miller, although of a snappish disposition, and somewhat offensive in the expression of his views as to my early enjoyment of tobacco, to be the greatest of living engineers.

My thoughts reverted to the old mill when I saw, sixty years afterwards, the wheel at Earl's Court, and again when I gazed on Niagara Falls, and recalled Professor Unwin's calculation that "they represent theoretically seven million horse-power, and for practical use, without appreciable diminution of the natural beauty, several hundreds of thousands of horse-power." The reference to a diminution of natural beauty caused a shudder when first I read it, but the agitation was brief as it was chill. There has been always, and is now, the most reliable evidence that, so far as human wisdom can provide, there shall be no diminution, no disfigurement of the glory of Niagara Falls.*

The contrast which I have drawn as to the motive power of water suggests an incident which, as a philanthropist, I am constrained to repeat. It was told to me and others some time ago by my friend Dr. Conan Doyle, and I run the risk accordingly of evoking from the critic who knows all stories the accusation, so odious to the author, especially when it is applied to a dear little anecdote of his own composition, of "Chestnut, chestnut;" but it is unknown to most men; and so, in the sure expectation of their gratitude, I provide an ointment for my wound:—

One who was born and lived close by the cataract, of course saw nothing extraordinary about it, but took it as a matter of course, and as a probable appurtenance of all villages. When he came to manhood he had the opportunity of reading Southey's poems, and the well-known verses on the waterfall of Lodore excited his curiosity. "Ah!" he sighed, as he put down the book, "what if some day I might see Lodore!" That day came. He crossed the Atlantic, and hurried from Liverpool to the Lakes,

* The State of New York and the Province of Ontario have made every provision and taken every precaution for the safe custody of the falls, by the appointment of superintendents with subordinate staffs. No less a sum than $157,000 was paid on the American side at one deposit for the purchase and removal of paper mills, etc., which marred the beauty of the scene.

made inquiries at Ambleside, and followed directions given; but he could neither see nor hear Lodore. Wearied by his wanderings on the hills, he sat down on a bank, and seeing a countryman approach, he addressed him: "Friend, I have come between four and five thousand miles to see your famous cataract. Tell me where—oh where!—are the great waters of Lodore?" And the rustic drew nigh and said, "*You be a-sitting on it!* But," he added, noting, it may be, a look of disappointment on the countenance of the pilgrim, "it'll be all right when the rain comes, and it comes reg'lar." The American replied with complete composure, and in a gentle tone, that, being in a somewhat delicate state of health, he thought that the exhibition might be almost more than he could bear. So he returned to the States, and persuaded a disagreeable neighbour, who had done him an injury, and whom he much disliked, to save up his money, and go and see Lodore.

We elderly gentlemen have been, and are, eye-witnesses of many other inventions and improvements which are now culminating in the application of electric power. I recall the dreary dimness of the oil lamps in the streets of Newark on the Trent when I was a schoolboy in that fair and loyal town, and took a prominent part in the elections—though I never received any recognition of my services—by shouting, "Red for ever!" whenever I saw a bit of blue ribbon, thus subjecting myself to much menace and many missiles, followed not seldom by vigorous pursuits with a view to *habeas corpus,* the latter always a source of high delectation, seeing that I was swift-footed as Achilles, and knew every yard and alley in the town.

How we exulted, how sure we were that we had attained to perfection as we walked in the glare of the gas, and the slow movements of the watchman in his cumbrous raiment were exchanged for the more brisk activity of the spruce policeman.

Again, I see the huge vans of Pickford crawling on the roads, and remember my yearnings as a child for admission into the small apartment, half filled with straw, at the end of the carriage, " to play at houses," and at travelling in foreign lands, with the little Pickfords, who, as I supposed, had no other habitation.

And the mail coaches! — the guard in scarlet splendour, with his long horn on one side, and his great blunderbuss on the other. Providentially these guards were not called upon to discharge their hideous artillery. I only remember one exception. Some mischievous young fellows, so the story ran, dressed up a dark hirsute figure, and, propping it against a wayside hedge, fired a pistol from the bank below as the mail went by in the moonlight. The result was that the guard was knocked off his perch by the recoil of his own blunderbuss, which he duly extricated and let off at a distance of one hundred and fifty yards from his object, that the horses ran away, and that, finally, no one was hurt.

Then there were the ordinary coaches, piled at

Christmastide with pyramids of white wooden barrels containing the delicious "natives" from Messrs. Lynn and Pim, at—weep, Epicurus,

> "Tears from the depth of some divine despair,
> While thinking of the days that are no more"—

something like six shillings a barrel. I have seen these pyramids sway to and fro more than once, when some young swell has tipped the coachman, and Phaeton, with the sun in his eyes and an erratic leader, has not been master of his team.

The iron horse superseded the four spanking tits, and, though the devious driver and his boon companions sang lustily—

> "Let the steam pot hiss till it's hot,
> Give me the speed of the Tantivy trot,"

the coach, as a public institution, with all its enjoyments of fresh air, exhilarating motion, pleasant scenery, and cheery conversation, and with all its miseries—biting sleet and nipping frost, scorching sun and choking dust, on the moor and on the mountain, the crowding and the cramps, the umbrellas dripping into the nape of your neck, until you felt, like Miggs, "as though water were running aperiently down your back;" the incessant putting on and taking off of skids, the man whose hat was always blown away as we descended the hill, and the tipsy man who sang rude songs with rasping discords, and fell asleep and snored, and seemed as though he would fall from the coach—but disappointed us—at every lurch—the coach, I say, as a conveyance for travellers has been expelled, with all its joys and sorrows, by the locomotive power of steam. It has been revived, nevertheless, in its most attractive form as an equipage of the rich, and a few enthusiasts still, as when we harnessed our younger brother and sisters with tapes and curtain rings, play at coaches.

Some think that steam, as a motive power, will ere long be superseded by electricity. I remember a remark which Sir Richard Owen made to me as we stood by the railway at Richmond—" The time will soon come when all this will be done by electricity." Babbage wrote more than sixty years ago that the source of steam-power—the fuel—was limited in quantity, and that a time might come when the coal-mines would be exhausted; and he spoke of the tides as an inexhaustible source of energy if means could be found for utilizing tidal action. This gigantic scheme, suggestive of an Atlantic Company Limited, makes the Niagara project to look "mean and poky" —as Martha Penny said of the Protestant religion in Hood's " Up the Rhine "—but it is not at present within the range of practical politics, whereas the work goes on at the Falls.

Qui va piano, va sano! And the engineer who is too ambitious may be hoist on his own crane or submerged in his ship-canal. All the splendid consummations of skill and industry, which appear to some so novel in conception and so rapid in completion, have been won by a combination of many minds, in many years, after many failures and mistakes. We stand upon the graves of those who discovered, and explored, and planned, and felled, and builded, and mined, and we say, "My arm, and the power of my might, hath gotten me this wealth."

The Rev. William Lee, vicar of Calverton, in the county of Nottingham, watched his wife knitting stockings—there seems to have been a time in England when all our ladies did some useful work— and her manipulations and her needles gave him the first idea of that "spinning-jenny" which was afterwards brought into successful operation by the Hargreaves, Arkwrights, and others. And so, in this matter of the utilization of water for the production and transmission of electric-power, we are informed by Colonel Turrettini, President of the Municipality of Geneva, and director of its public works,* that the town of Schaffhausen, on the Rhine, was the first in Switzerland to endeavour to use the river passing through it to procure power for driving the machinery of the manufacturers in the neighbourhood. At that time—twenty-one years ago—no other means of transmitting power were known than that of wire-ropes; and, for that purpose, very costly apparatus was set up in the middle of the river, the Rhine being dammed up so as to procure a fall to drive a set of turbines. About 1500 horse-power was

* See *Cassier's Magazine* for July, 1895—"Niagara Power Number."

obtained in this way, and was distributed to neighbouring workshops. Three years ago three new turbines were added, of 300 horse-power, driving dynamos which distribute the electric-power.

A few years later, an English company established a water-power plant, amounting to several thousand horse-power, at Belle Garde, on the Rhone; in 1878, at Zurich, and, about the same time, at Fribourg, companies were formed, and similar work was undertaken; but the chief enterprise was suggested by Colonel Turrettini himself, namely, the utilizing of the whole power of the Rhone as it issues from the Lake of Geneva and passes through the town. He made a special study as to the best system of distribution. Wire-rope transmission of power had been condemned by experience; transmission by compressed air gave unsatisfactory results; and transmission by electricity had not, in 1882, reached the degree of perfection which it has since attained. The only system which remained was that of water under pressure, and, though its efficiency in ordinary cases might have been inadequate, in this it was a satisfactory success. The water of the lake is absolutely pure, and could, therefore, be used as drinking water, as well as for general industrial purposes and motive-power. The same water-mains could also be applied for town purposes and for working private turbines. A credit of two million francs was voted by the Municipal Committee, 1883; and, in less than nine years from the starting of the machinery, seventeen turbines out of the eighteen contemplated have been erected, and the eighteenth is now being constructed. Financially, the work has done well, rendering in 1894 a net profit of $2\frac{1}{2}$ per cent. after deducting $3\frac{1}{2}$ per cent. for the interest on capital and the sinking fund for wear and tear of machinery. New works are, accordingly, in progress on an extensive scale, and will soon be completed, making another 18,000 horse-power available, and will be the most important in existence after those of Niagara Falls: "but"—to quote the modest words of the chief factor—"they will be very far from being rivals."

The power of electricity which might be generated and distributed from Niagara Falls seems to have been suggested to Sir William Siemens when he saw them in the autumn of 1876. We read in his biography, by William Pole, that in all his many journeys in different countries, nothing made such a deep impression on him as this wonderful natural phenomenon. The rushing of mighty waters filled him with fear and admiration; but he saw in them something far beyond that which was obvious to the multitude, for his scientific mind regarded it as an inexpressible manifestation of mechanical energy. And he at once began to speculate whether it was absolutely necessary that the whole of this glorious magnitude of power should be wasted in dashing itself into the chasm below; whether it was not possible that at least some portion might be practically utilized for the benefit of mankind. He had not long to think before a possible means of doing this presented itself to him. The dynamo-machine had just then been brought to perfection by his own labours; and he asked himself, Why should not this colossal power actuate a colossal series of dynamos, whose conducting wires might transmit its activity to places far away? This great idea, formed amid the thunderings of the cataract, accompanied him all the way home, and was a chief subject of his reflections long afterwards in the quiet of his study.

Ultimately, in 1877, he submitted to the public the results of his meditations in an address to the Iron and Steel Institute, of which he was president. He pointed out the dependence of the iron and steel manufacture on coal as a fuel. He alluded to the gradual diminution in the stores of the earth of this valuable commodity owing to the vast consumption of it for steam-power, and he urged that other natural sources of force, such as water and wind, ought to be made more use of. He said that although the immense advantage of water-power was not at present appreciated, it might, sooner or later, be called into requisition. They might take the Falls of Niagara as a familiar example. The amount of water passing over this fall has been estimated at 100,000,000 tons per hour, and its perpendicular descent may be taken at 150 feet, without counting the rapids, which represent a further fall of 150 feet, making a total of 300 feet between lake and lake. But the force represented by the principal fall alone amounts to 16,800,000 horse-power, an amount which, if it had to be produced by steam, would necessitate an expenditure of 266,000,000 tons of coals, at four pounds per horse-power per hour. In other words, all the coal raised throughout the world would barely suffice to produce the amount of power which daily runs to waste at this one great fall!

The tremendous power obtained must be distributed, the district being devoid of mineral wealth, or other natural inducements for the establishment of factories, and must be conveyed through large metallic conductors, and then be made to impart motion to electro-magnetic engines, to ignite the carbon points of electric lamps, or to effect the separation of metals from their combinations. A copper rod, three inches in diameter, would be capable of transmitting 1000 horse-power a distance of, say, thirty miles, an amount sufficient to supply one quarter of a million candle-power, which would suffice to illuminate a moderately sized town.

America may well rejoice in the practical realization of these great ideas, but Mr. Stillwell, who had under his supervision the entire installation of electrical apparatus at the Falls, candidly declares * that "she is in no position to claim exclusive credit." In the plans for the hydraulic plant, Switzerland, the land of water-powers, shows the way, while in the

* *Cassier's Magazine*—"Niagara Number," p. 253.

design of the great electric generators, the most powerful as yet produced, Great Britain is represented directly in the excellent general form of construction adopted, which was proposed by Professor G. Forbes, and indirectly in the works of Hopkinson, Kapp, Thompson, Mordey, and others, who have done so much to make possible the design of a machine far beyond the range of actual experience in full confidence of success.

Were it possible to trace to its true source each one of the great number of ideas embodied in the complete installation, it is probable that we should find nearly every civilized nation represented—England, America, Switzerland, France, Italy, and Germany—some in greater degree, some in less, but all co-operating to achieve what is beyond question one of the most significant triumphs of engineering skill in this nineteenth century.

There are delightful walks in the groves, avenues, and islands,* with ever-changing views of the rapids and the great cascades—the best being, from the American side, "Hennapin's View," so called after Father Hennapin, of whom tradition records that he was the first white man who saw Niagara Falls, in 1678. He described them as "a vast and prodigious Cadence of Water, which falls down after a surprising

* Goat Island, eighty acres in extent, is said to contain a greater variety of flora than any other locality of the same area, but when I was there those beauties were asleep beneath their counterpane of snow.

and astonishing manner, insomuch that the Universe does not afford its parallel. The Waters which fall from this horrible Precipice do foam and boyl after the most hideous manner imaginable, making an outrageous noise more terrible than that of Thunder." The reverend father seems to have been in an irreverent mood, with neither eye nor tongue for the sublime, and I have only heard one other disparagement of this magnificent creation, and that was drawled by an insipid youth with a receding forehead, who affirmed that "for the life of him he never could see what that sort of thing was for." Had he been aware that "the thing" was capable, by a somewhat elaborate and expensive process, of supplying a light for his cigarette, he might have criticized less severely.

The traveller must cross the Suspension Bridge into Canada, "when the sun is westering," to enjoy the most comprehensive and impressive view of the American and the Horse-shoe Falls. But they are always beautiful—in winter frozen into glaciers, in spring and summer with verdure clad.

When I first saw the American Falls a gorgeous rainbow spanned them with its arch from bank to bank, without a flaw or dimness, like a bridge made of precious stones; and solemn thoughts came to me of the waters abating, and the great flood going down, of the promise of mercy, and of the token of the covenant, and the rainbow of glory around the Throne of God.

At Prospect Point the visitor stands at the summit of the American Falls, close to the very brink, with only a low wall between. Here the waters of four great lakes—Erie, Huron, Michigan, and Superior—fall suddenly a hundred and sixty-seven feet. The first thought which occurs to the mind is of the swift destruction which must ensue to

NIAGARA IN WINTER.

all life which reaches that boundary and we are reminded, as we gaze upon the scene of the tragedy, of the pathetic story which tradition tells—how, in the old time, the Indians worshipping the great cataract offered yearly, with other sacrifices, the most beautiful maiden of their tribe. She was launched upon the rapids in a white canoe, decorated with flowers and laden with fruits, and was swept away to certain death. The last victim was the daughter of the chief of the tribe, a man of great renown and honour. When the selection was announced, he made no protest and showed no sign of grief, but when the time came for the sacrifice, and his child, lovely and beloved, went forth to meet her cruel doom, another canoe was seen to leave the bank for the rapids, and almost at the same moment the father and the daughter went down the falls.

Then the French took these districts from the Indians, and then the English took them from the French, and then the Americans took them, to a large extent, from the English. Peace prevails, but there are still tragic associations connected with Prospect Point. Not a few of *les misérables*, shattered in mind, body and estate, have here ignored their apprehensions of the "something after death," and have hoped to end their woes by suicide.

From the Canadian side, and on the Horse-shoe Falls, a strange weird sight was seen on the 29th of December, in the year 1837.* During the rebellion organized by the party calling themselves "the Patriots," against the ruling powers in Canada, there was a very strong suspicion among the English that arms and ammunition were supplied to the insurgents by their American neighbours. It was

* See Mr. Porter's "Niagara in History," *Cassier's Magazine*, p. 380.

asserted and believed that a small steamer, called the *Caroline*, under pretext of conveying passengers from Buffalo to the encampment of "the patriots," was furnishing them with weapons of war. A plan of retaliation was arranged, and at midnight on the date named, as the vessel was lying in dock, she was surrounded by six boats filled with British soldiers sent from Chippawa by Sir Allan McNab, was boarded, and, when her crew had been ejected, was cut adrift, set on fire, towed out to the middle of the river, and launched on her last voyage. "A glorious sight viewed merely from a scenic standpoint: ablaze all along her decks, her shape clearly outlined by the flames, she drifted grandly and swiftly towards the falls. Reaching the rapids, the waves extinguished most of the flames; but, still on fire, racked and broken, she pitched and tossed forward to and over the Horse-shoe Falls." This inflammatory proceeding had well-nigh kindled a conflagration; there was a wrathful outcry for war between America and England; but the counsels of wise men prevailed.

We saw the deep waters below Goat Island Cliff into which Sam Patch, the diver, twice leaped from a height of a hundred feet; the whirlpool rapids in which Captain Webb was drowned; and the heights from which Blondin crossed, in the presence of the Prince of Wales.

I did not visit the Cave of the Winds, *Rex Æolus Antro*. I met a man, attired in a suit of tarpaulin, who had recently passed through. He was a good man, a man of honour and veracity, superior to that silly self-conceit which will never acknowledge that it has made a mistake or been subject to imposition. So when I asked him what sort of a tenement the winds had taken, he simply said it was "beastly"; and he added, with appropriate and accurate humour, "that he would be blowed if he ever went there again." Blinded by mist and spray, he had seen nothing, but had felt much from continual collisions with the rock along which he crawled.

Ever since, I have respected that man, girt about with tarpaulin and truth, for there are few periods in our existence in which we feel so intensely our degradation of manhood, and realize so painfully our imbecilities of judgment, as those in which we find ourselves, when we have paid, and paid dearly, to be placed in situations of wretched discomfort, and are expected to bubble over with tears of thankful joy. I mean when we are laid out in a boat, and told that if we raise our heads we shall be scalped by the jagged roof above (I make one exception in favour of the "Blue Grotto" at Capri); when we are driven on a crowded coach, having previously noticed severe abrasions on the leaders' knees, with two of the wheels on the rim of a precipice; when we are creeping along some *mauvais pas*, or climbing among huge slippery boulders, with continual invitations to skip from one to the other as though we were goats, or with kind but ignominious offers to take the hand of the guide.

I went, when I was a long lad, with my father

through a cavern, dark and low, nigh unto Castleton, in the county of Derby. We passed through that miserable tunnel in the form of two notes of interrogation—? ? Water dripped copiously upon us, and the man who wrote that objectionable line, "Let some droppings * fall on me," would have been more than satisfied. When we emerged, stood upright, and breathed the air, my father turned to our conductor and inquired, "Well, my man, and what are we to have for this?" Nevertheless, the man got his half-crown.

I did not hear that any human being who had gone down the Falls had survived; but many animals —dogs, cats, and even pigs—have recovered. Dr. Rosen Muller, the Rector of Niagara, showed me a photograph of "Bismarck," a cocker-spaniel, who, jumping at a bird by the riverside, fell into the water, and was whirled down the cascade. No hope was entertained of his reappearance; but ten days afterwards he came back to the Rectory, unchanged, with the exception that he took no further interest in birds.

It only remains for me, ere I leave Niagara, to express my gratitude to the Honourable Mr. Welch, the Superintendent of the Reservation, for all his courteous consideration. Never shall I forget the sight which I saw when, after our descent on the inclined railway, he turned and bade me "look to the left," and the great wall of waters rose heavenward close to my feet.

* More recently amended to "drops."

CHAPTER XVII.

TORONTO, DETROIT, WHITEWATER, MILWAUKEE.

I RAISED my hat, with "God bless the President," as I left the States, and lifted it again with "God save the Queen," as I entered her dominion, and long may the two great nations behold how good and joyful a thing it is for brethren to dwell together in unity. America, so far as my information goes, has no wish to annex Canada, having, like other great landowners, quite as much on her own hands as she knows how to manage; and Canada has no desire to be annexed. If ever, in the ages to come, she should be unanimous in seeking independence, England will remember the 4th of July.

I had a most happy reception at Toronto; the bishop welcomed me at the station, the governor sent me a courteous message by his son and secretary, and a deputation of my brother-florists awaited my arrival at the hotel. So that Toronto was indeed to me, as the word means, "a place of meeting," with much kindness and many friends. After the usual interviews with the gentlemen of the Press, who were always in attendance, and always kind, the bishop took me to see the choir of his new cathedral, a stately building with clever carving in stone and in wood, and good painted glass by Heaton and Butler, and after dinner introduced me to a sympathetic audience of fifteen hundred people. A well-trained choir of a hundred and fifty voices discoursed excellent music at intervals, and Gounod's "Send out Thy Light and Thy Truth" was exquisitely sung. Among those who came to see me when the lecture was over were three emigrants whom I had baptized and taught forty years ago, in the little village of Caunton, who had never been more than six miles from their home before they set forth to travel between four and five thousand on land and sea, with just enough money to pay the costs of the journey, and only the assurance from some friend who had gone before that there was work to be had. They seemed to be doing well; but they had a wistful look, as we talked about old times and companions, and the lips quivered and the eyes glistened when we shook hands at parting. It was manifest in these, as in other cases, that, whatever had been the privations or provocations in the "old country," and whatever had been the prosperity in "the new," there were pensive yearnings for home.

I spent but a few hours in Canada, and left Toronto by order of my director—who had to arrange my lectures as best he could—by the midnight train for Detroit.

Detroit is a fine city, the chief city in Michigan State, with more than two hundred thousand inhabitants, with spacious streets, avenues, squares, and, in addition to a great public park, an abundance of trees.

The grass-plots in front of the houses, which are watered at the public expense, are a pleasing refreshment to the eye, and here, as elsewhere in the States, the absence of palisades, and walls, and fences of all denominations, is much to be admired, and an example which might be advantageously followed by many of my fellow-countrymen, who seem to think that their possessions are desecrated if visible to a neighbour's eye, and who immure themselves accordingly in genteel and lofty jails.

The lighting of the city is unique and effective, the electric lamps being placed at the top of metallic columns a hundred and fifty feet high.

I was amused to read in the newspaper notices, the morning after my lecture, an article headed, "Dean Hole's Calves," in which my form, features, hair, and wearing apparel were minutely described, and my general appearance was represented as that of a "Christian athlete, a whole-souled, genial, jovial man, an English Phillips Brooks."

More important topics were discussed by those interviewers who had asked my opinions, and now reported them, on subjects which were at that time under anxious discussion at Detroit. "Did I approve of the raid which had been made only a few nights ago, upon the houses of ill-fame at Buffalo? Should I advise a repetition at Detroit?" I replied that though the motive and intention had my hearty sympathies, I had no confidence in the method or results. By this sudden and cruel process of dragging women from their homes, what victories are won for Virtue? Is it not rather that in scattering the vicious, men are diffusing vice, dismissing the inmates of an hospital for infectious disease, instead of making new efforts to prevent and cure. To these, who seek rather to destroy than to save, the reproof is written, "Ye know not what spirit ye are of." They are wanting in tenderness as well as in discretion, there is something wrong both with the heart and with the head; they need patient continuance in well-doing as well as indignant zeal, love for the sinner as well as hatred of the sin. They must be asked, "Before trying such extreme severities, what has been done as to the reformatory and rescue work? What if Mary of Magdala had been driven out of Jerusalem? And are these women, whom we Christians call our sisters, to be expelled with no shelter but a prison, while they who betrayed them, and bribe them still, are free from hindrance and rebuke?" Surely these words of Tennyson should cause great searchings of heart—

> "One had deceived her and left her
>   Alone in her sin and her shame;
> And so she was wicked with others—
>   On whom will you lay the blame?"

"It is impossible to apprehend," so writes a great English divine, "the evil which may follow from one single seduction."

Then my interviewer asked me "what I thought on the subject of Sunday Closing?" I answered that I was an earnest advocate for the closing of drinking saloons on Sunday, but that I would insist on the same treatment for rich and poor, and that it should be as possible for the working man to get a jug of freshly drawn beer for his dinner at home as for the rich man to sip his whisky and soda or his liqueur at his club.

From Detroit I travelled to Whitewater, a pleasant little town with the broad breezy roads in which you can move and breathe, with their boulevards for beauty and summer shade, evoking envious admiration from the stranger, who is doomed to dwell in lanes and narrow streets sometimes described as "High," but having nothing high about them except their smell.

Here I was cordially welcomed by a most congenial brother-priest, Dr. Moran, the Rector, and by Mr. Salisbury, the Principal of the First State Normal College, which has its spacious buildings and complete staff and appliances for the training of schoolmasters and mistresses on the high ground adjoining.

I have previously spoken of the astonishing transformations which have been made in this great country during the last sixty years, and there can hardly be a more remarkable example than that which we find at Whitewater. Sixty years ago, where this College is at work on the distribution of scientific and useful knowledge (would that I could add of religious knowledge also!) with all the latest additions and helps to learning, there was no white man to be seen. Julius Berge was the first pale-face born here some fifty-four years ago.

The Indians have been displaced, but they are not neglected. If there was ever any truth in the ancient accusation that the pilgrim fathers first fell on their knees, and then fell on the aborigines, there is no suspicion of any such unkindness as concerns their descendants. Lo! the poor Indian's untutored mind is now taught the industrial arts, and to dig, and plough, and sow, and to speak the English tongue. But somehow or other civilization by itself does not seem to suit him. He is not happy in trousers, and seems to endorse the general opinion that this form of raiment is the most unsightly as yet designed by the tailor. Be this as it may, it is sad to see how he droops and fades, like some field-flower, uprooted, potted, and turned into a window plant, or some wild animal, caught and caged—an eagle in a box with iron bars, or a fox in a barrel with a chain.

Mr. Salisbury presided at my lecture, and sent a carriage next morning to my hotel, showed me the college, introduced me to the teachers, and then taking me to a large bright room, filled with the students, invited me to give them an impromptu address. I complied, of course, but refrained from uttering the first thought which arose in my mind, as I stood before that mixed audience of young men and maidens, all of that susceptible age which may at any moment be persuaded that there's nothing half so sweet in life as Love's young dream, namely, that there might be continual altercations between Venus and Minerva, and that the goddess of wisdom would get the worst of it. I was afterwards assured that such an antagonism did not interfere with the success of "the Co-operative System" (as it is termed); the familiarity of constant intercourse and the perpetual routine of study seem to suppress the more tender emotions; and I therefore considered it my duty to frown upon a flippant young man who suggested, on a subsequent occasion, that *coo*-operation would be a more appropriate term. But what was I to say to the students? You may have been accustomed for years to preach and speak without notes, but there is ever a perturbation and chill when you are invited to orate without a minute's preparation, a temporary sinking, until Faith whispers, "*Aide toi, Dieu t'aidera,*" and Hope pats you on the back.

I dare not turn away from such an opportunity, and I told them the reason why. Because, having visited my village school, when I was a country vicar, every morning of my life, when at home, for more than thirty years, I felt like a veteran among young recruits, and that I could tell them something about the scene of action, and the operations of war, their allies and their adversaries, success and failure.

They had chosen a vocation which had its special trials and temptations, which was irritating to the impatient, and wearisome to the faint-hearted, but which had infinite encouragements of recompense and reward to those who were brave and dutiful.

I told them how John Trebonius, the great schoolmaster, took off his hat when he appeared among his pupils, because he said there might be one in their number who would afterwards win great honour and renown; and how Michael Angelo had paused before a block of common marble, "because," he said, "there was an angel in that stone;" and I endeavoured to show that by a true education they might produce the greatest and best of men—men who should be not only good patriots, good citizens, good sons, good husbands and fathers on earth, but should be with the saints in heaven. For what was true education? It was not only the development of intellectual, scientific, technical attainments, it was the formation of character, of a Christian gentleman; and that can only be taught by "the wisdom that is from above, gentle, full of mercy, and good fruits;" that only gives "the gentleness which, when it weds with manhood, makes a man," keeps the child's heart in the brave man's breast, guards the chastity of honour, and can neither deceive others nor degrade itself.

Let them train athletes and rear philosophers, but let them try to endue the one with a strength which never fails, and to convince the other that "knowledge puffeth up, but charity edifieth."

I ventured to remind them of their great responsibilities, and of the question which we must all answer, "Where is thy flock that was given thee, thy beautiful flock?" and finally I exhorted them never to despair of those pupils who seem to be irrepressibly wild and mischievous, because I had already met two of these *mauvais sujets*, who, almost driven from their homes, and emigrating to the States, had presented themselves, with their wives, to my most hearty congratulations, as industrious and prosperous papas! You will find, if you seek, something good in all, and with this little leaven you may transform the whole.

Dr. Moran spoke very hopefully of the progress of the Episcopal Church in the diocese of Wisconsin, of the great increase in the number of clergy,[*] and of the popularity of the bishop, Nicholson. A rough working-man came to him at a station and said, "We like you, bishop, we all of us like you—*you make yourself the darnest commonest chap we know.*" Could he have received a more welcome encouragement?

---

[*] It is stated in the American Church Almanac and Year Book for 1895, "that the total number of clergymen in 4323 organized parishes and missions is 4870 ; and the present number of communicants 580,507; an increase of 17,429 over the previous year.

By such men, full of sympathy and affection, not appraising their neighbours by their dollars, but regarding all as brethren, and trying to make their lives happier and better, by such men is taught the only true and lasting Socialism, the only real union of hearts.

I had the privilege next day of making his acquaintance at Milwaukee, and of a personal share in his benevolence. He brought a carriage to my hotel, and introduced me before my lecture to an audience of 1500 people.

In one of the kind notices which appeared next morning in the Milwaukee papers it was stated that "when the Dean came forward to speak it was seen that he wore *the knickerbockers of his forefathers* and the other garments of the traditional dress of a Church of England clergyman. The talk was not deep, but nevertheless memorable and telling. He set the audience laughing with good stories, wit, and droll remarks, and then, almost while the laugh was going on, he thrust in a sermonette, an impressive little moral deduction or lesson."

The Rev. Dr. St. George, to whom I had an introduction, took me for a most enjoyable survey of the city and its surroundings, and to me it seemed that Milwaukee, on this lovely bay of Lake Michigan, was rightly named "the Cream City," not only with reference to the colour of the bricks of which it is largely built, but because it is *crême de la crême*. We went to the cathedral, which had originally belonged to the "Congregationalists," but had been transformed, after purchase, for the requirements of a Catholic worship. We drove through the fair avenues—Prospect Avenue, the West Grand Avenue —to North Point Tower and Park. We saw the Custom House and the County Court House and the enormous elevators which are said to hold 3,500,000 bushels of corn, and we saw, three miles from the city, the home for a thousand disabled soldiers in its extensive grounds and park.

But the most notable sight to be seen in Milwaukee is the brewery of Frederick Pabst. Imagine a dozen of the largest Lancashire factories collected and connected together, greatly improved as to architectural design and finish, and covering thirty-four acres of ground! There is a most charming and clever history of this the biggest brewery in all the world, published anonymously, with excellent photographic illustrations, and no author could have written more enthusiastically or attractively on his theme, however great, than he who has undertaken in these records to "chronicle small beer."

The fascinations of "nut brown ale," the praises of "John Barleycorn, who yields his blood for England's good and Englishmen's renown," have been told in poetry and prose, and an awful doom has been pronounced upon any person in authority if he tries to rob a poor man of his beer. When I was at Oxford, the poetical members of my college were annually invited to compete on the subject of

"Brasenose Ale,"* and every effort was made by the candidates to write from a persevering study and a full—very full—experience; but I can recall no success to be compared to that of this treatise on "Pabst." There is a solemn humour, a romance of reality, a decoration of facts, which either persuades the dull that the preparation and sale of beer is the noblest ambition which can occupy the heart and employ the brain, or leads him to believe that the whole account is an imposition; but which delights the *spry*, those who have a sense of the ludicrous, entertaining their fancy, and at the same time enlarging their knowledge.

"Fifty years ago, in the village of Milwaukee, now a city of two hundred and fifty thousand inhabitants, Philip Best and Sons had a tiny brewhouse. What to them was the result of a year's enterprise has now become the product of a single hour, and every ten seconds of the ticking clock equals in its results the effect of his longest day. The slowest of us can but admit that the world moves. Philip Best succeeded his father, *and inheriting from him the sterling characteristics which impel the descendants of the Teutonic race* to lay a solid foundation, on which shall rest the superstructure of coming progress, *he taught the world the virtue of an*

---

* Brasenose has been said to derive its name from *Brasen Aus* (King Alfred's brewhouse). If that learned monarch knew no more about brewing than he did about baking, there must have been some wry faces over the royal "cakes and ale."

honest brew, and won the respect and esteem of all who knew him. Industry, steadiness of purpose, and firm convictions actuated the development, which, in the previous sixteen years, had begun to prophesy *the mighty future which awaited the child of their creation*, and, after four years of tireless work, the two or three hundred barrels on which Jacob in early years had looked with pride became dwarfed beside the five thousand which was the honest brew of 1864.

"Destiny, with inexorable precision, marks for greatness, and Fate finds the man who shall minister to it; *yet by the blending of happy circumstances in the advent of Fred Pabst* into the brewing industry we can say with Schiller, *Fate had no voice but the heart's impulses, and he became the son-in-law of Philip Best!*

"Name a genius, and I will designate a self-made man. A youth, endued with ambition, and blessed by the freedom of America, crowned with noble purposes and high ideals, may climb to any altitude, and thus we find the self-sustaining boy of twelve the unimpeachable *protégé* of Captain Ward at fifteen, the mate on a Goodrich steamer at nineteen, and captain and part owner of the *Sunbeam* at twenty. In 1865 Captain Fred Pabst, as head of the firm of Philip Best and Co., showed the same unconquerable energy, industry, and business genius which had characterized his boyhood, and in 1873 the output of the company had reached a hundred thousand barrels! In 1889 the five hundred thousand barrel mark was left far behind, and, in recognition of a quarter of a century of tireless effort, and by an unanimous *vote the Philip Best Brewing Company, like the blushing bride of years before, with deep affection, proudly changed its name to Pabst!* In 1892, the capital stock was increased to $10,000,000, and, distancing all competitors, the race for the million barrel mark was passed, and the Pabst Brewing Company was proclaimed to be in all respects the greatest in the world!"

These records are followed by a quaint little allegory, which has some of the prettiness of Rudyard Kipling's style. It is "the Story which the Malt Told" to a gentleman, who, after enjoying a glass of "the amber beverage tipped with its snowy crown of foam," fell asleep, and dreamed a dream of the courtship of the elegant Miss Hop by John Barleycorn, and of the matrimonial alliance which, although it brought bitterness into his life, gave him character and a great success.

"In the spring of my life," said the Malt, "I grew rapidly, and rose in the world, and when my beard was grown I bowed and nodded to my companions, held receptions when the wind blew, and went through all the formalities of social life. One of my neighbours, named Hops, had a daughter, who had just blossomed into womanhood, and was tall and graceful as a vine. Our eyes met through a dear little bush which intervened. I fell desperately in love, and was seized with an irresistible desire to kiss her, when her father, a veritable old thistle, stood directly in the way.

"One day, however, with the assistance of the dear old wind, whom we all admired, though sometimes, like other travellers, he was noisy and gave himself airs, I leaned over and saluted the lady of my love. Unfortunately her father witnessed the interview, and blossomed out, all red with rage.

"Next day he had his revenge. I was cut down and bound. I was shocked, and not many days after I was threshed and deprived of my beard, and, having been clipped like a convict, was cast into a prison, called an elevator, but in my case most depressing. Then, in accordance with prison discipline, we had a bath of cold water, and became so clean and shiny that we began to swell and grow fat. But joy's full chords oft prelude woe, and our pride had a sudden fall to a great hard polished floor, on which we laid prostrate. Pretty soon I began to feel mighty good, just warm enough to be comfortable, and when the heat became unpleasant from our close proximity we were turned over by a kind gentleman with a big shovel. We actually began to grow, but we were on the eve of a terrible ordeal. We were transported to a chamber called a kiln, and placed upon a wire floor perforated with holes. The very look of the place took the starch out of me. Then the heat began to rise, and then the whole floor turned over and we fell upon another floor where it was fairly scorching. I became parched and dry, and thought that I must perish from combustion (anything but spontaneous), when I heard the head maltster say to a friend, 'You see when barley sprouts all the starch which it contains is transposed, so that it will become malt sugar when put in warm water, and the dry heat is applied to prevent any further change. The process is called malting.'

"And so we had become malt without knowing it; but our troubles were not over. We went through a long conveyor to the ground, crushed between rollers, which broke and tore our very hearts. We lost consciousness until we found ourselves in an enormous kettle, after having been tossed and turned, as I heard the brewer say afterwards, in a wash-tub, where we boiled, bubbled, and danced in ecstasy.

"Here I met again, to my intense delight, the beautiful Miss Hops! Words are inadequate to express our felicity. We were united. We were in a state of fermentation. Then, after a temporary coolness we realized our mutual dependence upon each other, our congenial dispositions, our power to make others happy, and we sparkled and effervesced with joy!"

The manufacture of cold from anhydrous ammonia, distributed in a liquid form over the storage cellars through some two hundred miles of four-inch pipes, the process of bottling (one hundred and fifty thousand barrels *per annum*), and the corking and labelling were admirably ingenious.

One hundred men are employed in washing the

barrels. The fire department is complete in all its details, and the firemen are regularly drilled. Visitors are received daily, guides are provided, and every part of the brewery is open to inspection.

When it is stated that the population of Milwaukee amounts to two hundred and fifty thousand, and that some two-thirds are Germans, it will be patent that the home consumption of Pabst's excellent lager beer is extensive. Tacitus informs us that even in his day the German nation had discovered the refreshing qualities of beer. "They make a drink of barley," he writes, "which has some similarity to wine."

CHAPTER XVIII.

CHICAGO.

BLESSED be the winds that come over Lake Michigan to murky, grimy, choky Chicago! And yet more blessed would the arrangement be if, ever and anon, the lake itself, like the beneficent Nile, would overflow its banks, and—notice being sent to such inhabitants as deserved the compliment to make for the first-floor—would give the city a swill! Even if certain tenements were submerged for a few hours, with their tenantry, there would be solace and compensation.

The main streets of Chicago resemble a numerous combination of New York Sixth Avenues. The rumble and the roar, the tolling of the locomotive bells, seem never to cease. Wake when you may in the night, you will hear the wheels in the street.

> "The forges glow, the hammers all are swinging,
>   Beneath its smoky veil
> The city, in its restless toil, is swinging
>   Its ponderous iron flail."

Chicago is a very large, and a very lively, but it is not a nice child, and nobody wants to fondle it much. It is a dirty child. It is a dark-complexioned child, and thereby hangs a tale, wherewith the reader may amuse himself at the expense of some impressible friend:—

"At the time of 'The World's Fair,' a large room was set apart, with attendant nurses, for the reception of babies, while their mothers were inspecting the Show. On one occasion a matron returned at a late hour to the *crèche*, when all the other mothers had departed, and being anxious lest—owing to the number of deposits—any mistake might have been made, eagerly inquired for her child. It was produced, after some little delay, and lo! *it was jet black!*"

Here, having related the history with solemnity and emotion, with the pathetic intonation which the French call "tears in the voice," you will pause to give your listener an opportunity to express the sympathetic sorrow which does so much honour to his Christian heart; and then you will remark slowly, and smiling sweetly, "The mother was also black."

Mr. Stead has told us, in his elaborate and eloquent essay "If Christ came to Chicago," that this child is abnormally black, naughty, and vicious. I should not myself venture to assert this pre-eminence in sin, because I believe that if such an investigation as that which Mr. Stead made—and such as was never made before—were to take place in New York, in London, Paris, or Naples, or any other great city, the scrutator would have revelations to make which, though varying in form, would be in every instance terrible; and it seems to me, moreover, that the degrees of guilt can only be determined by the Omniscient, Who knows all the surroundings, and to Whom the secrets of all hearts are revealed. None the less in proving—as he has proved—that this great metropolis of the world is corrupt and abominable, Mr. Stead has not only shown to those who live in it their peril and their responsibility, but he has reminded all Christian men of their duty to bear one another's burdens, and to overcome evil with good.

It is the easiest thing in the world to expel our application of such details to our own conscience by declaring that Mr. Stead exaggerates in denouncing Chicago as the *cloaca maxima* of the world; that he was rude to the ladies, and personal in naming the men; that he gives way to maudlin sentimentalism; that we don't want to hear details about vermin and disease, tramps and rogues, drunkenness and prostitution, blackmailing and bribery; that, after all, this misery and disgrace is the sure result and just retribution of sin; that it is a matter for parliament, parsons, and policemen; and that it seems too universal, too hopeless, for any individual effort. The simple question is, Is it true? And if it is true, dare we say, "I will do nothing to prevent or to reform?"

We may, but we must not call ourselves Christians.

When the poor man lay half dead on the road, the priest said, "I shall be late for service;" and the Levite said, "It is no affair of mine;" and the Samaritan might have said, "It is only a Jew," but he believed in Brotherhood and in GOD.

Mutual compassions and mutual recriminations supply us with convenient facilities for escaping from self-condemnation. New York and Chicago, for example, or Manchester and Liverpool, Sheffield and Birmingham, will furnish you with ample evidence that in making bargains which are not severely honest, in what is called " sailing close to the wind," there is no similarity whatever between them. Nathaniel is without guile, but Barabbas is a robber. There was a man in New York, I was told in Chicago, who was voraciously greedy of gold. It might have been said of him, as of Sam Brooks, when Brunel, the engineer, swallowed the half-sovereign, " Send for Sam; if it's gold, he'll have it." He was the autocrat of the breakfast and every other table. He was a lion in his house, a bear to his wife, and so harsh and unkind to his children, that at last one of his boys, who was high-spirited and sensitive of wrong, could no longer endure the tyranny, and ran away from home. Nothing was heard of him for many years, and then his father received a letter from him, in which he stated that he was dangerously ill, and desired to see him before he died. They met, and the son informed him that he had asked for the interview not only with a view to reconciliation, but because he was most anxious that his father should promise to grant his last request, assuring him at the same time that no expense would be incurred in the fulfilment of his wish.

The father solemnly pledged himself to comply; and then the son went on to say that he had been very prosperous in business, and had accumulated a large amount of wealth, but that he had seen so much of the evils of covetousness, of the waste and abuse of riches, that he would have all his money to be buried with him. The father again certified that he would follow his instructions, and saw his face no more.

By some means this strange agreement became known to others, and no long time after the funeral the father was accosted by one of his neighbours in New York with, "Well, Nabal, I just guess you're about the tallest fool in the States." And when an explanation was asked, it was given to the effect that no man in his right mind would bury money in the ground. "Perhaps," said the sire, with a grin on his cruel face which made him look like a gurgoyle, "I'm not quite such a fool as you think. *I paid it by cheque to his order!*"

There was a man in Chicago, I was told in New York, who came one morning to his office with such a radiant smile upon his countenance that his partner could not refrain from inquiring the cause of his exuberant joy. "My dear fellow," he replied, "my doctor, as you know, has ordered me to walk here from my house, and this very morning I have been able, in consequence, to do three splendid acts—enough, surely, to make any man happy. As I was passing one of the churches I saw a poor woman with a baby in her arms, weeping bitterly on the steps of the approach. I inquired the cause of her sorrow, and she told me that she had brought her little darling to be baptized, but that the priest said she must pay a dollar, and that she had no money. I told her that I had nothing in my purse but a ten-dollar note, but that she might take it to the priest, and I would wait outside for the change. She brought it, with such profuse expressions of gratitude and praise, that in my modesty I hurried away. Hear now what I have done, and refrain from envy, if you can. I have dried a poor woman's tears; I have placed her little one upon the heavenly road; *I have passed a false ten-dollar note, and have got the change in my pocket!*"

"But the stars shine o'er the cypress trees," however gloomy be the grove. In the first place, Chicago is not the place wherein to estimate the American character, and if any visitor will be at the trouble of perusing the police reports, he will be struck with the number of offenders whose names unmistakably announce that they belong to another nation.

And then, as there is much that is beautiful to the eye in the surroundings of smutty Chicago—in its spacious parks, pleasant boulevards, its lake-side avenue, its public buildings, sacred and secular, its private habitations—so is there much to admire not only in its industrious zeal, but in the refinements of society, and in the generosities of wealth.

I have seldom seen a brighter company of "fair women and brave men," whether judged by their appearance, their manner, or their conversation, than I met in the house of Mr. George Pullman, when I gave a lecture to the "Century Club," and also at a reception given to us by our Consul, Colonel Hayes Sadler, and elsewhere, nor will you find in the social institutions of Pall Mall and its neighbourhood more agreeable or able companions than in the Chicago Club.

As to generosity, there is only too much truth in the remark made by a working man, "Wealth has subjugated everything; it has gagged the Press, and bought up the Legislature;" and with a righteous pride I read Mr. Stead's remarks in favour of aristocracy, when compared with plutocracy, as to liberality in helping others and in recognizing its obligations; but we may not forget that the fewer men the greater share of honour, and knowing as we do the terrible power of money to make men misers or spendthrifts, we should be inclined to magnify rather than to disparage the offerings of the rich.

Whatever difficulties and disagreements may have ensued, I am convinced that Mr. Pullman, in building the town which bears his name, as when

Sir Titus Salt in England built Saltaire, was influenced by an unselfish philanthropy, and by a sense of duty, to provide for his workmen such commodious and healthful homes, such abundant means of recreation and instruction.

Of Mr. Marshall Field's munificence I heard from many sources, and of Mr. Armour's I shall have to speak. Such examples should be set on high, as the numbers of the hymns to be sung by a congregation, that more voices may join in the melody. One good deed dying tongueless slaughters a thousand waiting upon that, but new efforts follow appreciation and applause, and help to prove that a man's life, his true life, his honour and his happiness, consist not in the abundance of the things which he possesses, but in his use of them. They expedite the time, the good time coming, as we pray and hope, to Chicago, to America, and to the world, when men will have discovered that they may buy gold too dear, and that just in proportion as they injure or help their neighbours they injure or help themselves.

I went with Mr. Goodhart, a resident in Chicago, and the son of an old college friend, to see, under special and intelligent guidance, the Union Stock Yards, the great cattle market of Chicago, extending over four hundred acres of ground, and to Mr. Armour's famous slaughter and packing houses, in which he employs eight hundred men and five hundred clerks. Five thousand pigs and three thousand cattle were daily killed and prepared for exportation! Huge refrigerating carriages stood upon the railway outside.

I went, believing that the clergy should take a practical interest in sanitary matters, caring for the bodies as well as the souls of their flock—as a member of the Society for the Prevention of Cruelty, and also the Society for the Promotion of Kindness, to Animals, to ascertain whether the process was as

ARMOUR'S SAUSAGE MACHINES.

free as it could be made from cruelty and unnecessary pain, and with the hope of acquiring information which might be acceptable across the Atlantic, where, from want of supervision, accommodation, and expertness, from ignorance, haste, and ill-temper, much suffering is inflicted which might be prevented upon the animals slaughtered for food. I was speedily assured that, except by electricity or some

s

deadly poison, both of which would injure the meat, no more humane plan could be adopted than that which I saw in operation.

In a few seconds the pig, fastened by a chain on the hind leg, is raised by a pulley to a pole, which slopes over a large tank to the butcher. One blow severs the throat, and the life seems to go out with the copious outpour of blood. I only saw in one instance a spasmodic twitch, but the carcase must have been insensible to pain ere it was plunged without delay in a cistern of boiling water, divested of its bristles, scraped, cleansed, and passed on for future dissection, and for gradual adaptations in various forms to the taste of the eater and the convenience of the cook.

The beasts became beef by a method yet more summary. They were driven into a narrow passage, between thick boards of wood, and a strong man standing above with a pole axe, watching his opportunity, knowing the spot on which to strike, and hitting it with unerring aim, at one blow struck them dead—*procumbit humi bos*—and, by a mechanical contrivance, the floor on which they lay was lowered, and they rolled down the incline to be at once removed to the Company of Skinners.

There is no waste. The blood is used for manure, the horns and hoofs for glue, the superfluous fat for butterine and oleomargarine.

I commend the consideration of this important subject, in its connection with health, economy, decency, and mercy, to Parliament, to the Boards of Trade and Agriculture, County Councils, Church

DRESSING BEEF AT ARMOUR'S.

Congresses, Magistrates, Inspectors of Nuisances, and to private observation, and to public protest.*

* The public interest in this matter is rapidly increasing. During the Church Congress at Norwich in October, 1895, I was invited by the butchers of that city, as vice-chairman of the Church Sanitary Association, to witness an experiment and attend a conference. A beast was killed by a new instrument, "Greener's humane cattle killer," which, exploding noiselessly, sent a bullet through the brain to the spinal cord, and the animal fell without pain (in the opinion of the surgeons who were present), although there was some convulsive action of the limbs. The butchers, nevertheless, did not see any advantage over the old method of killing with the pole-axe, when it was properly handled. They admitted, at the same time, that there were some incompetent

There is a pathetic incident ever recurring in the establishment of Mr. Armour. Where the cattle reach a certain part of the premises, not far from the place of slaughter, there used to be from time to time a sudden panic and stampede. This has been prevented by the training of a huge and ugly steer to wait for the procession, place himself at the head, and slowly lead them on. Arriving at the entrance, he turns suddenly to a small space by the side, and the rest, pressing upon each other, pass on to their doom.

He is called "Judas," and reminds me of some toper enticing young men to drink, some gambler luring greenhorns to bet and play; Fagin, assisted by the Artful Dodger, teaching boys to pick pockets, the old decoy drake quacking at the entrance to the enclosure.

On one occasion Judas in his meditations went a little too far—they do sometimes, these traitors—and was irresistibly impelled to annihilation.

The Armour Institute, built, furnished, and sustained without restriction as to cost, is as perfect as money and brains can make it. The main object, described somewhat effusively in the words "to co-ordinate the theoretical principles underlying the work with practical exposition," is pursued by the

performers, and some inconvenient places of slaughter, and expressed their desire that these should be removed by authority. They rightly objected to interference, though not to supervision, when the premises were commodious and the work well done.

students, who must be over twenty years of age, and must have passed through some course of higher education, with every possible advantage. They are taught by the most accomplished tutors, professors, and lecturers, and with every appliance which can promote a thoroughly technical and mechanical education. They learn languages—Latin, French, and German; histories—Greek, Roman, English, and American; algebra, geometry, biology, physics, chemistry.

In the latter department we heard with indignant disgust that certain youths (not Americans) had been, as it afterwards transpired, to the Institute to learn the manufacture of explosives with a view to their destructive use.

There is a department, over which an expert presides, with a most complete modern apparatus, whereby young ladies can learn an art which will bring gladness to their homes, and which alone can satisfy a desire ever foremost in a father's, in a husband's mind—the art of cookery.

There is another department, the gymnasium, in which the scholars may combine *mens sana cum corpore sano*, and where a robust Englishman, who had served in our "Guards," was giving instruction in drill and gymnastics. He was risibly affected by an incident which occurred, on a scene which he knew so well, that of a small boy, looking through the tall palisades which surround the Wellington Barracks, and addressing a young officer, not much bigger than himself, but wearing the tall bearskin head-dress peculiar to his regiment : "*Now just you come out of that 'ere hat. I know you're in it, I see your legs a'-dangling.*"

The Armour "Elevators" for the stowage of corn should be inspected. During the year 1894, the company handled approximately 60,000,000 bushels of grain and flax-seed.

We went to the headquarters of the Fire Brigade, which has the reputation of being the best in the world. Chicago has learned, from a terrible experience, that "a burnt child dreads the fire," and has indeed beheld "how great a matter a little fire kindleth." From the fall of a kerosene lamp the flames spread among the wooden houses, and the timber piled in the yards, sweeping all before them, raging for three days, October 8, 9, and 10, 1871, and extending over an area of more than three square miles. The number of buildings destroyed was 17,450; of persons who were homeless, 98,500; of persons killed, about 200. It is estimated that the total loss occasioned by the fire was $190,000,000. Of this, $30,000,000 was recovered by insurance, but 57 insurance companies were ruined.

The marvellous energy and the indomitable courage of the people rose to the occasion. While the fire was still smouldering in the ruins, they began to rebuild. Business was resumed before Christmas in temporary wooden structures, and in private dwellings, which had escaped the fire. In a year a large portion of the city had been rebuilt, stone being largely substituted for wood, and it was calculated that, during the rebuilding, so rapidly was the work carried on, that one brick, stone, or iron edifice, four to six storeys in height, and with a frontage of twenty-four feet, was completed every hour.

We were highly favoured in being permitted to see the telegraphic and telephonic system by which the number and street of any house or building in which a fire breaks out is immediately communicated. We saw in a few seconds after the signal sounded a pair of horses and half a dozen men attached to the hydrant, and starting away at a gallop. Then we witnessed the agility of the firemen with the light ladders, which they moved from window to window, until they reached the highest chambers of the house, with other exercises and appliances for escape and rescue.

I had been present at a series of similar operations, conducted under the superintendence of Captain Shaw, of the London Fire Brigade, and it seemed to me that the only superiority in the American tactics (but it was a superiority of momentous importance) consisted in the rapidity and certainty with which the danger was announced.

One of the officials who accompanied us told me of a scheme, which was new to me, by which the action of fire on the ceilings, specially prepared, would set free the contents of large cisterns placed above them, and extinguish the flames; but neither he nor I were much impressed by the project.

Verily, these brave firemen may say, "My soul is always in my hand." Not many days after our visit, I read in a New York paper that two of their leaders, Battalion Chief Bresnan and Assistant Foreman Rooney, had been buried in the ruins of a fire, and eight other men seriously injured.

I have many pleasant memories of Chicago—of the reception committee, on which were more than fifty clergy, with the bishop at their head, nearly the same number of eminent laymen, and twelve distinguished ladies; of the welcome with which the florists greeted me, and their beautiful gifts of roses, lilies and chrysanthemums; of kind approbations from those who listened to my lectures; of carriages and horses placed at our disposal—*three* handsome vehicles, each with a pair, came to take us to church on Sunday—and, best of all, of hearty individual kindness. But I have in special remembrance a very happy evening which we spent, on the invitation of the president and members, with the "Chicago Church Club."

This society was formed some half-dozen years ago, under the auspices of the bishop, for the promotion of social intercourse between the members of different parishes and an increased interest in Church work; and, as a Churchman, I can think of no consummation more devoutly to be wished than such a practical and at the same time agreeable effort to unite the clergy and the laity in goodwill and good works.

The expostulation, "Sirs, ye are brethren," is often in these days opportune, and they who speak of candidates for holy orders as "going into the Church," suggesting that all but clergymen are outside, and have not been received into fellowship, are affectionately taught by such meetings as these that we are all members one of another.

Monthly meetings are held, at which papers are read and subjects are discussed. There are committees for the promotion of ecclesiastical, educational, and benevolent institutions, and for literary and historical studies. Two banquets are held during the year; and at one of them, kindly postponed for our convenience, we were welcomed with that *perfect* sympathy which exists only between those who are "one in faith and doctrine, one in charity."

And it should be noted here that another beneficent purpose of this society is to entertain strangers, and their club-room at the Masonic Temple is ever open to their travelling brethren. At this dinner there was a new adventure. Ladies were invited for the first time in the history of the club. They were not only the most ornamental, but, taking into account their opportunities and influence as compared with those of men engaged in business, the most useful members of our company.

Excellent speeches were made by the president, Mr. E. P. Bailey; by the secretary, the Rev. T. H. Snively; and an eloquent oration, humorous and instructive, by Mr. Sherman Boutell. He pretended to believe that the cordial treatment of Englishmen by Americans had its origin in the secret pride derived by the host in exciting the envy of his guest as he set before him the astounding magnificence of the country which he was permitted to see. " We like to get our visitor," he said, " by our hearthstone, with his feet under our mahogany, and to call his particular and intelligent attention to our splendid achievements. To inform him that we are seventy millions of people, and in possession of enormous wealth. That, while we claim an equal share in all the triumphs of the old country, he has nothing whatever to do with the splendid accomplishments of the new. And we say to him, 'Really now don't you wish—nobody at home can hear you—don't you wish that some ancestral spirit of roving had led your forefathers to settle in Massachusetts or Virginia two hundred years ago?'"

The guest is constrained to make an evasive answer, like the traveller in the Far West to the cowboys,* or Mr. Samson Brass, when Quilp made him smoke strong tobacco, and asked him, as he was slipping off a three-cornered chair, whether he did not feel like the Grand Turk? And Mr. Brass said that no doubt he did, but thought at the same time

---

* See p. 17.

MASONIC TEMPLE, CHICAGO.

that, if such were the case, the feelings of that potentate were not of an enviable description.

Then he—Mr. Boutell, not Mr. Brass—went on to state that it was never too late to mend, to be annexed by naturalization, and that he thought Dean Hole would make an excellent citizen of Chicago, a city which he described as being in area and population the largest city in the country—although this information does not seem to have reached the editor of "The *World* Almanac and Encyclopædia," who assigns to New York a trifling majority of more than 700,000 inhabitants, and predicts the addition of another million or so for the "Greater New York" now in contemplation—as the city which has more miles of railroad, more vessel tonnage, more freight, larger parks, dirtier streets, a sootier atmosphere, a more malodorous river, more gamblers, more good things, and more bad things, than any other city.

The speaker then revealed himself, without pedantry, as being thoroughly conversant with Rochester history—not only of the cathedral, but of the castle. He told how, in the reign of William Rufus, Gundulph Bishop of Rochester, who was a famous builder, in order to secure a certain estate for his Church in perpetuity, was required by the king to build a tower for Rochester Castle. It was to be 70 feet square at the base, the walls 12 feet thick, and 150 feet high, and the cost was to be £60. Is it not written in the "*Textus Roffensis*," and is not the great tower still standing? "Now, structures having a strong resemblance to this Gundulph erection are in great demand at Chicago; and if Dean Hole will show us how to raise these towers at £60 a-piece, I will promise, on behalf of Chicago, not only to restore his cathedral, but, in a new clubhouse of unparalleled size and splendour, to reserve a magnificent apartment for his use, his heirs and assigns for ever."

Next he spoke of the grafting and the growth of that branch of the Catholic vine which we venture to call the Church of America; of early missionaries from England in Puritan, busy Massachusetts and in Catholic Maryland and Massachusetts; of their toil and privations. One clergyman wrote that he preached every month in five different places, one hundred miles apart; another, that he had no food save that which he raised or caught, and no fuel save that which he cut for himself.

In Virginia, where there was a wealthier class of people—many of them English emigrants—the Anglican services were generally adopted; and there is a quaint picture of an old-fashioned Federalist, with powdered hair and long cane, three-cornered hat and top-boots, who remarked, in the course of a speech made to the Virginian Legislature, that "of one thing he was quite sure, that *no gentleman would choose any road to heaven but the episcopal*"—a remark which reminds me of a similar utterance made by a lady in New York to a friend who, on hearing that she proposed to leave the Christian community to which she belonged, and to join the Episcopal Church, had remonstrated, and asked an explanation—" Well, you see, it is so *toney*."

Alas! there's pride in religion as in everything else, down to the street-urchin delineated by Leech, and making, evidently to her own satisfaction, whatever may happen to the less enlightened, her declaration of faith, " Me and Mary Jane is Puseyites."

Mr. Boutell referred, in conclusion of his excellent speech, to the want of sympathy shewn in times past by the mother country, and to the consecration in Scotland of the first American Bishop, Dr. Seabury, of Connecticut, to which I have referred at length,* and which provoked the feeble sarcasm, " You Yankees have to go to Scotland for oatmeal, snuff, and bishops." And he spoke with faith and in hope, and with impressive eloquence of the Episcopal Church of England and America, as the future Church of the English-speaking people of the world, and that it was meanwhile their noble mission to foster and to increase those sentiments of mutual esteem and affection which ought to bind together the two greatest nations upon earth.

I must say no more about the church in Chicago, and yet I could not conscientiously refuse to share with my readers the enjoyment which I derived when I was told that a Roman priest, who had

* See chapter xi.

witnessed one of our services, in which the ritual was elaborate and dramatic, replied, on being asked what he thought of the ceremony, "that it was very beautiful, *but that on the whole he preferred his own simple worship.*"

CHAPTER XIX.

CINCINNATI.

I WENT from Chicago to Cincinnati, of which Longfellow wrote :—

> "And this greeting
> The winds and the birds deliver
> To the Queen of the West,
> In her garlands dress'd,
> On the banks of the beautiful river."

Again I was welcomed by flowers and florists, and one of the latter, an enthusiastic lady rosarian, took me in her carriage, after I had hastily inspected the grand fountain in Fountain Square, and seen from Eden Park the charming views of the city and the valley of the Ohio, to the famous Rookwood Pottery. I had an introduction from Mr. Alfred Parsons to Mr. W. H. Taylor, who presided over the works, and he most kindly and lucidly explained to me, as we watched, the whole process of manufacture, and then showed me the exquisite results in every variety of size and shape and colour, not to mention two hundred and twenty-five teapots, all of different patterns, from Japan.

I remembered the delight of the great poet whom I have just quoted when he saw in his boyhood the vessels formed by the hands of the potter at the old pottery in Portland, near Deering's Wood. I thought of Bernard Pallissy's genius and intense devotion. I repeated the quaint lines—

> "No handicraftsman's art
>   Can with our art compare.
> We potters make our pots
>   Of what we potters are."

And I mused on that wonderful verse of the prophet, in which we have the history of Paradise Lost and Paradise Regained, of the Fall and the Redemption: "The vessel that He made of clay was marred in the hand of the potter; so He made it again, another vessel, as seemed good to the potter to make it."

As soon as we had finished our most enjoyable tour of inspection, Mr. Taylor inquired what form of vessel I thought to be most suitable for the reception of cut roses, and when I replied, "The circular," and gave him dimensions, he at once instructed a workman to mould the clay accordingly, and in three or four minutes he produced the model which, when I had traced my signature with a pointed instrument upon the soft material, with the date of inscription, was designated by authority as "Dean Hole's Bowl for Roses." On my return from the States I received two specimens, highly finished and tastefully painted, and the proud proprietor—or rather his wife—has filled them with roses during the summer months,

T

and has lost no opportunity of exciting and exasperating the envy of his friends.

At a luncheon afterwards we had a lively interchange of reflections and experiences, grave and gay, and I made a note of a short poem in which tragedy and comedy are combined, and which I had not previously heard. Its title was

"LITTLE WILLIE.

" Little Willie from his mirror
   Sucked the mercury all off,
Thinking, in his childish error,
   It would cure his whooping cough.

" At the funeral, Willie's mother
   Smartly said to Mrs. Brown,
' 'Twas a chilly day for William
   When the mercury went down.'

Chorus—
"' Ah, ah, ah !' said Willie's mother.
   ' Oh, oh, oh !' said Mrs. Brown.
' 'Twas a chilly day for William
   When the mercury went down.'"

" I think it right to add," said the reciter, when we had dried our tears and suppressed our sobs, " as an American and as a patriot, in the presence of this distinguished Britisher, and lest he should have erroneous impressions as to a want of affection in our American mothers, and as to their unseemly behaviour at the grave, that the incident which you have just heard with such visible and audible emotion is absolutely unique, and must not for a single moment be regarded as a sample."

I solemnly assured him that, though his zeal for the honour of his country, which I had noticed in two or three other instances, was greatly to be admired, it was superfluous on the present occasion. That I had not met with any similar incident during my travels through the States, and that I was convinced that it was without precedent in this country, as also in the British dominions, Guernsey, Jersey, Alderney and Sark—(it seems desirable now and then to introduce these additions, in the presence of those who have such immense possessions that they are apt to form imperfect conceptions as to the extent of their neighbour's property, and the list may be occasionally enlarged by including the Isle of Wight and the Islands of the Upper Lake of Killarney, trusting that at such a distance no one will be aware that many of the latter are about ten feet in diameter) —and that I knew a multitude of mothers in both countries who regarded their little Willies as unrivalled in goodness, intellect, and beauty, and had believed it ever since they were born.

Not only from friends in private, but from the public press, I had at Cincinnati a most hearty greeting. Was it not written in a daily paper : " Dean Hole is certainly the finest specimen of Elizabethan ecclesiastical architecture that England has ever sent to this country " ? In another that " The reverend gentleman, seventy-five years old and over six feet tall, walked up two flights of stairs to his room in the hotel *with the hardy appearance and exact posture of a young Indian* in preference to using the elevator, notwithstanding that he had just endured the exhaustion of a ride from Chicago. He is as remarkable a man to look at as he is in the Church affairs in England, and his long grey hair is combed back from a strong Scotch cast of features." While a third described me as "large and ruddy, with white hair and very keen, kindly, quizzical eyes that are perpetually smiling, even when the rest of his face is serious."

CHAPTER XX.

VIRGINIA.

We passed through a most picturesque country from Cincinnati to Washington, when the sun revealed it to us, pilgrims of the night; "woods and cornfields and the abodes of men scattered at intervals;" solitary farms, and villages with tiny churches; cottages, with little niggers—papooses, piccaninnies—grinning at the doors, and reminding us of a man in "the Midlands" of whom it was said by a sarcastic neighbour, "They had some thoughts of widening his mouth, but they found that it would be necessary to move his ears, so they gave it up."

There is confusion in many minds as to the meaning of terms applied to the "darkies"—creoles, mulattoes, quadroons, etc. A creole is very commonly supposed to be an intermixture of the white and black race; but the word denotes, in the Southern States, one born of European parents. A mulatto is the offspring of a white and a negro; a quadroon—one-fourth white—of a white and of a mulatto.

A propos of colour, there is a very charming

contrast on our present route between the bright red and yellow soil and the dark-green foliage of the evergreen and the russet tints of the deciduous trees. Indeed, it seemed to me, as I woke in the morning light, and looked out from my cubicle upon the pleasant slopes, the woodlands and the plains, the hills and dales, the flocks and herds of Virginia, to be the most attractive site which I had seen in the States for a peaceful, restful home; and this impression was afterwards confirmed when, engaged to give a lecture at Charlottesville, wherein is the University of Virginia, I spent two delightful days in the country house of Mr. Sackville Caldbeck. Were I constrained to end my days in America, and the choice was given *where* the end should be, "Carry me back to Old Virginie" would be the burden of my song.

Enjoying, not long ago, one of the happiest of human enjoyments, a prowl round the shelves of a well-filled, well-chosen, well-warmed, well-lighted library, when the winds blow and the rains pour outside, I found a most interesting volume of travels in America, written by Archdeacon Burnaby, the great-grandfather of my host and brother-in-law, not long before the War of Independence. He describes Virginia as producing, in its natural state, great quantities of fruits and medicinal plants, with trees and flowers of infinitely various kinds :—

"Tobacco and Indian corn were the original produce of the country. Grapes, strawberries, hiccory-nuts, mulberries, chestnuts, and other fruit grow wild spontaneously.

"Besides trees and flowers of an ordinary nature, the woods produce myrtles, cedars, cypresses, sugar-trees, firs of different sorts, and no less than seven or eight kinds of oaks. They are always adorned and beautified with red-flowering maples, sassafras trees, dogwoods, acacias, redwoods, scarlet-flowering chestnuts, fringe-trees, flowering poplars, umbrella trees, magnolias, yellow jasmines, daphnes, Kalmias, pacoons, atamises lilies, May-apples, and innumerable other sorts, *so that one may reasonably assume that no country ever appeared with greater elegance or beauty.*

"The rivers are stored with incredible quantities of fish; in the mountains there are rich veins of ore; the forests abound with game—hares, pheasants, turkeys, woodcocks, and partridges; in the marshes are found soruses, a particular species of bird more exquisitely delicious than the ortolan, snipes also and ducks of all kinds.

"In the woods there are a variety of birds remarkable for their singing and their beauty: the mocking-bird, the red-bird or nightingale, the blue-bird, the yellow-bird, the humming-bird, the Baltimore bird, the summer duck, the turtle, and many others. The fruits introduced here from Europe succeed extremely well, particularly the peaches, which have a very fine flavour, and grow in such plenty as to serve to feed the hogs in autumn.

"The horses are fleet and beautiful.

"The established religion is that of the Church of England, and there are very few Dissenters. There are at present between sixty and seventy clergymen, men in general of sober and exemplary lives. They have each a glebe of two or three hundred acres of land, *and a salary, established by law, of* 16,000 *lbs. of tobacco, and an allowance of* 1700 *lbs. more for shrinkage.* This is delivered to them in hogsheads, ready packed for importation at the most convenient warehouse. *The diocesan is the Bishop of London.* He is also the Chancellor of the College of William and Mary, the only public place of education.

"The inhabitants are indolent, easy, and good-natured, extremely fond of society, and given to individual pleasures. *The progress of the arts and sciences is inconsiderable.*

"The women are, generally speaking, handsome, and though fond of society, and especially of dancing, are industrious and domestic also, spending their days in sewing and in household duties, like the Roman matron, *domum mansit, lanam fecit,* and make as good wives and as good mothers as any in the world." Their husbands, according to the archdeacon's experience, were always in a position to speak with great boldness to their enemies in the gate. "We called," he writes, "at the plantation of Colonel Symes. His wife, a very beautiful woman, was said to have just attained her twenty-first year, and was at that time the mother of seven children, all living."

Then follows a most significant and suggestive passage :—" Their authority over their slaves makes them vain and imperious. In regard to the Indian and the negro, they scarcely consider them of the human species, so that it is almost impossible, in cases of violence, or even of murder, committed upon those unhappy people by any of the planters, to have the delinquents brought to justice.

"They are haughty, and jealous of their liberties, impatient of restraint, and can scarcely bear the thought of being controlled by any superior power. Many of them consider the Colonies as independent States, not connected with Great Britain otherwise than by having the same Queen, and being bound to her by natural affection."

Do we not see in these characteristics the fuel and the sparks of that terrible conflagration, the American Civil War? It may be said that the War for Independence was a rebellion against authority; but it was righteous and inevitable, for that authority was overstrained, and its maintenance impossible. "Thrice is he armed that hath his quarrel just." America, moreover, was almost unanimous in her desire and determination; but, in the war between the Northern and Southern States, her unity was broken. A man's foes were those of his own house, for brothers fought against each other, and one chief cause of this deadly disunion—which brought desolation to thousands of happy homes, to the mothers, the widows, the loving maiden hearts, which flooded the land with blood like a red Niagara, so that everywhere was heard the poet's wail,

> "There's not a flock, however watched and tended,
>   But one dead lamb is there;
> There's not a household, howsoe'er defended,
>   But hath its vacant chair;"

—one main argument for the continuance of this suicidal strife was the defence of slavery!

I heard in Virginia, wherein the bitterness of all that hatred and suffering still sours the spirit of those on whom it was entailed—and as I looked upon the statue of the soldier in the uniform of the Southern army, in the centre of the burial-ground at Charlottesville, surrounded by hundreds of his comrades slain in battle, I felt that so it must be until the mourners were gone to those whom they mourned, and that cruel severance had ceased to throb—I heard in Virginia, as I had heard elsewhere, that, before the war, the slaves were content and happy; that during the war, so far from fighting for their emancipation, they sympathized with their masters; and that, before the statue to which I just now referred was publicly unveiled, a negro came to the committee who were making the arrangements, and informed them that he would die in resisting any attempt which might be made to raise the flag of the Stars and Stripes upon that ground. Some maintain that the negroes were happier before the war than now. It was so in many of the plantations. Successive generations of kind masters were beloved by their willing slaves, and they were as one family together. There were cases in which slaves, to whom freedom had been given for good conduct, returned and entreated that they might continue their work. These arguments were asserted by many, before and during the war, as an insuperable answer to the accusations brought against slavery, and to them we are indebted for Lowell's caustic lines :—

" It's coz they're so happy, that when crazy sarpints
    Stick their nose in our business we get so darned riled ;
We think it's our dooty to give pooty sharp hints
    That the last crumb of Eden on earth shan't be spiled."

"Says John C. Calhoun, sez he,
    'Ah!' says Dixon H. Lewis,
    'It perfectly true is,
That slavery's earth's greatest boon,' sez he."

The same author had previously described Uncle Sam of the United States as "the loudest boaster of liberty and the largest owner of slaves."

Many, nevertheless, would not listen to the rebukes of ridicule or of scorn ; and some still speak, as though all that has been written and spoken and preached against slavery was mere verbiage and vain imagination — Lincoln's eloquence, Longfellow's pathetic verse, Dickens's denunciation of "that most hideous blot and foul disgrace," and Beecher's " Patriotic Addresses " were mere romance ; and the great multitudes who heard and read and glowed with righteous indignation, or shed tears of sorrow and of shame, were all under a delusion. There are some who to this day will tell you that " Uncle Tom's Cabin " was a fiction and nothing more.

It is true that thousands of slaves were kindly treated, and well fed, and danced and sang. But were there no markets in which they were bought and sold, grouped for inspection, as cattle now, lauded by the auctioneer, criticized and depreciated by the buyers, jeered at by the crowd? Were there no manacles, no cruel overseers ever repeating the cry of the Egyptian taskmaster, " Ye are idle, ye are idle?" Were there no drivers' whips, no bruises, and no sores? Might it not have been said in bitter mockery that the banner of those bondmen was *Scars* and Stripes.*

It is true that slavery was not the first provocation at the beginning of the war,† though it

---

* The flag of the Stars and Stripes was adopted by Congress on the 14th of June, 1777, when it was resolved "that the flag of the Thirteen United Colonies be thirteen stripes, alternately red and white, and that of the Union thirteen stars, white in a blue field, representing a new constellation. Some have thought that the arms of Washington, which contain three stars in the upper portion, and three bars across the escutcheon, may have suggested the American flag.

† It was maintained by the Southerners that America was not one nation, but a number of nations, of states, united for convenience, but each having a right to secede. The Northerners denied this right, and declared it to be every man's duty to preserve the integrity of the empire, and to obey the Supreme Authorities.

became afterwards inseparably associated, but there are many who regard the war as the retribution of Slavery. At the Lincoln banquet, held in Colorado Springs, February 12, 1895, Mr. Grafton said, "God's ways are not our ways, and His instruments and instrumentalities are not of our choosing. His wrath was not to be appeased except by sufficient sacrifice. The wealth piled up by the bondman's unrequited toil had to be destroyed. The young men just budding into manhood, the flower of the land, their blood alone could wash the guilt away. The sacrifice had to be as great as the sin."

It is a common question, What will become of the negroes? According to the census of 1890, their number in the States is 7,638,360. They seem to have no desire to return

> "Where Afric's sunny fountains
> Roll down their golden sands,"

but rather to have adopted the Hanoverian motto, "*Vestigia nulla retrorsum:*" "We don't intend to go back again." It is better so than that they should fret themselves with a desire so hopeless as an exodus to their native land. Nevertheless, the good Bishop of Sierra Leone reminds us, with a righteous zeal, "that these black people were transported forcibly and utterly against their will, and that it was only to be expected that an impossible state of things would sooner or later be created. The true solution," he affirms, "is repatriation. Why talk of planting British Indians in Africa, when so many expatriated

Africans will colonize it far more satisfactorily? I contend that limited repatriation, wisely directed, can be made a success."

There is no probability of amalgamation between the blacks and whites; no hope that the negro can be raised to the intellectual platform of the American race, although his education might be greatly improved. What, then, should be done? I have heard another suggestion, but it was made by a gentleman whose theories seemed never to present themselves in working order, that the negroes should have a State assigned to them, with special privileges and adaptations, and with the sole restriction that they never emerged beyond their boundaries. Encouraged by applause (of a fictitious character), he proceeded to enlarge our conceptions, and to illuminate the future with a further revelation of his political schemes, announcing his conviction that it would be for the mutual advantage and accommodation of all parties if a separate and spacious allotment could also be apportioned and awarded to the Irish nation, in which all its ancient glory should be revived, and there should be no more Saxons, no more landlords, no more policemen, but an absolute freedom from restraint, and "Home Rule," with the slightest possible modifications—such, for example, as a friendly consultation with the Federal Government in case of any differences of opinion which might arise, and which were not unknown to close students of history even among the peaceful, unimpassioned brethren of United Ireland.

I was not much impressed by the architectural presentments of the University of Virginia. The Rotunda * is pleasing, but the dormitories adjoining are small and low. Nevertheless, the undergraduates who occupy them are a bright, cheery brotherhood, and the learned and genial professors were most kind and hospitable to me. The University and I are coeval, for it was founded by the famous Jefferson, whose home and grave are at beautiful Montecello, four miles away, in the year 1819.

After my lecture to a congenial audience,† I was conversing with one of the "potent, grave, and reverend" Dons of the University, and was making the most of my classical reminiscences, affectionately referring to the Greek and Latin authors, as though they had been the playfellows of my boyhood, the dearest friends of my manhood, and were now the sweet solace of mine age; I was earnestly eulogizing the "Agamemnon" of Æschylus (what an exhibition I should have made if he had produced a pocket-edition, and had solicited my views upon certain lines of the chorus, which I had not seen for half

---

* The Rotunda and the Public Hall were destroyed by fire on October 27, 1895.

† I was more fortunate than Emerson, of whom we read that he went to lecture to the literary societies of the University of Virginia, and that there was so much noise that he could not make himself heard, and, after contending with the din for half an hour, concluded.

a century, and which always brought my Pegasus down!); and I was declaiming upon the superiority of the Greek over the English language, in the musical grandeur of its tones, contrasting in proof the account of the Greek tragedian of the lighting of the beacons, which announced the taking of Troy to the sentinel at Argos, with the verses of Macaulay (splendid as they are), upon a similar illumination on the arrival of the Spanish Armada, when a pleasant voice addressed me with, "Dean Hole, we know that you are a sportsman, and we propose to have a special meet of the hounds to-morrow morning in your honour."

"Agamemnon" vanished, and my good friend the professor reminded me that we should meet at supper, as I suddenly and joyfully transferred my thoughts from the stage to the stable, from the mournful drama to the merry horn. I had been interested in the country as I travelled on the rails, not only by its beauty, but by its relations *pro et contra* for the chase (every man who has ridden to hounds for many years of his life amuses himself now and then with imaginary runs beside his train, and feels himself personally aggrieved when, having distanced all competitors and taken a commanding lead, he is suddenly confronted by a broad river, a tunnel, or a town), and I had come to the conclusion that the irregular arrangement of the wooden fences in Virginia would require the careful handling of a clever horse, when lo! I was face to face with the secretary and manager of the hunt. I could not accept his complimentary and congenial invitation, for I was a guest that tarried but a day, but we had a most refreshing though brief conversation—(remember, dear reader, that the Very Reverend the Dean had only just concluded an effort to raise funds for the restoration of his cathedral, so that business went first and pleasure after), and he told me that though, as I saw, the country, with its continuous woodlands and immense spaces of uninclosed land, had neither the facilities nor the excitements of the English fox-hunt, with its miles of pasture and every variety of obstacle in hedges and ditches, banks and brooks, rails of strong wood and walls of stone, that they had nevertheless some capital sport, plenty of foxes, red and grey, and a goodly company of fair dames and gay cavaliers.

The American gentleman is somewhat heavily handicapped as to the enjoyment of field sports. As a rule he devotes his energies to business, and has only just begun to discover that all work and no play makes Jack a dull boy, and that if you apply no oil to the wheel the friction may set it on fire. When I gave up hunting years ago that I might devote myself more exclusively to ecclesiastical and literary work, my health failed, and my doctor commanded " horse-exercise." So I invested in a stout high-stepping cob, and I called him " Taraxacum," for he was as medicine to my liver, and as a tonic to all around.

If the millionaires and all who can afford the recreation would leave their Wall Street, their banks, and bureaux for a gallop once a week after hounds, they would do as much work as before in a shorter time, that is, with a constant supply of new vigour both to body and mind.

In England all the surroundings are favourable to the hunting of the fox. The landowner is a sportsman, with a few melancholy exceptions (the vulpicide and the man who puts barbed wire in his fences occupy about the same position in the esteem of his fellow-countrymen as a garroter or a ticket-of-leave man), and he has woods and coverts, sometimes specially made for the comfortable reception of the fox, and he and his tenants are of one mind that the sacred animal shall be strictly preserved until the time comes when he must meet that which the old huntsman declared to be his " natural death." In America the land is occupied by its owners, sometimes to a small extent, and any one of these proprietors may of course forbid and oppose the sport.

Against these disadvantages the American, inheriting such a love of horses and of sport that he has shown us in the far West, and in England by the performances of Colonel Cody and his troupe, the most difficult of all horsemanship, the breaking and the riding of the buckjumper, and has bred the fastest trotters in the world, is now developing a vehement desire for the chase. Developing, not originating, for there has long been foxhunting in various parts of the States.* *Lord Fairfax and George Washington kept a pack of hounds in Virginia*, and not only in Virginia, Maryland, the Carolinas and Georgia has there always been a more or less unorganized fox-hunting by farmers and others, but Philadelphia and Baltimore have also an ancient renown. There are twenty-five American and Canadian hunt clubs of various dates, chiefly modern, and yearly increasing.

From Harper's Magazine.   Copyright, 1895, by Harper & Brothers.
AMERICAN MIDDLE-WEIGHT HUNTER.

They have been established and are supported by wealthy citizens, who, having sporting proclivities, thoroughly enjoy their holidays in the happy hunting-grounds not far from their cities.

The men turn out in the good old style, in "pink"

* A most interesting article on "Country Clubs and Hunt Clubs in America," with excellent illustrations, appears in *Scribner's Magazine* for September, 1895.

and in "tops," and though their steeds may not be quite so highly bred or highly groomed as in England, and their hounds may not be quite so shapely or so swift as the "Belvoir" or the "Quorn," and the cavalcade may consist of twenty instead of two hundred horsemen, the *tout ensemble*, as faithfully represented by photographs, fully satisfies the sportsman's eye. The easy "seat" of the man who can ride, the caps and coats of the huntsmen, the well-made habit of Diana —all are there.

Fox-hunters are inclined to be sternly severe in their condemnations of those who hunt a drag, and philosophers have declared that a millionaire, riding as for his life, after a red herring, was mad, and should be under restraint. There is some argument in both these allegations. There is an element of comedy in the anxious, elaborate, and costly preparations for the chase of a fox—in the feverish, frantic excitement evoked by his appearance, and it can hardly be denied that the sudden presentation to a foreigner, having no previous information, of a gentleman on horseback, clad in scarlet, and shouting "Tally-ho!" (meaning of the words unknown to linguists) at the top of his voice, would suggest insanity. But has not the Latin poet said wisely, *Dulce est desipere in loco*—life cannot be all philosophy? As to hunting a drag, there is a perfect unanimity on both sides of the Atlantic that it is a process very inferior to that of hunting the fox, and that it more resembles a race of horsemen than a run with hounds. The American sportsman and the American fox have the same *esprit de corps* (the words admit a double translation with reference to the fox) as the English; but what is to be done in districts where the wily animal cannot be induced to leave the great woods, in which there are no roads, or in districts where he is not to be found? And so it comes to this, "*recte si possis,*" hunt the fox if you

From Harper's Magazine.   Copyright, 1895, by Harper & Brothers.
PURE-BLOODED AMERICAN HOUNDS.

can; "*si non, quocunque modo,*" but if this be impossible, *hunt something.*

The American man of business has no time to waste in a tedious and uncertain search for his quarry, which may end in a "blank day," and so he gets the best sport and exercise within his reach, just when and just where he pleases, and just as much as he likes. And in this latter arrangement he inherits from his forefathers their relish for a moderate amount of danger, a few of those impediments which we love the most when we arrive on the other side.

The most scrupulous sportsman, who retains his nerve, will not deny, when he has tasted them, the fascinations of the drag, although he may doubt their orthodoxy! In my college days, when we felt it to be a duty which we owed to our country, to our parents, and to ourselves, to keep our minds and bodies unimpaired by excessive study and close confinement; when there were no near meets of the hounds, and yet we knew that strong exercise and pure air was absolutely essential to health, we were wont to organize a drag. We had about four couple of hounds, principally contributed by the sons of the M.F.H., to the great joy of the kennel huntsman, who was thus relieved of his reprobates. They were not to the eye of the connoisseur what is termed a "level lot," because we could not afford to repudiate beagles, and, therefore, our pack somewhat resembled the army of a country theatre, low and lanky, emaciated and obese. They were weak in those "points" which are required at a hound-show, but they were strong in their resolution, and they would run, and they would eat any mortal thing.

A curious incident occurred in connection with our drag.* As a rule we confined our recreation on horse-

* I wrote a full account of this small drama in an early volume of *Once a Week*, and it was accompanied by one of the cleverest illustrations which John Leech ever drew.

back to several farms over which we had permission to ride, covenanting to pay for damages, which were very rarely laid to our charge, as the farmers were sportsmen also; but on one occasion our dragoman had diverged into adjoining fields, and was caught in the very act of trailing his odoriferous compounds (chiefly aniseed) by the owner and his gamekeeper, who were shooting in a wood hard by. The proprietor, a retired colonel, was furious, and astutely ordered the unhappy trespasser to accompany him, still leaving a line of scent, to the Hall. Poor old "Badger Bowles," the superintendent of the drag, used to delight us afterwards with vivid representations of his captors, the colonel marching along as straight as a plumb line, turning round from time to time to scowl and sneer and sniff, and exclaiming, "Bah! Beastly! Cursed impudence! Have 'em all expelled;" and his keeper, with a gun under each arm, "trying to look as if he'd never smelt nothing stronger nor cowslips, and had never cut up a putrid 'os for his dogs." Bowles was taken to an unoccupied coach-house, and was locked in.

By-and-by the hounds, having astonished the

From Harper's Magazine.—Copyright, 1895, by Harper & Brothers.

AN EMBRYO M.F.H.

master and his company by racing over a private park, and past a stately mansion, rushed at full cry into the stable-yard, and besieged with howls of angry disappointment the coach-house door. Then the colonel appeared upon the scene, and, raising his hat, with a politeness which bordered on humility, and speaking with a suavity of tone which was almost feminine, he asked "to whom was he indebted for the honour and the privilege of that most charming interview?" But this dramatic effort was too much for him, and, without any further sparring, he went for our highly esteemed but depressed master, and let his thoughts flow in impassioned language. In still amazement we heard our revered leader (idol of his college, heir to a peerage, and a thorough sportsman) denounced as an "electro-plated impostor, a pestiferous poacher, and a disgrace to the University, from which he hoped to remove him at the earliest available date. As for your delectable friend," he remarked, in conclusion, "the skunk in the coach-house, he will be prosecuted according to law. And now, sir, I must demand your card"—it was given with profuse apologies—" and ask you to remove your elegant retinue, so that these premises may be fumigated without delay."

Now comes the strange *dénouement*. Our dejected chief had scarcely gone a mile on his homeward way when a groom came galloping up, with a note in his hand, and therein was written, "Come back at once. Know your father. All a mistake." He returned to an enthusiastic welcome. "So sorry, my dear boy. I see from your card that you are the son of my dearest friend—in the Guards together, fought side by side. Come in! Dobson, take some food into the dining-room. Bottle of Champagne. Young fellows like champagne. Let me introduce you to my wife and daughters."

The Country Club is a more recent and rapid development of American delight in *al fresco* exercises,

OLD QUAKER INN AND PINE-TREE CLUB-HOUSE.

on horseback and on foot, in the winter and in the summer also. The club-house is a large, commodious building, with rooms for reception, dancing, dining, dressing, and billiards. Outside there are lawns for tennis, golf-links, grounds for races, steeplechases, polo, and base-ball. The club is situated within the distance of a drive from the city and its suburbs, and gives to the coachman, as well as to the rider and the athlete, every opportunity for the display of his equipage and his skill—his four-in-hand, his tandem, or his trotting steed. It is a centre of cheerful, healthful, social intercourse, and so far it has not been degraded by the paltry and cruel practice of shooting pigeons from traps.

Reverting to the negroes—when they "get religion" they are much more serious in their demeanour and devout in their worship. Some of their hymns, strange not seldom and unsound in doctrine, quaint sometimes in their language and in their association with common things, are stirring, pathetic, and harmonious. For example :—

"DE GOSPEL TRAIN.

"De Gospel Train's a-coming, I hear it just at hand,
  I hear dem car wheels movin', and a-rumblin' through the land;
  I hear de bell and whistle—she's a pulling on de curb;
  She's playing all her steam-power, and she's straining every nerve.

Chorus—

"Get on board, children; get on board, children;
  Get on board, children, for dere's room for many more.

"No signal for another train to follow on that line;
  O sinner, you're for ever lost, if once you're left behind!
  She's nearin' now the depôt, O sinner, don't be vain,
  But go and get your baggage checked, and be ready for the train.

"De fare is cheap, and all can go, de rich and poor are dere.
  No second-class aboard dem cars, but all go first-class fare;
  And all alike are equal, and all alike are free,
  And de white man and de black man is all one familee.

"Dere's Moses, Noah, Abraham, and all the prophets too,—
Our dear departs are all aboard, O what a happy crew!
We soon shall reach the depôt, how den we all shall sing,
And wid all the heavenly armies, we'll make the roofin' ring!"

In appropriate sequence I transcribe an epitaph from the grave of an engineer (our English term is engine-driver), named Valentine, who was killed on the Chesapeake and Ohio Railroad in Virginia, and was buried in Hollywood Cemetery, Richmond:—

"*In the crash and fall he stood, and gave his life,
that he might save many.*"

"Until the brakes are turned on time,
　Life's throttle-valve shut down,
He waits to pilot in the crew
　That wear the heavenly crown.
On schedule time, on upward grade,
　Along the homeward section,
He lands his crew at God's round house
　The morn of Resurrection.
His time all full, no wages docked,
　His name on God's pay-roll,
And transportation through to Heaven,
　A free pass for his soul."

Some may regard these analogies and expressions as verging on profanity, but to the pure all things are pure.

Another epitaph engraved upon a tomb in Virginia is remembered as having evoked a brilliant repartee. A famous author resident in that State was bereaved of his wife, and inscribed upon her gravestone, "The light is gone from my life." Time not only modified his distress, but kindly and wisely suggested a renewal of conjugal bliss. An acrimonious neighbour had the bad taste to banter him on his engagement, and to express a surprise that he had so soon forgotten his words of lamentation. "So far from forgetting them," he replied, "I remember and repeat them now, as originating and confirming the intention which you are pleased to criticize. I declared that *the light was gone from my life*, and it is for this reason that I propose to *strike another match*."

There are in Virginia a few of the crazy folk who go by the name of Spiritualists. One of them died, and his relations, who were rational beings and Christian people, buried him with his fathers. But when his brother lunatics were informed of the fact they were filled with indignation, and hastily convened a committee of inquiry to consult with the spirit of their departed friend, to ascertain his views upon the subject, and to act accordingly. An answer was returned by the usual process from the deceased, "That no attempt had been made to ascertain his wishes, that he had had nothing whatever to do with the arrangements, and that" (as the Scotchman said at his execution) "he was disgusted with the whole affair." Whereupon a deputation waited on the officiating minister (I do not remember his denomination), and assailed him in opprobrious terms. He listened patiently, until they had exhausted their ammunition and ceased firing, and then said, "Ladies and gentlemen, for a long period of years I have conducted funerals in strict accordance with the usual order and services, to the satisfaction and consolation of the survivors, and *this is the first time that I have ever been sassed by the remains!*"

And yet another memoir ministerial :—An elderly village dame was talking to her neighbour in disparagement of their pastor, who was a good farmer but a bad preacher. "Well," replied the counsel for the defence, " I guess he is a bit dry in the pulpit, but in the *grasshopper and caterpillar season he's mighty in prayer!*"

Farewell, beautiful Virginia! Peace be in your kind hearts, and health in your happy homes, bright as the sunshine on your hills and dales!

CHAPTER XXI.

WASHINGTON.

ARCHDEACON BURNABY, from whose "Travels in North America," published some 130 years ago, I have already quoted, was the friend of Washington, and was his guest at Mount Vernon more than once. "From Colchester," he writes, "we went about twelve miles to Mount Vernon. This place is the property of Colonel Washington. The house is most beautifully situated upon a high hill on the banks of the Potomac, and commands a noble prospect of water, cliffs, woods, and plantations." And again, "On the 19th of December, 1759, being on a visit to Colonel Washington at Mount Vernon, upon the river Potomac, where it is two miles in breadth, I was greatly surprised to find it entirely frozen over in the space of one night, when the preceding day had been mild and temperate."

He relates to us an incident in the early life of Washington which indicates, as clearly as the dawn the day, the rise and splendour of his fame. "On the 1st of November, 1753, Lieutenant-Governor Dinwiddie, having informed the Assembly in Virginia that the French had erected a fortrees upon the Ohio, it was resolved to send a messenger to M. St. Pierre, the commander, to claim that country as belonging to his Britannic Majesty, and to order him to withdraw. Mr. Washington, a young gentleman of fortune, just arrived at age, offered his service on this important occasion. The distance was more than four hundred miles, two hundred of which lay through a trackless desert, inhabited by cruel and merciless savages, and the season was uncommonly severe. Notwithstanding, Mr. Washington, attended by one companion only, set out upon this dangerous enterprise, travelled from Winchester on foot, carrying his provisions on his back, executed his commission, and, after incredible hardships and many providential escapes, returned safe to Williamsburg, and gave an account of his negotiation to the Assembly on the 14th of February following."

On July 27, 1761, he wrote this letter to his friend:—

From GEORGE AUGUSTUS WASHINGTON
(*Afterwards* **President of Congress**, *and Commander-in-Chief* **of the Forces of the United States of America**,)
To ANDREW BURNABY
(*Archdeacon* of Leicester.—*Of Bagyrave Hall, in the County of Leicester, Great Britain.*)

"Mount Vernon
"27th July 1761

"Dear Sir,
"Your obliging favour of the 14th of April I had the pleasure to receive about the 10th inst.— The news of your safe arrival in London was often

confirmed to me by the Governor and others, or else
I should have felt a very singular pleasure in the
account of it from yourself.—If apologies are necessary, I certainly have the greatest reason to make
one, for my silence till now—a silence really occasioned from the doubts entertained here of your
returning again, or with more justice I might have
said, from a belief that you certainly would.—I must
own, that after the Death of the poor Commissary
and other changes which both preceded, and followed
that Event, I was in hopes that something had
cast up Introductory to your return; but as I
am perswaded your resolution's of remaining in
England are founded upon very solid motives
your Friends in Virginia must acquiesce to the
loss of your Company, and endeavour to avail
themselves of an Epistalory Correspondance with
you.—This is my plan, and in your power to render
it effectual.—

"I deal little in Politic's, and what to advance
under the article of news I really know not; This
part of the Country as you know, affords few
occurrences worthy of remark, and as to the Transactions of Climes more distant,—but let me speak
more intelligibly—of our neighbouring Colonies, you
have letters transmitted to you with more regularity
and certainty than we have, tho' perhaps with not
quite so much Expedition—The perfidious conduct of
our Neighbours the Cherokees, have occasioned the
sending Major Grant with a detachment of His
Majesty's Troops, and what Forces the Carolinaens
coud Muster into their Country on that side; while
Colonel Byrd with the Virginia Regiment is ordered

to penetrate it on this—what may be the Event of these Expedition's is difficult, and perhaps may be improper to conjecture; but they afford matter of speculation, and while some think the Indian's will make the most abject submissions rather than come to blows, there are others of very different opinions, and fearful of the Consequences; but so it is in all doubtful matters of Importance.—

"His late Majestys Death having occasioned a general Election of Burgesses in this Colony, many new members are chosen; among whom Col. Mercer supplies the place of my late Colleague Col. Martin, who thought proper to decline.—Phil: Johnson turns out Ben Waller—Bernd: Moore, and Cartr: Braxton, Peter Robinson and Harry Gains; and so with, many others whom you know.

"You must in some measure Sir have misunderstood my account of the Cavern near Winchester; or I greatly aggravated the Circumstances in giving a Relation of it—true it is, that within 16 miles of Winchester to the North East hand of it, in a plain flat Country no ways contigious to any Mountain or constant running Water, there stands a natural Cave or Well, which at times a Person may go down into, to the depth of 100 or 150 Yards, and at other time, the Water rises to the Top and flows of plentifully, but I never observed any regular Flux or reflux, or that this happened at any fixed periods; on the contrary, I always concluded, and have been so informed, that the dry and wet Season's was the Sole and only occasion of these Changes—However, as it lyes within two miles of my Plantation in Frederick I will, when next I go up there, make

x

a more minute Enquiry of the most Intelligent
People of the neighbourhood, and give you a further
account thereof in my next; and this journey I
propose to undertake so soon as my health will
permit, which at present is in a very declining way,
and has been so in spite of all the Esculapian Tribes
eversince the Middle of May; occasioned by a violent
Cold I then got in a Tour to Winchester etc.—I have
found so little benefit from any advice yet received
that I am more than half of the mind to take a
trip to England for the recovery of that invaluable
Blessing — Health.—but enough on this subject
for the present.—Mrs. Washington, who takes pleasure in hearing of your Welfare, desires her Com-
pliments may be presented, along with the sincerest
wishes of

"Dear Sir
"Your most obedient and most humble Servant
"Go: WASHINGTON

"P.S. Your little white horse departed this life
soon after you did the country."

How strangely the words sound now, "I deal little
in politics . . . . think of taking a trip to England!"

Englishmen are reticent in the presence of
Americans as to their estimate of Washington, not
because in a just cause he defeated their armies, but
because they fear lest their praise should seem to
be exaggerated by a courteous desire to please; and
I sometimes doubt whether the depth and sincerity
of our admiration is realized by our Transatlantic
friends. Be this as it may, we believe, with our

historian,* that "no nobler figure ever stood in the foreground of a nation's life. Washington was grave and courteous; his manners were simple and unpretending; his silence and the severe calmness of his temper spoke of a perfect self-mastery; but there was little in his outer bearing to reveal that grandeur of soul which lifts his figure with all the simple majesty of an ancient statue out of the smaller passions, the meaner impulses of the world around him. It was only as the weary fight went on that the colonists learned, little by little, the greatness of their leader, his clear judgment, his heroic endurance, his silence under difficulties, his calmness in the hour of danger or defeat, the patience with which he waited, the quickness and hardness with which he struck, the lofty and severe sense of duty which never swerved from its task through resentment or jealousy, that never through war or peace felt the touch of a meaner ambition that knew no aim beyond that of guarding the freedom of his fellow-countrymen, and no personal longing save that of returning to his own fireside when that fruition was secured. It was almost unconsciously that men learned to cling to Washington with a trust and with a faith such as few other men have won, and to regard him with a reverence which still hushes us in the presence of his memory. Even America barely recognized his true greatness till death set its seal on the man first

* Green's "Short History of the English People." Illustrated Edition, vol. iv. p. 1700.

in war, first in peace, and first in the hearts of his fellow-countrymen."

Of all the tributes of praise and gratitude expressed by his own countrymen, I like the best, so far as I have read them, that of Jefferson, who knew him intimately and thoroughly. While he does not hesitate to speak of him as "slow in action, though irritable in temper, sometimes tremendous in his wrath, in conversation not above mediocrity, called upon for sudden opinion unready and embarrassed," he declares him to have been "incapable of fear, inflexible in justice, in every sense of the word a wise, a good, and a great man, warm in his affections, handsome in his appearance, graceful in his manner, the best horseman of his age; and it may be truly said that never did Nature and Fortune combine more perfectly to make a man great. It was his singular destiny and merit to lead the armies of his country successfully through an arduous war to the establishment of its independence, and to conduct its councils through the birth of a government until it had settled down to order and peace."

The city which bears his name is worthy of it, with its beautiful avenues and squares and parks, its stately public buildings, Government offices for the State, War, Navy, Treasury, Patent and Postal departments, its galleries, museum, and monuments, the Washington Obelisk, said to be the highest masonic structure in the world, 555 feet (I did not ascend the nine hundred steps, having acquired during my sojourn in the States a strong preference for the elevator system), made from the white marble of Maryland at a cost of $1,300,000; and, dominating all, the magnificent Capitol, with a frontage of 750 feet, its grand Chamber of Representatives, its splendid library with nearly half a million books, and erected at an outlay of $16,000,000. Further

THE CAPITOL, WASHINGTON.

improvements are in progress or contemplation, and when these are completed, and a park supersedes the buildings which now occupy "the Division," it will take that precedence in appearance as well as in authority which becomes the capital of the United States.

Compared with New York or Chicago, Washington,

though it is full of animation and energy, is a city of rest and peace. The inhabitants do not rush onward as though they were late for the train or the post, or as though the dinner-hour being past they were anxious to appease an irritable wife who was waiting at home for her food. The ear is not deafened by the clanging of bells, the roll of the cars, and the tramping of feet which never seem to pause. It was a busy day (December 3) on which we arrived, the first day of the meeting of Congress after vacation, and we had come from the tranquillities of a village in Virginia, but, though there was a great gathering of Representatives, there was no commotion nor din.

As to politics, I failed signally to grasp the divergent opinions which separate the Democrats from the Republicans, and, unable to identify myself with either party, I became what in America is called (it is not a pretty or euphonious title, and I do not propose to place it on my visiting-card) "a Mugwump." The etymological derivation is obscure, but the term is applied to persons who, not having been persuaded by satisfactory arguments to attach themselves to one side or the other, maintain their right to vote as they please—for measures and not for men, for principles and not for parties. In England the Mugwump would be denounced as "a Trimmer," and in America he has a second title, being sometimes known as "a Bolter."

The information which I received on this subject from gentlemen both competent and willing to give it was meagre. The chief differences seemed to be, that after the Revolution the Democrats were very zealous for State rights and independence, the Republicans were more anxious for the unity and honour of the nation; but that since the Civil War, the abolition of slavery, and the settlement of the constitution, there have been no very special questions to emphasize the division of parties. At present the Republicans are said to be the advocates of Protection and the Democrats of Free Trade, but it was observed that, when the latter had the power and opportunity for a definite and practical manifestation of Free Trade principles, there was such a complication of different interests among producers and manufacturers that nothing was done. These two great political parties do not seem to be led, as with ours, by men pre-eminent above their fellows, whose names are familiar in our mouths as household words—Salisbury and Balfour, Devonshire and Chamberlain; but in other features there is a strong family likeness. Both parties are alike convinced that the greatness of the nation depends upon their supervision, and that the moment they leave the helm of government the ship drifts away to the rocks.

Washington represents the characteristics as well as the constituencies of America. In a population of 230,000, there are 18,000 persons foreign born, a very small proportion compared to other great cities; and, as in our House of Commons, these characteristics are displayed in a variety of types and phases. Of course, the representatives are as a rule of a high class, as to culture and deportment, but exceptions may be introduced from distant States, and these, with their wives and daughters, may require in Washington, as in London, some slight adaptations to the refinements of modern society. Many years ago the "Guards" quartered in Dublin gave a ball, which created a great sensation. Mothers came with their fair daughters from remote parts of the country, in which the serene elegance and the severe etiquette of the *élite* were altogether unknown, and during one of the dances a mamma was seen to approach her daughter, and was heard to say, "Jump, Judy, jump, the Guards are looking at yer."

I could not have hoped, at that busy season of the opening of Congress, for an interview with the President of the United States (Mr. Cleveland) had I not been highly favoured by a letter of introduction from His Excellency (some of my readers may object to titles, but all who know the man will agree that in this instance the prefix is strictly accurate) the American Ambassador in London. This secured for us a most genial reception at the White House from one of the most able, reliable, hard-working rulers of the world. When I was asked the usual question, "What sort of a man does he look?" my answer was, "He looks the sort of man who would give all his mind and heart and soul to those questions which seemed to him to be of chief importance to his nation, would study the statistics, and weigh the evidence, and then would fearlessly act in accordance with his convictions, whether thwarted by friend or foe." On fixed and frequent dates he welcomes all alike, and, in proof of his popularity, has had as many as six thousand visitors a day. He mentioned that Mrs. Cleveland had found these receptions too fatiguing; and when I told him that I had the pleasure of meeting that lady not long ago in New York, he seemed perplexed, as well he might be, for the simple reason that she had not been there. He was amused by the explanation— Mr. Sarony, long famous as an artist in photography, has cleverly discovered a method by which he secures a pleasant expression on the countenance of his "sitter." He places in his view a likeness of Mrs. Cleveland, one of the most beautiful women of her day, and a smile of admiration at once illumines the lineaments of the spectator.

The White House, or "Executive Mansion," does not display any special grandeur without or within. It is a large, substantial, handsome building, but, with the exception of some most interesting portraits of former Presidents, and the spacious conservatories adjoining, there is no remarkable ornamentation. It is in every way suitable to the purposes for which it was designed, but men of rank and of riches have built far more stately homes. Nevertheless, there is a simple dignity, an intimation of power, a reality of business, which impresses some minds as forcibly as "the divinity which doth hedge a king."

After my interview with the President, and after my lecture in the evening, I had another memorable introduction, namely, to Edgar Wilton—sometimes called "Bill"—Nye. Does there seem to you, my readers, a startling antithesis, a great gulf between these two men—the statesman and the humourist? Let me suggest that it is not so great as it seems. While we give all due precedence and highest honours to those who lead us with a faithful and true heart, and rule us prudently with all their power, to those who govern us, think for us, fight for us, instruct us in knowledge, science, and art, let us not forget that they, too, are our benefactors who expose cowardice and meanness and idleness and ignorance to ridicule, to shame, and scorn, and who make sunshine in this dreary, doleful world with their bright imaginations and their sparkling wit. It is written, moreover, let the righteous be merry and joyful, and the best men whom I have known, inclusive of most reverend and reverent divines, have been cheered and have cheered others with this joy. And when the mind is dull, and the spirit depressed by long and laborious efforts, what a relief and refreshment we find in the writings of the humourist. A chapter of Dickens, a poem of Hood or of Lowell, a lecture by Artemus Ward, doeth good like a medicine; and in all the Pharmacopœia of comic literature I find few tonics so invigorating as "Bill Nye's History of the United States of America, with coloured illustrations by

F. Opper." Let the man who is not moved by the humour of that book write me down an ass, but let it never be my misfortune to spend a day with the scribe! It would resemble a like period of time referred to in a correspondence between father and son. The son, desirous to enlighten his father (having previously finished the education of his grandmother as to the most enjoyable method of sucking eggs), and to instruct him in virtuous living, exhorted him to abstain from all alcoholic stimulants, and assured him that in addition to many other blessings, teetotalism would prolong his days; and the father replied that, while he failed to recognize the force of the preceding arguments, he promptly and heartily accepted the final plea. He was convinced that total abstinence would prolong his life —he had tried it for a day, and it was the longest he ever spent!

Next morning I had a visit from the Historian, and we parted as sincere and faithful friends. Some weeks afterwards I received from him the following letter, which expresses so exactly and incisively the justification of humour which I have tried to confirm, that I asked and received his permission for publication :—

"Christmas Day, Washington, 1894.

"MY DEAR DEAN HOLE,

"Your very welcome 'Memories' are here, and I have already enjoyed one volume, with the other in reserve.

"You do not realise, perhaps, that you had a mission to America, which I am going to appropriate mostly to myself.

"I have always sort of wondered why 'the children of a king' should 'go mourning all their days,' and I have often tried to settle in my own mind the question why the clergyman and the man who rides a bicycle should never smile.

"It seems to me that if I could be as good as many preachers appear to be, I would be radiant with gladness all the time.

"You have proved to me that a clergyman may have a good time, good health, and long life, without injury to his piety.

"It is fully as unjust to put down all clergymen as enemies to humour as it would be to assume that all humourists were destitute of religion. So, you see, my dear friend, that the general public has a wrong idea of us both.

"I have rebelled more perhaps over this assumption than 'most any other. Why should one who sees and describes the ridiculous side of life be necessarily vulgar and Godless?

"On the other hand, why should one whose mission it is to proclaim the gladdest of all glad tidings, as did the angels 1894 years ago, be habitually dejected and bilious?

"To me your life, as revealed in your 'Memories,' seem almost ideal, and I am proud and happy if, along with those delightful friends of whom you write, on the shelf devoted to your American acquaintances, you may find room for

"Your sincere friend,
"Edgar Wilton Nye."

We know, of course, that there are surroundings, such as difference of climate and of scene, as well as innate diversities of disposition and temper, which stimulate or suppress hilarity and humour. The Scotch, for example, are said to be obtuse in their appreciations of comedy, though this does not agree with my own experience, and E. W. Nye told me that he was gratified by an illustration of this defect, solemnly related by a member of the Savage Club in London, at a social meeting which he joined as a guest.

The narrator stated that a report had reached him (not having travelled from afar, because every one knew that it had originated in his own imagination) that our beloved Queen had been recently afflicted by a sudden, strange, and incessant monomania. "From morn to noon, from noon to dewy eve," her Majesty gave utterance to an infinite variety of puns and jokes, so sadly inconsistent with her usual dignity and habit that the Court was astonished and alarmed. The Lords and Ladies in Waiting were distressed beyond measure, because they had to listen, and it was not etiquette to yawn, to sigh, or to gasp. They were men of truth and maids of honour when they declared openly that they had never before heard the like, and when they added inwardly that they would rather not hear it again. Every effort was made to arrest and to divert the stream, but the flood was irresistible and carried all before it. The doctors prescribed in vain, until one, more sagacious than his brethren, discovered the remedy. "We can readily persuade her Majesty," he said, "to reside for a time in Scotland, and there this habit will not be noticed." His treatment was a rapid and complete success. The puns and the jokes went on for a time, but Scotland did not move a muscle. There was no perception, and therefore no acknowledgment, of humour. It was not even suspected that the Queen meant to be funny; and when she had to do all the laughing herself, and there was no sympathy, no surprise, no opposition or interruption, the river subsided, and gradually dried up as in times of drought!

I made another pleasant friendship while I was in the States—and, as friend after friend departs, it is a solace, as welcome as it is rare, to find some new congenial presence in their vacant place—with Monsieur Paul Blouet, a brave soldier, who fought and well-nigh lost his life for his country in the Franco-Prussian war, a scholar, a most successful writer and lecturer, a brilliant, caustic, but kindly humourist, the author of "John Bull and his Island" and "Jonathan and his Continent," commonly known as "Max O'Rell." We had cheerful conversations, in which he reproduced, with a dramatic and delicious fidelity, the incidents of his long and large experience. He may require them for his own use, but he has such a vast accumulation that I cannot resist two small peculations.

He was travelling in the gold diggings, and seeing the advertisement, I think it was at Bendigo, of a meeting of Irishmen, to be addressed by some famous agitator, he joined the assembly. It was presided over by an elderly gentleman, small in stature, meek in demeanour, low and slow in utterance, wearing spectacles of an abnormal size. He called upon the famous orator and noble patriot, Mr. Rory O'Something, and O'Something proceeded to roar. The usual "Hereditary bondsmen, know ye not," "the bloody Saxon tyrant," "the bloated Saxon thief," "the virtuous, suffering Celt," "must rise as one man," "break chains," "hurl oppressor into the sea," etc. When he had finished, and the acclamations had ceased, the chairman, adjusting the big spectacles with much deliberation, and with a voice which sounded after the oration and the uproar like a sparrow chirping after a thunderstorm, inquired whether any other gentleman was desirous to address the meeting. The invitation was immediately accepted, but the new speaker had only got so far as to say that he differed entirely with some of the statements which they had just heard, when an excited individual rose from his seat, rushed at him, and knocked him off the platform! He was badly hurt, and was taken in a dilapidated condition to the hospital, but during his removal, and for some time afterwards, there was such a shouting, shoving, struggling, striking, and general scrimmage as none but Home Rulers can organize and sustain. At last, from the interference of the police and from a general feeling of fatigue, order was restored, and once more the diminutive president assumed the large binoculars, and, smiling sweetly, "wished to know whether any other gentleman was anxious to speak?" The company seemed to think that it was about time to go to bed—and they went.

Petty larceny No. 2. He related that, in a certain city in which he was giving a lecture, the head-mistress of a large school of girls was informed by his agent that the pupils would be admitted at half-price, and the governesses without payment. At the commencement of his lecture, and surveying his audience, he saw that four scholars and eleven teachers had availed themselves of his invitation, and it struck him, as a man of keen perceptive power, that the number of the shepherdesses was excessive in proportion to the lambs!

Max O'Rell keeps his friendships in good working order. We were together in a large town when, as he was alone in his private room, his solitude was suddenly invaded by a biped, evidently under alcoholic influence, and smoking a cigar. "I'm told that you are a friend of Dean Hole," he began, abruptly. "I am," replied Max O'Rell. "Tell him," said the invader, "that we don't like that dress of his, and advise him to change it." "Dean Hole is a free man, from a free country, and can dress as he pleases." "Oh, indeed—our opinions seem to clash." "Yes," said my friend, "and our bodies will clash also if you don't leave this room." And then, noticing a doubt in his intention and a debility in his locomotive endeavours, he assisted and expedited the departure.

Y

CHAPTER XXII.

PHILADELPHIA, PITTSBURG, BALTIMORE.

DR. CONAN DOYLE, another delectable companion, who was also giving lectures in America, but whom I only met for very brief interviews—too few and far between—declared Philadelphia to be by far the finest city in the States. He saw it in its best clothes, on Thanksgiving Day, when all were keeping festival, and when his brother athletes (grand athletes! eleven of whom afterwards defeated in one innings a like number of our Oxford and Cambridge cricketers) were contending on the football field; but I venture to doubt whether, seen in its ordinary aspect, and regarded as a place of permanent residence, he would have so readily awarded this supremacy over Washington or Boston.

Greatly to be admired at all times, and by all, is this Quaker city, the city of brotherly love. Founded by William Penn, from England, some two hundred and fifty years ago, this acorn has grown into a gigantic oak. At the beginning of the last century it had between four and five thousand inhabitants; now it has over a million, the largest population in the country, except those of New York and Chicago. In 1725 the places of worship were three Episcopalian, three Quakers, two Presbyterian, one Roman, one Lutheran, one Swedenborgian, one Anabaptist, and one Moravian. Now there are five hundred churches, so called; and these seem true to their title of Philadelphians, and in brotherly love to agree to differ. At the lecture which I gave in their city, there were assembled on the platform the bishop of the diocese and many of the clergy, a Roman Catholic priest, several Presbyterian ministers, a Methodist "bishop," and a Jewish rabbi.

Bishop Whitaker entertained us affectionately in his "Episcopal Rooms" in Walnut Street—several of the streets have the names of trees: Walnut, Chestnut, Spruce, and Pine, as if, as Longfellow suggests in "Evangeline"—

"As if they fain would appease the Dryads whose haunts they molested,"

and lovely bouquets, and tall pyramids, and bountiful, beautiful boxes of roses awaited me in his happy home and on the platform from which I spoke. And I may mention a small incident which pleased me much. As I was leaving the hall after addressing a large audience, "with a broad English accent," according to a newspaper report, a dollar note was placed as unobtrusively as possible into my hand, and the donor said, *sotto voce*, "I'm only a working man, but I come from the old country, and should like to give a trifle to your restoration work."

Next day, there was a fresh outpour of this

brotherly kindness. Dr. Edwards, a friend's friend, with a couple of carriages and pair, came to show us the city and suburban sights. The great City Hall, covering a larger space ($4\frac{1}{2}$ acres) than any other building in the States; the stately tower surmounted by the colossal statue of William Penn; the post office, the custom house, and mint; and interesting above all, and famous for ever in the history of nations, the hall wherein was read on July 4, 1776, the Declaration of Independence,* which was afterwards proclaimed from its steps.

The first sensation of the Britisher as he contemplates this eventful scene somewhat resembles that of a hunting man who goes at his leisure to survey a fence at which he got, during the heat of the chase, "a tremendous cropper." His collar-bone has been skilfully adjusted, his other bones have ceased to ache, his flesh is no longer discoloured, and the slight feeling of discomfort induced by the recollections of his disaster is quickly superseded by the consciousness that he was the victim of his own temerity and that he was riding for a fall.

We drove to Fairmount Park, which is said to be the largest city park in the world, eight miles in extent, and might be the most beautiful. We passed the pretty Elizabethan house built for the English

* "That these United colonies are, and of a right ought to be, independent States; that they are absolved from all allegiance to the British Crown; and that all political connexion between them and the States of Great Britain is, and ought to be, totally dissolved."

INDEPENDENCE HALL, PHILADELPHIA.

officials at the Centennial Exhibition in 1876, the Memorial Hall and Museum, the Grand Horticultural Hall, which contains one of the best, if not the best, collection of stove plants, both as to selection and culture, which I have ever seen—palms, musas, alocasias, marantas, cyanophyllum, *et id genus omne;* but of all the ornaments which adorn that fair city, the brightest and the purest are those which make her most worthy of her name—her charitable institutions, her hospitals and homes, her asylums and penitentiaries for the sick and the poor, for widows and orphans, for the demented and the fallen. May this charity which never faileth bring upon Philadelphia not only the blessing of him that was ready to perish, but that promise of a far more glorious benediction, which was given to the city, which first bore her name when Saint John wrote to the Churches.

Pittsburg would be more enjoyable as a home if the inhabitants were favoured with occasional glimpses of the sky, but it is at present to be more admired for its industry than for its atmospheric surroundings. But there are

"Smiles which make a summer
Where darkness else would be,"

and these I received from episcopal, floral, and other friends, with wreaths of roses which might have been more appropriate, but could not have been more appreciated, if they had been offered to a young *débutante* instead of to an ancient Dean. Bishop Whitehead most kindly presided at my lecture, and next morning my horticultural allies conveyed me on a tour of inspection to the Allegheny Court House, said to have cost half a million pounds; to the magnificent library, museum, etc., nearly completed and built by Mr. Andrew Carnegie for presentation to his fellow-citizens. "The Iron King," who has mounted step by step from the ground to the throne—" Every American," writes my friend Nye, "except Dr. Mary Walker, was once a poor boy"—has a royal munificence (American and English millionaires, "please copy"), and has written a splendid treatise, which he calls "The Gospel of Wealth." In this essay he asserts, and he has reason and Revelation on his side, that it is disgraceful for a man to heap up riches and to die, instead of dispensing them abroad and giving to the poor, and lightening the burdens of his fellow-men. Whereupon, it is reported that he received a letter from a sarcastic neighbour, in which the writer stated that, having read "The Gospel of Wealth," he was so overpowered by the terrible apprehension that the preacher, whom he greatly revered, might be removed by some sudden vicissitude before he could extricate himself from his accumulations, and so might himself incur the dishonour which he had denounced, that he lost no time in offering to relieve him of $500,000, and if the sum named was inadequate, he had friends, on whom he could rely for assistance, with regard to a further reduction.

We saw the splendid range of glass, well stored with stove and greenhouse plants, presented to his fellow-citizens by Mr. Phipps, a partner of Mr. Carnegie. Here again there is not only excellent culture with the inseparable element of cleanliness, but, large and numerous as the houses are, there is an admirable economy of space. A tank, some eighty feet in length, occupied at an earlier season by aquatic plants, was covered over with boards, and on them were placed a charming collection of cyclamens in pots. With their mitre-like flowers they resembled an œcumenical council of fairy bishops, but I saw neither cardinal nor pope.

There was what we gardeners call "a nice lot" of Waterer's rhododendrons outside one of the houses, looking as fresh as when they left the nurseries at Bagshot.

Baltimore is named after an Irish baron, one of its original founders, but his memory is not cherished in the "monumental city," which claims for a triumvirate of more illustrious benefactors our sympathy and homage. First for Washington, who is ever in just pre-eminence throughout the States, "Stylites," the Pillar Saint, and has in Baltimore a noble statue, sixteen feet in height, and raised upon a Grecian column and basement nearly two hundred feet from the ground. And so—

> "He doth bestride the narrow world
> Like a Colossus; and we petty men
> Walk under his huge legs, and peep about
> To find ourselves dishonourable graves."

In the square below there is a lion in bronze, supposed

WASHINGTON STATUE, BALTIMORE.

by some to represent the Lion of England, which, when the war began, said, "We've treed you, Yankee George," but when the war was over said nothing.

Hard by is a statue from Story's studio—a replica of that which we have in London—of another great American (and where within the same range of opportunities shall we find a greater?), George Peabody; and, something to be far more admired than statues, because a man's good deeds are his best monuments, the Peabody Institute, which he built and endowed, with its art galleries and academy of music, and the most fascinating library I ever entered, six tiers or galleries of books between floor and roof, containing 120,000 volumes, with every accommodation for readers and writers, every help to guide them to the various subjects of their search.

The learned and beloved president of the Johns Hopkins University, Dr. Gilman, kindly called upon me and took me—pointing out as we went a house still occupied by members of the Buonaparte family, being descendants of Jerome, brother of Napoleon I., who married Miss Patterson of Baltimore—to see the college of which he is chief. Johns Hopkins, with the same magnanimity, if not with the same imposing appellation as King Alfred the Great, gave three million and a half dollars to found a university, and the same sum for a hospital!

The Americans say, and they prove from history that they have a right to say, that whenever there arises an extraordinary crisis or an extraordinary enterprise, they have always in readiness an extraordinary man to solve the one or to lead the other. In this instance a master mind was most urgently needed for a work of vast proportions and importance—to make the most of seven millions of dollars—to build on an enormous scale, with elaborate arrangements, the most suitable structures that could be erected for teachers and pupils, physicians and their patients, surgeons, dispensers, and nurses—to establish systems, and to select from a crowd of candidates those who were most qualified to maintain them well. There might be some among a people who are not hampered, as a rule, by abnormal bashfulness who would gaily volunteer to boss the show, but to put the right man in the right place—that was the question.

Then appeared the *Deus ex machinâ*. He came, saw, and conquered, and my eyes endorsed that which my ears had heard of the president's complete success. I was greatly impressed by the brightness, order, and adaptation of all I saw, especially by the rooms set apart for the study of particular subjects, with exhaustive collections of the best books thereupon, and visited from time to time by erudite professors who gave lectures to the students. I was informed that the standard of medical education is higher than elsewhere, being prolonged beyond the usual period for those qualified and disposed to continue their studies, when others are satisfied and have satisfied their examiners with the knowledge which they have acquired, and proceed to practise.

It is recorded that at a dinner-party at Baltimore many years ago, at which these two noblemen, George Peabody and Johns Hopkins, were present, that some one inquired, "Which did you enjoy most, Mr. Peabody, making your money or giving it away?" "Well," answered Mr. Peabody, and Johns Hopkins was observed to be deeply interested in his answer, "I enjoyed making money. I think it is a great pleasure to make money; and when the idea was first suggested to me that I should give money away it did not please me at all—in fact, it distressed me. But I thought the matter over, and concluded that I would make an experiment on a small scale. So I built the first of the model tenement houses in London. It was a hard pull, but after it was done I went among the poor people living in the rooms, so clean and comfortable, and I had quite a new feeling. I enjoyed it very much. I gave more, and the feeling increased; and now I can truly say that, much as I enjoyed the making of money, I enjoy far more the giving it away."

I met with other genial and generous friends, clerical and lay, who took me to see the exterior of the Hopkins Hospital, the Women's College, the City Hall, and the pretty park on Druid Hill. I regard Baltimore city, with its attractive scenery, its grand institutions (sacred and secular), its clever sons and fair daughters (the latter well sustain their ancient reputation for beauty), as one of the most charming cities in the States.

CHAPTER XXIII.

UNIVERSITIES AND COLLEGES.

ALTHOUGH the happy satisfaction which I enjoyed in visiting the Theological Seminary at New York was greatly diminished in the Universities and colleges not in communion with the church to which I belong, and which I believe to be of all churches the most primitive and pure, I found so much to admire, so much intellectual brightness and erudition, such complete systems of education, didactic and practical, such grand libraries and technical appliances, such genial courtesies from those in authority, and such cheery smiles—of all sights the most refreshing—on the dear, honest faces of those in obedience, that my regret was overwhelmed in my rejoicing. I was delighted with Young America, and I beg respectfully to offer to the nation in general, and to parents in particular, my heartiest congratulations.

Of all the educational institutions which I saw in the States, Princeton is by far the most picturesque, with its massive, beautiful buildings, not crowded together, but with ample surroundings, in a fair ground or "campus," with grass and trees and a pleasant view of the country beyond—like the University in Tennyson's "Princess"—"half garden and half town."

Some time before my visit I had received an announcement from the corresponding secretary of the Cliosophic Society that "I had been unanimously and most heartily elected an honorary member," and soon after my arrival I was welcomed in the Clio Hall, a classical and charming edifice, resembling a Grecian temple, in white marble; and, after kindly speeches by the president and two of the professors, was received into the society. Then, as we left the building, the young alumni,* standing upon the steps, gave me such a greeting as only undergraduates can, shouting my name with the college cheer,

> "Hooray, Hooray, Hooray!
> Tiger-Sis-Boom-ah!
> Princeton-Dean Hole."
>
> *Da Capo.*

Their colours are the same as those of my own college, Brasenose, and I seemed suddenly to ignore the last half-century of my life, and to feel as boyish as the merriest of them all. Reluctantly I returned to my inn, though it was one of the most agreeable hostelries which I have found in the States, in a delightful position, bright and clean, with good fare

---

* In the year 1770 a traveller wrote: "At Princetown there is a school and college for dissenters, about twenty boys in the school, sixty in the college." There are now eight hundred students.

and excellent attendance, the head-waiter actually inquiring whether we had all we wished, and recalling the good old times which I thought had "departed, never to return," when the landlord or landlady of the hotel came to you at your breakfast to express their hope that you had found your bedroom comfort-

CLIO HALL, PRINCETON.

able, and that the viands provided for your morning meal were acceptable to your palate.

Mr. Rutherford Trowbridge met me at the station, Newhaven, and took me in his carriage to see the University of Yale, the Campus, with its grand old elms and spacious buildings, the dormitories (large blocks in which the students have apartments, not only for the night, but for the day, two of them sharing the same sitting-room), the libraries, lecture rooms, and the Peabody Museum. The most imposing of these edifices is the Vanderbilt Memorial Hall, raised by Mr. Cornelius Vanderbilt as a monument to his son, who was a student at Yale, and closely resembling one of our Colleges at Oxford or Cambridge. Mr. Vanderbilt, whom I had the pleasure of meeting on board the *Majestic*, kindly gave me an engraving of this Memorial Hall, and told me that his son, when on a visit to England, had so greatly admired the architecture of our Universities that he determined to reproduce it in association with his name.

We went through the art studios, containing statues, busts, and carvings in wood (including three huge confessionals from Ghent, preposterously out of place), and the picture galleries, in which were some excellent portraits of Washington and his generals by Trumbull; and then Mr. Thorne, the captain of the football team, showed us the largest and most complete gymnasium which I have seen, with its running track in a raised gallery, and every possible appliance for bodily exercise. He showed us the stationary boats in tanks of water, where the collegians are taught to row, and then the beautiful baths of white marble, where, slightly altering Hood,

> There were some that leapt, and some that swam
> Like troutlets in a pool.

Let no man, therefore, doubt the testimony which

YALE UNIVERSITY BUILDINGS.

I bring to the physical qualifications of Young America, and which fully prepared me to admire, without surprise, the splendid proofs of athletic prowess in the "Trophy Room" of triumphant Yale. *Væ victis!*—woe to its adversaries! And so we read in the newspaper accounts of the last football match with Harvard, "Wrightington's collar-bone was broken; Hallowell was carried off the field disabled; Murphy lay bleeding and insensible on the ground; Brewer was hurt in the first half, but was able to resume play, though subsequently retired by the physician's order."

A zealous advocate of all manly games and sports, I protest—although I was informed that, three hours after the match, the wounded, owing to their healthful condition, were little the worse—against an excessive violence, which has been attended by fatal results, and which has been and must be modified if such contests are to be continued.

The uses and abuses of athletic competition have been admirably demonstrated by Professor Eliot, President of Harvard University, in one of his annual reports. He states that there has been a decided improvement in the average health and strength of the students during the last twenty-five years; that athletic sports have supplied a new and effective motive for resisting all sins which weaken or corrupt the body; they have quickened admiration for such manly qualities as courage, fortitude, and presence of mind in emergencies and under difficulties; they have cultivated in a few the habit of command, and in many the habit of quick obedience and intelligent subordination; and, finally, they have set before young men prizes and distinctions, which are uncontaminated by any commercial value, and which no one can win who does not possess much patience, perseverance, and self-control, in addition to rare

YALE BOAT-HOUSE.

bodily endowments. The president rightly asserts, on the other hand, that if these exercises and competitions are *carried to excess*, they are destructive of the chief purpose of University life—that is, study. No student can keep up his studies and play his full part in any one of these sports as at present conducted. The faithful member of a crew or team may, perhaps, manage to attend most of his lectures, but he rarely has any mind to give to his studies. Wantonly aggravated, athletic sports convert the student into a powerful animal, and dull for the time his intellectual parts; they present the colleges to the public, educated or uneducated, as places of mere physical sport, and not of intellectual training; they make familiar to the student a coarse publicity, which destroys his rightful privacy, while in training for intellectual service, and subjects him to insolent and vulgar comments on his personal qualities; they induce, in masses of spectators at interesting games, an hysterical excitement, which too many enjoy, but which is evidence, not of physical strength and depth of passion, but of feebleness and shallowness; and they tend to dwarf mental and moral pre-eminence by unduly magnifying physical prowess. Strong bodies with weak brains are as bad as large heads and little hearts, and without culture of mind or formation of character, the captain of the eleven or of the eight with his team, in two or three years are clean forgotten, as dead men out of mind. Let the Universities contend with a noble emulation, intercollegiate and international, for mental as well as manual or pedal excellence; and let it not be said of their sport, as once of Rugby football, "It is a game in which the players carry the ball and kick each other."

Yale University was founded at Saybrook in 1701, and was removed to New Haven in 1718, where it was named after its chief benefactor, Elihu

Yale. In the churchyard at Wrexham, North Wales, his monument has this quaint inscription:—

> "Born in America, in Europe bred,
> In Africa travelled, and in Asia wed,
> Where long he lived and thrived, in London dead.
> Some good, some ill he did, so hope all's even,
> And that his soul through mercy's gone to heaven."

In my anticipations, before I started to America, Boston was always in the front as the chief scene of my enjoyment. I longed to see the homes and haunts of its famous men, "the modern Athens," * with its parks and gardens, to meet my brothers as an honorary member of the Massachusetts Horticultural Society. I was sadly disappointed. I had an engagement to preach in Trinity Church, but when I returned on the previous Saturday from a long series of journeys and lectures to New York I was so much out of condition that my doctor forbade me to leave the city. Restored by rest, I set forth two days afterwards to deliver a lecture, which I had also promised, and had a great reception. I was embowered in evergreens and roses. The Bishop presided, and the platform and hall were crowded. I was compelled to leave next morning, after reading most gratifying notices of my lecture as "brimful of wit and humour, mingled with pathos," but with the

* Lord Coleridge remarked to an American who was speaking somewhat contemptuously of England with regard to comparative size, "You must permit me to remind you that an acre of ground at Athens has produced a multitude of infinitely greater men than have been produced in all your continent."

determination, and under promise, to repeat my visit at the first opportunity. I was especially anxious to renew a most congenial acquaintance with Professor and Mrs. Sargent. Shortly afterwards I received a Boston newspaper containing an abusive accusation that, contrary to an agreement with the Episcopal City Mission, I had appropriated all the profits, that my lecture was a mass of nonsense, that I had only "left a Hole in the ground," with other specimens of refined thought and elegant diction. My agent, Major Pond, wrote immediately that I had made no engagement, nor had any communication with the Mission committee, and that all the pecuniary arrangements were fixed by himself. I was reminded, moreover, that curs would bark, and donkeys would bray, and geese would hiss, but it was the first insult which I had received in America, and I declined to risk a repetition. Subsequently an attack was made in a similar spirit, and probably by the same accuser of the brethren, though not in the same publication, upon Dr. Conan Doyle. "The brawny Englishman" was accused of barbarous rudeness to his host and hostess, refusing to join them, eating his dinner alone, devouring several plates of roast beef and frequent relays of vegetables with lightning rapidity, and, after the lecture, pocketing his $300 fee, and hastening to the train. No one who knew Conan Doyle could be deceived by such impossible rubbish, but why should they, who do not know him, be subject to delusion, and believe a lie?

Although the weather was severe, and my visit was short, I found time to cross the river to Cambridge, and to make a brief survey of Harvard College. These two names remind me that the reverend and revered John Harvard, a member of Emmanuel College, Cambridge, was the founder of the University of Harvard. In the year 1638 he bequeathed half his property and his library for its first establishment. It is a pleasant, peaceful place,

OLD BUILDINGS, HARVARD UNIVERSITY.

and there is a quiet dignity about its solid, spacious buildings which indicates their intention—*work*. In the spring, when the trees and the grass in "the Yard" are green, the contrast between the old red brick walls and the new verdure—the sunshine and the shade—must be delightful, and "fair Harvard" can never be forgotten by those who have found a home within her walls. In that gallery of pictures, which Memory constructs for us all, the places and faces which we loved in our youth are the most precious, and the imagination of the Harvard collegian will delight continually to roam amid its halls and dormitories, to play base-ball and football and to handle the oar, to gaze upon the long lines of portraits of men that were famous and of friends that were dear. Most prominent of its famous heroes are " *Vir illustrissimus Georgius Washington Armiger*," on whom Harvard conferred the degree of Doctor of Laws ; Adams, Prescott, Emerson, Motley, Longfellow, and Lowell.

Harvard has not been faithful to its original dedication, " *Christo et Ecclesiæ*." It has, on the contrary, been permeated with a heresy most repugnant to the Christian faith, by that subtle form of Antichrist, the foe who pretends to be a friend— Unitarianism. It is no longer predominant, but it is largely represented. In 1878 the president stated that "the Harvard Divinity School was not distinctively Unitarian, either by its constitution or by the intention of its founders, and that the government of the University could not undertake to appoint none but Unitarian teachers, or to grant any peculiar favours to Unitarian students." In 1887, of the six professors in the theological faculty, two were Baptists and one a Congregationalist; while of the eleven members composing the visiting committee not half were Unitarians. Let us pray and hope that the influence which Bishop Phillips Brooks was empowered to impart may increase more and more, until "we all come in the unity of the faith to the knowledge of the Son of God."

At Cambridge the first printing press known in North America issued, in 1640, its first publication, a metrical version of the Psalms. May the time come when Christians, with one heart and voice, shall sing, "Behold, how good and joyful a thing it is, brethren, to dwell together in unity."

The college at Amherst is very charmingly placed on its tree-clad hill, and though it is small in comparison with those I have described, it has between four and five hundred members; it is under most complete and able ministration, and has large sums at its disposal, which are generously used in diminishing the expenses of the students generally, and in helping those especially who have the smallest means. The expenses of an undergraduate at Amherst vary from $268 to $413 per annum.*

Here again my spirit was refreshed by the bright aspect, the fresh sincerity, the free yet courteous manners of Young America. Returning after my lecture from the college to my hotel, I was invited to one of their habitations, a bright, prettily furnished home, in which fourteen of them lived together without supervision or restraint. They were to be trusted,

---

* In America many of the poorer collegians will occupy themselves during vacation, greatly to their honour, in some profitable employment, so that they may be enabled to defray the expenses of their education.

or they would not have desired the presence of an elderly ecclesiastic. I seemed to read upon each honest face "*integer vitæ, scelerisque purus,*" and was never in a more happy company.

Henry Ward Beecher was a student at Amherst, and Oliver Wendell Holmes speaks of him as being in after years " the same lusty, warm-hearted, strong-fibred, brave-hearted, bright-souled, clear-eyed creature as he was when the college boys acknowledged him as the chiefest among their football kickers."

At Schenectady we had a happy sojourn in the pleasant home and genial society of Professor Raymond, but had not time to visit Union College, of which he is president, nor the great works of the famous Edison hard by. Apropos of Edison, I heard at Schenectady of the only good result which, to my knowledge, ever came from betting. It is said that one of Edison's first chief experiments in electricity was the result of a bet. When he was doing telegraphic work, his midday meals and those of his companions were conveyed to them in tin cans. These were invaded by cockroaches, and all attempts to expel them were failures until Edison made his bet. He collected the cans together, and then, having placed around them two circles of a narrow tinfoil ribbon, about a quarter of an inch apart, he connected them with the electric current. The roaches on their journey to the cans placed their hind legs on one piece of foil and their fore legs on the other, and, thus completing the circuit, perished abruptly.

CHAPTER XXIV.

HARTFORD AND ALBANY.

"THE Arsenal at Springfield" is situated between Boston and Hartford, and suggested to an admiration which never tires some of the grandest verses which Longfellow ever wrote. When we are told that eight hundred thousand guns were made here during the civil wars we may well sigh as we read—

"Were half the power that fills the world with terror,
  Were half the wealth bestowed on camps and courts,
 Given to redeem the human mind from error,
  There were no need of arsenals nor forts."

Of Hartford I would repeat the words which Dickens wrote in his American notes: "I shall always entertain a very pleasant and grateful recollection of Hartford. It is a lovely place, and I had many friends there." Soon after my arrival Dr. Bristol, the rector of the Church of the Good Shepherd, a church erected in memory of Colonel Colt, the inventor of revolvers, by his wife, called on me, accompanied by Mr. Charles Lincoln, an enthusiastic rosarian, who brought me a large box filled with lovely blooms of the "Mrs. Pierpont Morgan" rose. They drove me to see the city, and took me through the Soldiers' Arch to the capitol of capitols—for it seemed to me the most beautiful of all—where I was introduced to the Governor, the Speaker, and other members of the Senate. Governor Vincent Coffin showed me the ancient charter granted by Charles II. to the colonists of Connecticut in the year 1662. In July, 1687, a meeting was called to resist the attempts of Major Andros, the British governor, to interfere with the privileges given by this Charter, and during the discussion the lights were put out, the document was removed from the major's custody, and was concealed in the hollow of an immense oak, until its intentions were no longer opposed. The Charter, framed in wood from the tree, which was blown down in 1856, is now in the State Library.

Among other interesting portraits, there is a likeness of General Washington, which has this remarkable attribute, that from whichever side you see it the left foot of the hero always seems to be in advance of the right. I was unable to accept invitations to visit Trinity College, to my great disappointment, but my lectures and interviews and long journeys absorbed nearly all my time.

I passed the home of Mrs. Beecher Stowe, and was again reminded of Longfellow's words, written in his diary, May 22, 1852, "Every evening we read ourselves into despair out of that tragic book, 'Uncle Tom's Cabin.' It is too melancholy, and makes one's blood boil too hotly." Also the house of Mark Twain,

CAPITOL AND SOLDIERS' MEMORIAL, HARTFORD.

but he was non-resident, or I should have asked leave to thank him for the joy which I have had from his books. The gardens in the suburbs of Hartford seemed to me, so far as one may speak of horticulture in January, to have a special prettiness and care.

From Hartford to Albania Felix, Albany the Blest—blessed in its location by the banks of the Hudson river and on its terraced hill, exalted and enthroned as the queen, the capital of the State of New York; blessed in its industries and prosperity, in its public buildings and mansions; but above all in its chief pastor, the Right Reverend William Croswell Doane, for twenty-six years Bishop of Albany. His father was Bishop of New Jersey, and, if I have not misread the history of the American Church, and have not been misinformed by her sons, no two men have done more to maintain her dignity and to extend her usefulness. Through years of fierce controversy, vacillation, surrender of the truth to expediency, to ease, false doctrine, heresy, and schism, they have contended earnestly for the faith once delivered to the saints, and by their eloquent exhortations and patient continuance in well doing, have overcome evil with good. Very rarely are such splendid possessions as persuasive oratory and persevering energy, as in this instance, strictly entailed. I have never forgotten the impression which was made by the father when, fifty-four years ago, he preached at the re-opening of the parish church of Leeds; and, speaking to an archbishop, several bishops, three hundred clergy, and a great multitude of the laity, he said, "Brethren, right reverend, reverend, and beloved, it is written in the elder records of our faith that when the ark of God was on its progress to the hill of Sion, it rested once for three months in the house of Obed-Edom. And it was told to King David, 'The Lord hath blessed the house of Obed-Edom, and all that pertaineth unto him, because of the ark of God.' And as I have gone from scene to scene of highest interest and rarest beauty in this most favoured land of all the world, contemplated its arts, its industries, its wealth, enjoyed its comforts and refinements, and shared with a full heart the peace and happiness of its dear Christian homes; as I have thought of its attainments in science and in letters; as I have recounted its feats of arms and fields of victory; as I have followed through every ocean and through every sea its cross-emblazoned flag, and seen that on the circuit of its empire the sun never sets—I have asked myself instinctively, whence, to so small a speck on the world's map, a sea-beleaguered island, sterile in soil and stern in climate, Britain, cut off in ancient judgment from the world, such wealth, such glory, and such power? And this answer has come spontaneous to my heart, 'The Lord hath blessed the house of Obed-Edom, and all that pertaineth unto him, because of the ark of God.' Yes, from my heart I say, the strength of England is the Church of England. Your wealth, your glory, and your power, is but God's blessing upon your kingdom, as the home and shelter of His Church."

He wrote as impressively as he spoke in defence of sound doctrine, and he was a poet as well as a preacher. He pleaded and worked successfully in the cause of Christian education, and the first Church boarding school for girls was in his diocese. He was

BISHOP DOANE'S WORK, ALBANY.

the bold advocate of free and open churches, and had a powerful coadjutor in Dr. Muhlenberg, who wrote—

> "If the Saviour drove out of the Temple of old
> Poor ignorant Jews, who bought there and sold,
> Alas! for the Christians, so given to pelf
> That traffic they make of the Temple itself!"

The Bishop of Albany is one of those of whom it is written, "The good works of some are manifest beforehand." They surround him. Under his auspices, by his efforts, and largely through the munificent generosity of Mr. Corning and his son who gave the land on which the buildings stand, have been established the school of St. Agnes for girls, which has already sent out nearly four hundred graduates; the Child's Hospital, where in bright rooms and with loving tenderness all is done that

BISHOP'S THRONE AND OLD CROZIER, ALBANY.

kindness and skill can do to restore health and alleviate pain; the St. Margaret's Home for Babes; the Christina Home in Saratoga Springs, which is not only for the convalescence of invalids, but has an industrial school; the Sisterhood of the Holy Child Jesus, and the Orphan Home in Cooperstown.

2 A

His *magnum opus*, his most noble enterprise, is his cathedral, which, although it is very far from completion, is already the most imposing ecclesiastical structure of those which I saw in the States. It is built and it is used in the spirit which feels that " the Palace is not for man, but for the Lord God," and that the mother church of a diocese should be a model of beauty and of worship. A bishop is a governor and a judge, and as such should have his capitol, his hall of justice, his *sedes episcopi*, for what is a cathedral without a cathedra? He should have his robes, his insignia of office; and Bishop Doane is not one of those who think that a mitre should only appear on forks and spoons and livery buttons; he wears it upon his head.

I had happy days with the Bishop; saw and heard much that was delightful within and without his home: his neighbour, Mrs. Puyn's, treasures of antiquity and art, including the beautiful " Camp Service" of the first Napoleon; Mr. Corning's collection of precious orchids, accompanied by his " grand old gardener," Mr. Gray, with whom, as he showed me his favourites with all the affection of a fond father among his children, I had much genial talk about famous flowers and florists; and a memorable afternoon in the library and garden of Mr. and Mrs. Sage. The latter showed me the collection which she had made of the flowers mentioned by our king-poet, after reading Canon Ellacombe's charming book upon " The Plant Lore of Shakespeare," and I was amused to hear of the difficulties which she had encountered in the culture of our common gorse, preserving it under glass during the winter, and tending it with anxious care. Before we left, this accomplished and generous lady made my heart glad by presenting me with an autograph letter from Oliver Wendell Holmes, together with a copy of his poems.

Although the capitol of Albany is said to have cost more than a million of our money, it did not evoke my admiration so much as the unpretentious City Hall below. The exterior is huge and monotonous, the interior is dreary and dark, always excepting the government and senatorial rooms, with their wainscots and roofs of carved mahogany, and their rich adornments of Mexican onyx, and the library containing 150,000 books. Among its curiosities are the dress sword of General Washington, and surveying instruments which he used in his youth; also two links of an enormous chain which was stretched across the Hudson to hinder the passage of the British fleet.

I preached in the Cathedral on the Sunday morning of my visit, and in the afternoon addressed a large congregation of the little ones, who are so lovingly tended and taught in Albany. Asked by the Bishop's daughter to give her an epitome of my discourse for her children, I put my thoughts into verse as I travelled in the train.

CHRIST TO HIS CHILDREN.

"I was a child, that you
    Might learn from Me,
From My life, pure and true,
    God's child to be.

"Might from the Manger take
    Heart to endure
Hardship, and for My sake
    Pity the poor.

"I, as a servant, learned
    Obedience due;
My daily bread I earned;
    You must work too.

"'Learn from Me,' learn the Truth,
    Growing in Grace;
Love, as I loved, in youth
    God's Holy Place.

"You, child, must bear your Cross;
    Soon there must be
Sorrow and pain and loss—
    Share them with Me.

"Come, tell Me all thy woe,
    When thou art sad,
And in thy gladness, know
    I too am glad.

"Fear not, for I am nigh.
    Asking my aid,
Faith hears My voice, ''Tis I,
    Be not afraid.'"

CHAPTER XXV.

ROCHESTER.

ARRIVING at Rochester in America from Rochester in England, I received the heartiest and happiest of many welcomes which it was my privilege to enjoy in the States. There were synonymous sympathies between old Rochester and the new—new Rochester, by the way, has far more ancient possessions than ours; for what are the Roman walls in my Deanery garden, and the remains of Ethelbert's Saxon Church adjoining, but mere novelties compared with the tusk of the mastodon found in the valley of the Genesee, and nine feet in length? But these were subordinate to stronger attachments, ecclesiastical, floral, and masonic. Two large committees (honorary and active), with representatives of the Masonic Lodges, arranged our reception on arrival, and, after a short rest at our hotel, we were conveyed in a stately carriage, lined with white satin, having an electric lamp, and drawn by a pair of greys (there had been a discussion whether we should have two, four, or six) to the Chamber of Commerce, where some three hundred of the principal citizens, invited by the committees, were assembled to greet us with such a cordiality as made that day "a green spot on the path of time."

Rochester is known as the "City of Flowers," chiefly because the most famous nurseries of America are in its suburbs, and Mr. William Barry, one of the two proprietors (Barry and Ellwanger), appropriately bade us welcome. I had met him in England, where he was accompanied by a son of Mr. Ellwanger, Henry Brooks, a young man of great promise, author of a delightful book on the Rose, and an accomplished musician, but taken in his early manhood to a garden fairer and a music sweeter than those which he had known on earth. His grave, with a monument of beautiful sculpture, is in the cemetery of Mount Hope.

Of course I paid a visit to the nurseries, very extensive and in admirable order, and had a delightful interview with the head of the firm, conversing about old friends and fruits and flowers.

After my lecture I was escorted to a conclave of my brother Masons assembled in lodge, and was introduced to the members individually by a brother—not only in Masonry, but in the ministry also—the Right Worshipful the Rev. Warren C. Hubbard, Chaplain of the Grand Lodge of the State of New York.

In the records of Rochester * are two sad

* A copy of "Rochester, a Story Historical," a most interesting book by Jenny Marsh Parker, was presented to me at the reception by the lady to whom it is dedicated, Sarah R. A. Dolley, M.D.

tragedies: William Morgan, a free accepted mason, failing, it is said, to obtain some masonic work which he desired, wrote in a revengeful spirit a book in which he professed to reveal the secrets of the craft. Soon after its publication the author suddenly disappeared. Two Rochester men, Burrage Smith and John Whitney, were suspected of having effected his abduction, and they left the city and went to New Orleans, where Smith died. Whitney returned in 1829, was tried and imprisoned for one year and three months. Before his death he made the following confession :—" Morgan had been enticed by false pretences to the unoccupied magazine of Fort Niagara. Simultaneously the instalment of an encampment of Knights Templar at Lewiston drew together a large number of friends, of many of whom the question was asked, 'What is to be done with Morgan?' But the matter was so perplexing that no one seemed willing to act or to advise. In the evening, however, after we had been called from labour to refreshment, Colonel William King asked me to step into another room, where I found Mr. Howard of Buffalo, Mr. Chubbuck of Lewiston, and Mr. Garside of Youngstown. Colonel King said there was a carriage to take us to the fort, into which we stepped and were drawn hastily away. As we proceeded Colonel King said that he had received instructions from the highest authority to deal with Morgan according to his deserts, and that, having confidence in their courage and fidelity, he had chosen them as his assistants. On their arrival at the fort they assured Morgan that arrangements had been made for his removal to a farm in Canada, and he accompanied them from the fort to a boat which awaited them. The boat was rowed in a diagonal direction to the place where the Niagara river is lost in Lake Ontario. Here, either shore being two miles distant, a rope was wound several times round Morgan's body, at either end of which a large weight was attached. Up to that time Morgan had conversed with them about his new home, but when he saw the rope and the use to be made of it he struggled desperately and held firmly with one hand to the gunwale of the boat. Garside detached it, but as he did so Morgan caught his thumb in his teeth and bit off the first joint."

A body was subsequently found in Lake Ontario, which Mrs. Morgan declared to be the body of her husband; and a Rochester committee, attending the inquest, made a like affirmation. Others believed it to be the body of Timothy Monro, who was drowned near the spot where Morgan was said to have been murdered.

This cruel act, alleged to have been done by a few demented men, was repudiated and denounced by the Masonic body, "the Grand Chapter," individually and collectively, disclaiming all knowledge or approbation in relation to the abduction of the said William Morgan.

The other catastrophe was that of Sam Patch, to whom I referred as having twice leaped from a height of one hundred feet into the deep waters below Goat Island Cliff, not far from Niagara Falls, and who, on his return, issued a notice in the Rochester papers that, on Friday, November 13, at two o'clock, he would jump from a scaffold erected on the brink of the Genesee Falls into the deep below, a distance of one hundred and twenty-five feet.

It was a chilly, miserable November day, when shivering thousands from all parts were crowded on the banks of the river. Sam was "fond of a glass," but was not a sot; and his friend William Cochrane, who accompanied him, stoutly maintained that he had had no more than one glass of brandy to keep out the cold, and was not affected by drink. He climbed up the pole to his platform hand over hand, and there made the following speech: "Napoleon was a great man and a great general. He conquered armies and he conquered nations, but he could not jump the Genesee Falls. Wellington was a great man and a great soldier, and he conquered Napoleon, but he could not jump the Genesee Falls. That was left for me to do; and I can do it, and will."

He sprang from the scaffold, but in a form, they said who had seen him in his successful feats, quite different to his usual mode, awkwardly and heavily, so that from the first moment of his descent a horrible dread overwhelmed the spectators, and an awful presentiment was shrieked in piercing tones by a woman's voice, "That is a dead man!" In five minutes that huge multitude, stricken with sorrow and with remorse, had dispersed. Search was made day and night, but nothing more was seen of him until the next St. Patrick's Day, when his body was found in a block of ice near the mouth of the river. Cochrane always believed that Sam attempted to swim back under the cataract, and so became entangled in the great tree which was there for many years after.

Rochester has another pleasant title, "The City of Homes," and it is so called because it is said to have more houses occupied by those who own them than any other city in the States. It is an honourable ambition among American working men to have a home of their own, and to economize, with a view to such an acquisition, the money which is too often wasted in drink. There is some risk of their being tempted by jerry-builders to buy houses badly built from inferior materials, but this should be prevented by some authorized supervision, and every encouragement should be given to an enterprise which evokes a new interest and makes it easier to be content.

A third appellation has been bestowed on Rochester, "The City of New Beginnings." It claims to have originated "The American Bible Society," and it was recorded in 1884 that "General Riley still has the cane with which he marshalled the first Sabbath School Convention held in Rochester, when two thousand children with their teachers were gathered in Washington Square."

In its village days it was celebrated for its mud, of which at times there was in Buffalo Street a rolling stream. An adventurous youth, seeing a good hat on the surface, started on a plank to secure it, but as he neared his object, was startled by an angry expostulation, "Can't you let a man cross the street without trying to steal his goods?" Whether this mud has had any influence in muddling the brains of the weaker brethren, I am not prepared to say; but there have been some eccentric proclamations and performances by those who designate Rochester as the "Bethlehem of the New Dispensation," who believe in tappings, and are on intimate terms with "Spooks." I did not meet with any citizens of Rochester whose weak physiognomy suggested these hallucinations; but I enjoyed, on the contrary, in the public receptions and in hospitable homes, the wise and witty discourse of intellectual and rational men. Of many I may say that "we took sweet counsel together, and walked to the house of God as friends," when, on the invitation of the rector, the Reverend Algernon Crapsey, who was one of the first to suggest my visit to the States, I worshipped and preached in his church.

The snow was two feet deep in the streets, and my visit was so brief, that I was unable to visit the Theological College, the University, and other institutions. The sleighs were gliding over the frozen canal behind their splendid trotters at the rate of fifteen miles to the hour. A timid tourist, about to make his first journey in a carriage upon the ice, was informed by the waiter in his hotel that "he had put a buffalo" (referring to the "robe" or skin of that animal) "in the sleigh." "Oh, thank you," said the stranger, "but, if it makes no difference, I think *I'd rather have a horse.*" His remark reminds us of the little boy who, when asked by a mamma with anticipations, "whether he would prefer as a playmate a little brother or a little sister?" replied, after consideration, that, "if it made no difference, he should prefer a pony."

CHAPTER XXVI.

CLEVELAND, ST. LOUIS, DENVER, AND THE ROCKY MOUNTAINS.

CLEVELAND, on Lake Erie, founded by General Moses Cleaveland, is a handsome city with more than 260,000 inhabitants, well-built and spacious, with such an abundance of trees in its parks, cemeteries, squares, avenues, and lawns that it has been called "The Forest City." Alas! it is another fair victim offered in sacrifice to the demon smoke, and its atmosphere is polluted by its bituminous coal. It is divided by the river Cuyahoga, and connected by a magnificent viaduct which cost more than two millions of dollars.

For those who are interested in good food, well cooked (deans, of course, only notice these minor details for the gratification of others), the Hollenden Hotel will be a happy home, but it is difficult to discover the hours of feeding. There is a great disagreement among the working clocks, though they are not simultaneously on strike. There is "the standard time," "the city time," and "the railway time," and none of them correspond with "the New York time," so that there is a complication and perplexity which remind us of the sailor's chronometer, as described by Mr. Albert Smith, from the words of its proprietor: "You see, when the hands of this 'ere machine is a-pointing at half-past three, it strikes eleven, and I knows as that means a quarter to six; but it's just like a woman, don't yer see, you've got to study her ways, and get to know what she means, or she won't tell yer nothink."

Between Cleveland and St. Louis we pass by remains of old log huts and by stumps of trees left there by the brave pioneers, who made the desert smile and the valleys to stand so thick with corn that they seem to laugh and sing.

Crossing the Mississippi, which is there a muddy, sluggish stream, and, "like the wounded snake, drags its slow length along," you enter the railway station, or depôt, of St. Louis, which claims to be the largest in the world, covering 497,920 square feet, or eleven acres. The architecture of the exterior is very imposing.

The Southern Hotel is one of the largest and best in the States. The great entrance-hall is built in the form of a Greek cross, with four entrances from four different streets. There is only one coloured servant in the establishment, and he is also exceptional in his wonderful power of associating in his memory every man of the crowds, who three times a day leave portions of their apparel before they enter the dining-room in his custody, with the hats and coats which they wear.

We were cordially welcomed by Bishop Tuttle and his wife, who invited a distinguished company to meet us, and the latter took me, the day after my lecture, to the Missouri Botanical Gardens, of which Dr. Asa Gray, a supreme authority, has said, "This park and the botanical garden are the finest institutions of the kind in the country; in variety of foliage the park is unequalled." Extending over seventy-five acres of ground, they were the noble offering of a noble mind to the citizens of St. Louis, for their pleasure and instruction; and they were also designed to provide adequate instruction, theoretical and practical, for young men desirous of becoming gardeners. The donor was Mr. Henry Shaw. Born at Sheffield, he came from England to St. Louis with a small stock of cutlery in the year 1819. He rented a room, in which for a time he lived, cooked, and conducted his business. He made a large fortune, and came to London in 1851, to the First Great International Exhibition, a millionaire. Walking with Sir Joseph Paxton in the grounds at Chatsworth, the question came to his thoughts, "Why should not I have a garden also?" On his return, he corresponded with Sir William Hooker, engaged the services of Mr. Gurney, from the Royal Botanical Gardens in the Regent's Park, and devoted the rest of his life to the development of this grand conception. From his boyhood he had been a lover of the garden, and his fondness for flowers was expressed by his reply to a lady who said to him, as they were inspecting the Missouri collection, " I cannot understand, sir, how you are able to remember all these different and difficult names!" "Madam," he replied, " did you ever know a mother, who could forget the names of her children? These are mine."

Professor Trelease, formerly a pupil of Dr. Asa Gray, and an enthusiastic and most learned botanist, showed me the very valuable library, the laboratory, the herbarium, engravings, etc. I was specially interested—because the idea was new to me, and revealed a source of delightful information—in a collection of drawings which the professor had in progress of trees as they appear in winter, enabling the observer to recognize them at once, and to increase his knowledge of their habits and diversities. I went through the houses, which include a remarkable collection of agaves, and some good specimens of palms, cycas, cacti, etc.

Mr. Shaw was a lover of music also, and a band played in the Gardens on the Sunday evening. He had such a love for his old home in the city that he ordered its transportation and re-edification, brick by brick, in the grounds of the Missouri Gardens, and not far away he erected a mausoleum, in which he placed a statue of himself, carved at Munich some years before his death. The expression on the countenance and the posture of the recumbent figure are those of sleep rather than of death, and the right hand holds a rose above the heart.

I was conducted through the brewery of Messrs. Busch by one of the brothers, and was amazed, as at Milwaukee, by the infinite extent of the premises, granaries, malthouses, and cellars, the size of the mash-tubs, and the "kettles," many of them holding 450 barrels of beer. The great chimney, 275 feet in height, is said to be the tallest in "the States."

St. Louis is the chief mart for mules in the world, but the market was closed during my visit. I was consoled by an appropriate anecdote. Many years ago, and in a diocese which I may not name, a young American bishop was somewhat unduly impressed by a sense of his dignity, and was tempted to magnify his office. Travelling to a distant part of his diocese, he was met at the end of his journey by a farm help, who had brought an ancient and shabby conveyance, drawn by a mule, for his use. The bishop imprudently asked whether *that thing* was for him, and the driver promptly replied—"Your Master rode on a donkey, so you need not be so skeered at a mule."

The sun rose as we drew near to Denver, "the Queen City of the Plains," and changed the infinite expanse of prairie, with its yellow herbage, into a golden sea. In the recollection of many living men the buffaloes swarmed where now the silence and the solitude is only disturbed by the rush of the railway train, and the Indian was monarch over all. Not that we are to attribute his exodus entirely to the advent of the stranger; the tomahawk and the poisoned arrow were suicidal. Mr. H. M. Stanley writes, in the book of his early travels in America, "that while the fire-water and rifles of the white man have done much, the Indians have themselves done more for their own extermination by internecine wars."

After a first view of the Rocky Mountains, majestic in their grandeur, raising their hoar heads towards heaven like patriarchs in adoration, we arrived at the capital of Colorado. Forty years ago there was no Denver. In 1858 there was a camp of miners. In 1870 the population was 4759; in 1890 106,713. It is a complete and beautiful city. The public buildings, especially the Court House and State Capitol, are spacious and imposing; and it has more picturesque and varied private residences in its suburbs than those seen elsewhere. The views of "the Rockies" from different points, especially when seen at the end of a long street, as through a vista or avenue, are exquisite.

Again we had the happiness of a most genial welcome, of the kindest hospitality, in the house of Dean Hart, whose reputation has long ago reached England as a foremost champion of the Church, as the founder of a beautiful cathedral, as a most energetic priest, brave in his faith, but tender in his kindness, an accomplished gentleman, musician, artist, doctor, sportsman—a real sportsman, with no resemblance to an individual whom I saw in Denver on the afternoon of Sunday, riding a bicycle, with a jack-rabbit dangling in front, and two villainous mongrels of the lurcher genus "lorping" (as we say in Nottinghamshire) behind their proprietor, who assumed such an expression of successful prowess as might have been excused if he had slain and brought home a lion or a man-eater which had long been the terror of the town.

Bishop and Mrs. Spalding, Judge and Mrs. Lefevre gave us Receptions, and the Denver Club gave me a dinner. The weather was bitterly cold, and my lectures were not numerously attended, though they were warmly applauded.

"Chill though the wind blew, and threatening the storm,
Those hearts, full of kindness, beat kindly and warm."

A Denver audience is notably benevolent, and it is said that a chairman, after a depressing address, assured the speaker that his discourse was "moving, soothing, and satisfying." When reproved next morning as having commended a dismal failure, he denied the charge, and maintained that he had uttered no approbation, but only simple facts, namely, that the lecture was "moving," because a large proportion of the audience fidgeted in their seats, and several left the room; it was "soothing," because many fell asleep; and it was "satisfying," because there was not a single person present who had not had quite enough.

I went to see a very near and dear relative. I

refer to my visit because there was not only the joy of reunion, but because there was in her house the best sermon I ever heard—no, I mean (for not a word was spoken on this subject) the best illustration I ever saw—of the text, "The voice of joy and health is in the dwellings of the righteous." She was born and "raised" in a lovely country home, with servants and carriages and every comfort. Now she has a comparatively small abode, and must live frugally, without a **conveyance**, without a servant. And yet I never saw a happier home! No tiara of diamonds is so bright as the eyes of those who love and help each other, no service of gold plate has on it more wholesome food, no powdered footman waits upon guests with such graceful diligence as the daughters of that house. We cannot buy happiness, but we can create it. It is all home-made.

The early history of Denver would be a rich feast to those who crave for startling incidents. Dean Hart informed me that of twenty-one entries on the first page of the registry of burials in Denver Cathedral, nineteen were records of death by violence. Among the miners were many experts in crime. A friend of mine, not an expert, was with them some forty years ago, and one night, as they were smoking their pipes around the camp fire, he mentioned in conversation that he came from South-well. "Southwell, in Nottinghamshire?" exclaimed a neighbour, not of prepossessing aspect, but with much animation. "Yes," my friend replied; "do you know it?" "Know it?" said the inquirer, "know it? I should think I do. The best jail I ever was in!"

Evidence was not easily obtained, and when forthcoming was contradictory. The judicial authorities were merciful to a fault, after the sudden removal by violence of some of their learned brethren, who had recklessly proceeded to administer justice. Two men, one the owner of a mine and the other of a ranch, were engaged in litigation. The case was ultimately decided by the Supreme Court at Washington. Soon after the decision, the principals met, and one inquired of the other, "Did you say that I perjured myself at Washington?" "Yes," was the answer, "I did." No further remark was made, but in the evening they met again, and the same question was repeated, with the same reply, whereupon the accused drew his revolver and shot his accuser dead. The jury brought in a verdict of "Not guilty," and when one of them was asked the reason why, he said, "We have never yet hanged a man in Leadville, and we are not going to begin with an old 'un."

The services at the cathedral are daily and reverent, and the music, vocal and instrumental, is excellent. Dr. John H. Gower, who took the highest musical degree, when he was only twenty-five, at Oxford, is the organist and precentor. He most kindly played for us, and his descriptive performance of "The Storm" and "The Procession of the Blessed Sacrament" was most impressive.

From Denver I went to Colorado Springs, and, through the kind introduction of Dean Hart, was the guest of Dr. Solly. His father's work, "Solly on the Brain," is well known, but the son's work is "Solly on the Heart," for he has won the gratitude and affection of his patients. He came to the Springs many years ago suffering from lung disease, and with faint hope of recovery; but this migration, humanly speaking, not only prolonged his own life, but that of many others. Several of the residents told me that they had found here the relief and restoration which they had sought elsewhere in vain. The small city is laid out with much taste, and with broad avenues and delightful houses, from which there are beautiful views of the mountains, including the famous "Pike's Peak," named after Colonel Zebulon Pike, an early pioneer, in 1806, and also Monte Rosa, so designated in honour of Rose, the daughter of Charles Kingsley, the first lady who climbed to its summit. These mountains are easily reached by carriage or by electric railway, and there is a sublime and awful grandeur in the stupendous cañons—narrow gorges cut through the solid rocks, the perpendicular walls on either side rising to the height of 1000 to 1500 feet. The game has been banished to more quiet and distant lairs, but in these the sportsman will find deer, elk, wapiti, the mountain-lion, the antelope, wild cat, wild turkey, grouse, and quail.

One of many delightful drives is to the picturesque residence of General Palmer, called "The

THE MOUNTAIN MONARCH, COLORADO.

Eyrie," and still having in its grounds the huge nest, long forsaken, of the eagle, high on the rocks, and thence to "The Garden of the Gods," which is entered between two gigantic columns of red granite

BALANCE ROCK, GARDEN OF THE GODS.

330 feet high. It contains about 500 acres of ground, and the surface is diversified by fantastic and grotesque, though natural, formations of red and white sandstone, in which striking resemblance

may be traced to human figures, animals, and buildings, and which contrast delightfully with the vegetation around, the dark firs and cedars, and the bright blue sky overhead. We returned by Manitou, renowned for its delicious waters, and much frequented as a summer resort.

The underground wealth of Colorado seems to be infinite: gold, silver, lead, iron, and coal; and its quarries supply in abundance every diversity of stone—marble, onyx, granite, lava—white, pink, blue, and grey, in natural colours.

Wild flowers are lovely and numerous. They were, of course, invisible in January—(the thermometer went down one night during my visit to 24 below zero)—but I had the privilege of inspecting their portraits, faithfully and charmingly painted by Mrs. Hill—anemones, aquilegias, gentians, œnotheras, cacti, and every variety of Alpine plants.

A touching tribute of sympathy was offered to me at Colorado Springs. A new golf ground, "The Prairie Links," had been recently laid out, and one of the apertures was named "Dean *Hole*."

There is good sport for the angler. "Old Sammy," a keeper, died not long ago. The clergyman who visited him in his last sickness, making inquiry as in duty bound as to his spiritual condition, asked him whether he had any special burden upon his conscience. Sammy, being weak and hazy, does not seem to have realized the solemnity of the question, and replied, after some consideration, that "There was one thing he should alter, if he had to live his life again—he thought he should fish more wi' bait, and less wi' fly."

A more satisfactory incident is recorded of an old man, whose home was high up on the Rockies, and who, strong in faith and hope, said shortly before his death, "Well, I guess we're over nine thousand feet above the sea level, so when I come to quit I'll not have far to go."

I heard from ranchmen and others more details of The Dawn of Civilization in Colorado. Like old Sam, it was hazy, and when the sun shone through the fog it glittered on bowie-knives and six-shooters. "I had a young fellow in my employment for some time," said one of my informants, "and I took a great fancy to him, he was always so cheerful and ready for any amount of work. He was a youth of undaunted courage, and you would infer from his flashing eyes that he was sudden and quick in quarrel, but he loved to play with children, and was a favourite with all. It transpired, nevertheless, that this bright, attractive young fellow was a murderer. Working in New Mexico, he owned some horses. The Mexicans stole them. He followed and overtook them; a fight ensued, and he killed two of them. The sheriff came to arrest him, and, instead of giving himself up and standing his trial, he killed the sheriff! He repented of the act, but, knowing that if he was captured he must either be hanged or imprisoned for life, he always declared that no man should take him alive."

Among his other friends was a Frenchman, living alone on the mountains, a trapper, a guide to hunting-parties, and a splendid cook. He was full of mirth, good-humour, and hospitality, but if any reference was made to the Germans, whom he hated (he had been a soldier in Garibaldi's army), or to kings and queens, he was furious, and suggested immediate decapitation for the lot. When he was engaged in preparing his venison and mountain trout, with a scientific manipulation which France alone can teach, his visitors were careful as to their topics of conversation. A remark having the remotest connection with Germany or with royalty evoked an utterance of ferocious words, accompanied by gesticulations which, in the case of a man with a frying-pan in one hand and a pepper-box in the other, were fatal to culinary success.

Clay Allison, a notorious desperado, was followed by a detective officer from Chicago, who introduced himself as a stranger travelling through the country, entered into friendly conversation, and proposed that they should ride together to a town not far distant, where he intended to make the usual announcement, "You're my prisoner." As they were passing through a silent and dismal gorge, Allison suddenly reined in his horse, and, surveying his companion with an admiring smile, blandly addressed him, simultaneously touching the handle of a revolver in his belt:

"*Mr. Jones, of Chicago, you would make a beautiful corpse!*" Ultimately, Mr. Jones went home.

Zan Heckler, a Dutchman, sold the Government a large lot of corn, and with the proceeds went down to Maxwells, New Mexico, where he met a gambler from New York. They played poker for some hours, and when the New Yorker had lost his "pile," he accused the winner of cheating, and challenged him to fight. The Dutchman assented, and, having his choice of weapons, and having spent many years among the Indians, he chose bows and arrows on horseback. At daybreak the challenger, looking out from his bedroom window, saw the Dutchman practising his archery, shooting at a post as he galloped round a yard adjoining, in which the combat was to be fought, and when he hit his mark, as he almost invariably did, uttering, after the manner of the Indians, triumphant yells. As he gazed, he remembered a domestic engagement, which irresistibly constrained him to take advantage of the early coach.

Alas! I was myself impelled to depart, like the bereft and intimidated gambler, from the West to New York, for my term of absence was nearly over, and I was over five thousand miles from home. I brought from Colorado one—only one—sorrowful thought, and though it is but as a little cloud no bigger than a man's hand on my memory's American sky, it sometimes casts a shadow on my path. I refer to those of my countrymen who, in the last thirty years, have gone with brave hearts and bright hopes to invest their money in the ranch and the farm, have spent the best years of their manhood in arduous toil, and are working at this time in the daily monotonous drudgery of mean employments—cutting wood, making fires, cooking, cleaning and mending, to supply the necessaries of life. I warn young English gentlemen that there is no room for them as farmers in America.

The day before I sailed from New York I received this telegram from the Bishop of Albany: "God speed you and yours home, my beloved brother. May you take with you as delightful memories as those you leave behind."

THE END.

www.ingramcontent.com/pod-product-compliance
Lightning Source LLC
Chambersburg PA
CBHW032026220426
43664CB00006B/383